Pitt Series in Policy

and Institutional Studies

THE DEVELOPMENT OF THE DUTCH WELFARE STATE

From Workers'
Insurance
to Universal
Entitlement

Robert H. Cox

Pittsburgh and London

UNIVERSITY OF PITTSBURGH PRESS

Published by the
University of Pittsburgh Press, Pittsburgh, Pa. 15260

Copyright © 1993, University of Pittsburgh Press

Manufactured in the United States of America

Printed on acid-free paper

Library of Congress Cataloging-in-Publication Data

Cox, Robert Henry.
    The development of the Dutch welfare state:
from workers' insurance to universal entitlement /
Robert H. Cox.
        p.   cm. — (Pitt series in policy and institu-
tional studies)
    Includes bibliographical references (p.   )
and index.
    ISBN 0-8229-3760-3 (alk. paper)
    1. Netherlands — Social policy. 2. Netherlands —
Social conditions — 1945–   I. Title. II. Series.
HN513.5.C67   1993
361.6′1′09492 — dc20   93-6667
                                 CIP

A CIP catalogue record for this book
is available from the British Library.

Eurospan, London

Contents

Preface   vii
Abbreviations   xv

1   The Comparative Position of the Dutch Welfare State   3

2   Reconsidering the Development of the Welfare State:
    Suggestions from the Dutch Case   27

3   The Evolution of the Dutch Corporatist State: The Role
    of Religious Forces   58

4   Reasons for Late Development: False Starts after
    World War II   96

5   Reasons for Rapid Growth: Changes in Corporatist
    Relationships   133

6   The Politics of Retrenchment   171

7   Conclusions: Lessons from the Dutch Case   202

Appendix One: Chronology of Social Legislation   227

Appendix Two: Major Political Parties   230

Appendix Three: Cabinets, 1945–1989   231

Appendix Four: Composition of Parliaments,
1946–1989   236

Bibliography   237

Index   253

Preface

Foreign observers, especially Americans, are amazed by what they find in the Netherlands. Tourists often discover the social permissiveness of Amsterdam. Add to this an afternoon of staring at Rembrandt's *Nightwatch* in the Rijksmuseum, and they've "done" the Netherlands. Most Dutch lament that their country's international image is produced of such limited and narrow experience. But it is not just tourists who are at fault. Scholars often commit a similar sin. They tend to look briefly at the Netherlands (if they look at all), then move quickly to the more important countries of Europe.

Indeed, it is not just the Netherlands that gets overlooked. The study of European politics is characterized, almost defined, by a tendency to focus attention on the larger countries and ignore the smaller ones. There is good reason for this sort of selection. The larger countries encompass the greatest number of citizens. All of the "Big Four" (Great Britain, Germany, France, and Italy) have populations in excess of fifty million. With the exception of Spain, none of the others can boast fifteen million citizens. Size also lends world stature. For example, the languages of the larger countries are more accessible than those of the smaller ones. Over time, the greater attention given to the larger countries tends to reinforce their importance, and the relative neglect of the smaller countries underscores their obscurity.

Though it is natural to lavish more favor on the larger countries, there is a problem with this bias, especially for the social scientist. Social scientists are creatures with a proclivity for theorizing, an endeavor inspired by a desire to make sweeping generalizations about a very large world and to provide parsimonious explanations of extremely complex phenomena. Good social science theory should be encompassing in the things it explains. In other words, the analysis should include all relevant cases. If the theory is good, it should explain most cases. If it is great, it will explain all of them. It is precisely this concern with creating social science theory that makes the ignorance of the smaller European democracies so perplexing.

The handful of scholars who dare to venture out and explore the smaller countries often find the theoretical models that work for the larger ones to be inappropriate for the smaller ones. The welfare state is a case in point. Much of our understanding of the development of European welfare states is based on the experiences of the larger nations. Sweden is one of the smaller countries that has been included in comparative studies of the welfare state because it stands out as the most advanced. On the basis of the bulk of such studies, we assume two basic premises to be true of the development of European welfare states: that they developed slowly during the twentieth century, and that they grew the most in countries where the social democratic left has been a powerful political force.

To the extent that attention is paid to the welfare states of the smaller democracies, the approach tends to be descriptive rather than comparative. Though this is useful in providing a great deal of information, it is time to include the smaller countries in the theoretically informed comparative studies. This book represents a modest attempt to do this: It is a case study of the development of the Dutch welfare state. Desiring to provide more than a descriptive account, I use the Dutch case to examine some of the general themes in the comparative development of the welfare state. Indeed, on many counts the Netherlands is a crucial test case for assumptions about the welfare state. Its system is one of the largest in the world, rivaling Sweden's as one that devotes the greatest share of public spending to social welfare. Yet it did not develop slowly. For the first half of the twentieth century, the Dutch welfare state was a comparative laggard; then it quickly mushroomed in the 1960s. Nor was it constructed by the social democratic left. Centrist religious parties presided over its development.

Preface

Where, then, does the Dutch case fit in comparison with other countries? Is it unique, or does its history point toward the need for a new way of conceptualizing development of the welfare state? I believe our present theories can adequately account for the Dutch case but that they need to be rendered in more general terms. One problem that needs to be addressed is the tendency toward reductionism. Too often, theoretical explanations tend to be monocausal. Other important factors are assumed to be intervening variables that explain deviance when they often are important enough to be central factors in the analysis. Consequently, the whole empirical world gets shoved impolitely into the model. My answer to this is to develop a synthetic theory.

To be more precise, there are three important components of the development of the Dutch welfare state that receive little attention in the comparative literature. The first is the influence of ideas from abroad, an important theme for anyone interested in why policies in different countries look similar. The problem is that we often assume that convergence of policy is a result of exogenous factors. In other words, macrochanges in society, such as industrialization or literacy, force all countries that experience them to adopt the same types of policy. Less attention is paid to how ideas move across national borders. Yet this is an especially important factor if one wishes to explain, for example, why the Dutch welfare state developed so much later than its social and economic modernization. The study draws attention to the active search by Dutch policy makers of other countries for solutions that they adapted to their own circumstances.

The second major factor is the extensive development of a welfare state in a country where the left is relatively weak. This fact challenges the basically ideological bias of scholars who assume welfare states are the pet projects of social democratic governments and are resented by centrist and rightist political forces. To explain how the Dutch welfare state could be built by confessional rather than social democratic forces, I argue that it is more important to examine the dynamic of collective action to explain why political groups adopt the types of policy programs they do. Focusing on how organized political forces interact in their efforts to influence policy seems a preferable way of conceptualizing the role of parties and other organized groups. Especially for building theory that has comparative application, it seems inadequate to assume how a particular group behaves before looking at the political environment it operates in.

The third and final component is the extent to which corporatism in the Netherlands gives particular shape to policy. Scholars of the welfare state have not been very rigorous in examining the role institutions play in shaping policy. Though corporatism as an institutional structure has received a great deal of attention over the last two decades, the efforts to relate it to specific outcomes have been scant, especially in the area of social policy.

None of these factors is of my own devising, and I therefore can make no claim to breaking new theoretical ground. I have merely taken three themes that have been inadequately explicated in the comparative literature, rendered them more amenable to comparative application, and tested them in the Dutch case. Though the theorizing is synthetic, there is a unique contribution in this book. Since no comprehensive study of the Dutch welfare state is available in the English language, it would be useful simply to have a sound descriptive history of it. This study strives to go a step farther by offering an account of the Dutch experience that simultaneously places it in comparative context.

Another aspect of this study is its historical focus. It traces the development of Dutch social welfare throughout the last one hundred years. I make this effort at a time when historical investigation is only beginning to return and is still a relatively marginal activity in political science. Since the behavioral revolution took hold of the discipline in the middle of this century, theory has replaced description, but the empirical focus has come to emphasize observable events, often without consideration of their historical context. The new wave of scholarship strives to integrate these two activities. Especially for those who study comparative politics, the concern is with developing a theoretical understanding of history.

There is, however, a difficulty with this integration of theory and history. Developing an abstract theory to explain a few isolated events works fairly well for the behavioral approach, but for the historical approach such abstract explanations work more convincingly for some time periods than for others. This concern only underscores the need for theory that is general and flexible rather than narrow and focused. For this reason I have endeavored to recognize that the institutions and processes under consideration are not static. But because they change over time, it only becomes more important to cast the theoretical concerns at a sufficient level of abstraction to be amenable to application to different historical periods. Corporatism is not the same in all countries, and in the Netherlands its form has changed over the last century. It is only by allowing for flexibility in putting concepts into operation that the theory can remain true to the historical context.

Some may find fault with this approach because it does not provide for a tidy, parsimonious explanation. The only defense I can muster is that few things in the world lend themselves to simple explanation. The welfare state is an incredibly complicated entity. It is a difficult creature to define, much less explain in simple terms. No two welfare states in the world look exactly alike. A rigid explanation may work well for one case, but only a flexible one will work for them all.

In addition to developing a theory flexible enough to be adapted to specific historical periods, efforts to provide logically coherent explanations of complex historical phenomena must be made with a sensitivity to the fallibility of human beings. There is a tendency to attribute too much intention and rationality to the activities of participants in a historical event. It is easy to distill logical coherence after the fact, but this does not mean that it was there to begin with. This point is crucial for understanding the Dutch case. In conducting this research, I found that one point Dutch politicians continually stressed was that they never intended to create the world's most expensive welfare state. Their objectives were more limited, and more immediate. That theirs is now one of the largest welfare states is a result of a number of unintentional consequences that policy makers either were unaware of or chose to overlook. The lesson for comparative study is that it is important to distinguish between the welfare state that was meant to be and the one that exists.

Examining the political history of the welfare state renders it easy to make this distinction. The political process more often produces bargains and compromises than winners and losers. Recognizing this is crucial to understanding how the policy that is finally formulated can deviate from the objectives of the actors in the policy-making process. This study focuses primarily on the politics of social welfare in the Netherlands. It examines how the attitudes and ambitions of various actors structured their behavior. It explores the obstacles they confronted and the compromises they made. Though Dutch policy makers were aware of how their welfare state compared with those of other countries, their struggle was not with the rest of Europe but with political opponents at home. Hence the Dutch case lends itself to comparison, but only when the comparative themes are rendered in general terms and much allowance is made for contextually specific factors.

The findings in this study are based primarily on my interpretation of the historical record. Though they do not depart substantially from much of the understanding Dutch scholars have of the development of their welfare state, I endeavored not only to rely on the wealth of academic literature available in the Dutch language but also to verify claims with primary sources. To a great extent, these consisted of archival materials kept on file by Dutch ministries. The great advantage of the archival records is that they contain all memos and correspondence pertaining to the development of legislation. In addition, they include meticulous collections of the position papers of various advisory bodies, contemporary newspaper clippings, and related publications. Numerous interviews with Dutch academics, politicians, and public officials have also helped me distill the major themes out of the myriad of details.

I am grateful to many people for their support of this project. My greatest debt is to Norman Furniss and Alfred Diamant. Nor-

Preface

man Furniss first brought my attention to the peculiar position of the Dutch welfare state. Both he and Alfred Diamant helped me turn the project into a doctoral dissertation. The project has also benefited from the input of numerous individuals who offered advice on various chapters, and in some cases the full manuscript: Douglas Ashford, Jacques van Doorn, Erich Frankland, Russell Hanson, Arnold Heidenheimer, Peter Katzenstein, Percy Lehning, Ilja Scholten, Keith Shimko, Timothy Tilton, Theo Toonen, David Wilsford, and Steven Wolinetz.

Financial support for the project made it possible for me to conduct research in the Netherlands. The Department of West European Studies at Indiana University funded the first trip during the 1986–87 academic year. A research assistantship from the Department of Public Administration at Erasmus University allowed me to extend that initial visit. A follow-up visit in summer 1990, supported by the Research Administration of the University of Oklahoma, allowed me to collect information for the chapter on retrenchment. During each of these trips, the Department of Public Administration at Erasmus University provided generous, and greatly appreciated, institutional support.

My greatest personal debt is to many Dutch friends whose warmth and hospitality helped me build a second home in a foreign country and who afforded me insights into the social dimension of the Dutch welfare state that cannot be gleaned from dusty texts or formal interviews. Paramount among these stands Hanneke Mastik, to whom I owe a debt that cannot be repaid and who remains a most esteemed and true friend.

Abbreviations

ARP	Antirevolutionary party
CDA	Christian Democratic Appeal
CHU	Christian Historical Union
JMS	Joint Medical Service
KVP	Catholic People's party
NIB	National Insurance Bank
NVV	Dutch Federation of Trade Unions
POO	provincial reconstruction organization
PvdA	Labor party
SER	Social-Economic Council
VVD	Liberal party

The Development of

the Dutch Welfare State

1

The Comparative Position
of the Dutch Welfare State

"The Netherlands surpassed all Common Market countries by 1970."
— Harold Wilensky (1975, 12)

"In no other West European country has the welfare state expanded to such an extent after World War II."
— Peter Flora (1986, xix)

"That the Dutch have constructed the world's most extensive welfare state is not that well known and fits rather uneasily into current explanatory frameworks."
— Göran Therborn (1989, 196)

The growth of the Dutch welfare state has been remarkable. Throughout the postwar period, all western countries experienced growth in levels of spending on welfare. One characteristic of this trend has been disproportionate growth of the welfare state among countries. Welfare leaders (e.g., Britain, France, West Germany, and Sweden) exhibited sharp growth, while laggards such as Switzerland and the United States grew at a slower rate. Expansion of the welfare state exacerbated the distinction between leaders and laggards in all but one country — the Netherlands, which during this time, went from one of the lowest- to one of the highest-spending welfare states (Flora 1986, xix; Wilensky 1975, 11–12). Figure 1.1 illustrates this differential growth in welfare states.

Certainly there is something unique about the growth of the Dutch welfare state. But studying this growth also raised universal questions about the factors that contribute to it and especially to transformations from laggards to leaders. That the Nether-

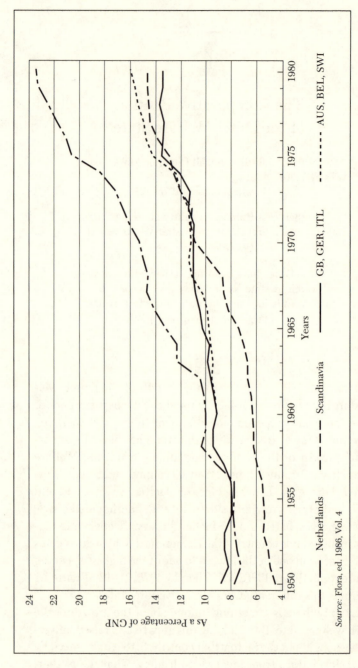

As a Percentage of GNP

24 22 20 18 16 14 12 10 8 6 4

1950 1955 1960 1965 1970 1975 1980

Years

——— Netherlands   — — — Scandinavia   ——— GB, GER, ITL

·········· AUS, BEL, SWI

Source: Flora, ed. 1986, Vol. 4

Figure 1.1 Income Maintenance Spending Netherlands Compared with West Europe

lands caught up with the other countries does not reflect some broad convergence among western countries. Were this true, then we should expect to have witnessed the same catch-up in other countries. Nor does a slow start determine that a country will remain behind. Had this been the case, the Netherlands would continue to be a welfare laggard. What it does indicate is that the Dutch experience presents a comparative puzzle and a challenge to theoretical explanations of development of the welfare state.

Another remarkable aspect of the Dutch case is that it has received relatively little attention from scholars who study the topic. That is to say, the Dutch case has been overlooked in the English-language literature on the welfare state.[1] Even in the Dutch language there are few comprehensive accounts. Those that exist are generally out of date (e.g., Hoogland 1940; Gosker 1970; Veldkamp 1980). The bulk of research by Dutch scholars has appeared as collected volumes or as doctoral dissertations on the histories of individual programs (e.g., Beus and Doorn 1984; Jansen and Berben 1982; Peper 1972; Rieken 1985; Schuyt and Veen 1986; Valk 1986). Moreover, they generally have not addressed the concerns of the comparative literature on the welfare state.

In the comparative literature convergence and divergence stand apart as perhaps the most important themes. Scholars who study convergence note that similar pressures, such as industrialization, urbanization, and the breakdown in traditional community relationships, account for similarities in the development of welfare states. Other scholars, by contrast, emphasize the divergence in development. For them, the welfare state is a unique phenomenon in each country, since the specific debates and discussions that influence a country's response to social issues are contextually bound. The truth probably lies somewhere between these two extremes. Accepting that as the case, I would further assert

1. The only recent studies in the English language that have focused on the Dutch case are not comprehensive accounts but merely underscore its importance as an exceptional case (Swaan 1988; Therborn 1989). A similar statement can be made about the German literature (Becker and Kersbergen 1986).

5

that some synthesis of the two perspectives could also go a long way to explain the Dutch welfare state. Perhaps the Dutch case will become less exceptional when viewed through a synthetic lens.

But what are the important elements of such a synthesis? In answering this question, I point to the peculiar position of the Netherlands within the current literature. First, the Netherlands poses problems for the convergence school because the emergence of its welfare state bears little correlation to its pattern of socioeconomic development. Indeed, the Dutch welfare state came rather late because politics was more determinant of the timing and character of welfare policy than was socioeconomic development. Lateness also brought with it one decided advantage: at the time Dutch policy makers became concerned with adopting social welfare programs, there were already a myriad of foreign examples to choose from. In fact, the historical record shows that they borrowed extensively from their neighbors, specifically Germany and Great Britain. Thus, for understanding the peculiar Dutch pattern of convergence, the accent should be placed on the manner in which policy makers learned from the policies adopted by their neighbors, rather than on their reaction to socioeconomic developments.

Since politics is crucial to understanding the apparent convergence in the development of the Dutch welfare state, it becomes all the more salient for understanding where the Dutch experience departs from those of many other western countries. There are basically two prevailing explanations for divergences: one focuses on partisan politics, the other on political institutions. For the first explanation, leftist political power is viewed as a factor that accounts for the extensive development of a welfare state in a country where the left is strong, and for limited development where the left is weak. This poses another perplexing issue for the Dutch case: the Dutch welfare state was not built by the political left. Though the left contributed, the centrist religious parties were largely responsible for its development. The Dutch case suggests that we must abandon the assumption that only the left can build an extensive welfare state and instead concentrate on the reasons why mobilized political groups — whether of the left, right, or center — pursue expansion of welfare provisions.

Though recognizing that centrist parties may be just as important as the left in fostering development of the welfare state helps us understand who built the Dutch welfare state, it leaves unanswered a crucial question: Why was it built so late? The religious parties dominated Dutch politics throughout this century. Why, then, did they resist expansion of the welfare state for the first half of this century but then become dramatic proponents of it in the 1960s? In part this question is answered when we explore the history of religious political mobilization in the Netherlands.

But, to explain divergence fully, an understanding of the institutional context within which policy is made is essential. Institutional explanations are the second way of explaining welfare state divergence. But institutional analysis has not been applied to the Dutch case.

It is peculiar that the Netherlands has been overlooked by institutionalists, because its policy institutions are perfect examples of a type that has drawn the attention of scholars who study other European countries. In the Netherlands, corporatism characterizes the structure of the institutions that formulate and administer welfare policy. Though there are many studies of the corporatist experience in Europe, most do a poor job of handling countries like the Netherlands, where religion was an important force in the development of corporatism. Moreover, the corporatist literature also concentrates heavily on explaining economic policy and only weakly on explaining social policy.

The Dutch corporatist institutions, which were built at the beginning of this century, were originally designed to prevent the expansion of the state's role in social welfare. Corporatism persisted until the mid-1960s, at which time the changing institutional context allowed welfare reformers to push through their policy preferences. Hence concentrating on the changing nature of corporatist policy making in the Netherlands makes it possible to answer another perplexing question: Why did welfare provisions expand so rapidly in the 1960s?

To answer the three perplexing issues of convergence, lateness, rapidity, I propose recasting some of the major theoretical premises in ways that make it possible to include the Dutch state in comparative analysis. First, to address the issue of convergence, I place a greater emphasis on the international transfer of ideas, or borrowing of policy, rather than on socioeconomic conditions as the factor that accounts for cross-national similarities in development of the welfare state. To account for the role of the religious parties, I abandon the assumption that expansion of social welfare is favored only by the political left. Instead, I concentrate on the dynamics of political mobilization and the way this influences the policy preferences of societal organizations. Finally, to account for the institutional context of Dutch policy making, I argue that the Dutch case makes it necessary to refine our understanding of what corporatism is and how it operates.

The three themes that comprise this effort to explain the Dutch case were designed to address certain lacunae in the literature. Though I propose to recast them in order to encompass the Dutch case, this should not be confused with what Giovanni Sartori (1970) has called conceptual stretching. Rather, I propose that concepts must be explicated at a more abstract level of analysis. The reason the Dutch case appears not to fit within our current understanding the development of the welfare state is that the assumptions scholars currently work with are generalized from the experience of a few European cases.

At the same time the three themes neatly encompass the basic three levels of theoretical analysis: the individual, the organizational, and the structural. The use of a theoretical framework that operates on different levels of analysis is necessary for historical investigation, since the importance of specific factors waxes and wanes during different historical epochs. In addition, identifying different levels of analysis implies that relationships exist among the levels, and good theory should specify these relationships. A detailed outline of the theoretical framework is the subject of chapter 2. For the remainder of this chapter, I wish to demonstrate just how puzzling the Dutch case is within the comparative literature and to outline the basic argument.

THE INADEQUACY OF SOCIOECONOMIC EXPLANATIONS

Generally, socioeconomic explanations of the development of the welfare state assume that it expands in response to broad changes in society. And though the processes that bring about these changes cannot be controlled, they require policies that attend to their consequences. Scholars who apply this model to the welfare state argue that its development follows from the attainment of a certain level of modernization in a society.

Harold Wilensky's (1975) path-breaking book was one of the first to employ this theme. Wilensky demonstrated that much of the expansion of welfare programs can be accounted for as a function of "economic growth and its demographic and bureaucratic outcomes" (Wilensky 1975, xiii). In other words, once societies attain certain thresholds of economic development, all begin to pass social security, health, and other forms of welfare legislation, and over time they devote an increasing share of the public purse to these programs.

Though the Netherlands was one of the countries in Wilensky's study, applying generalizations from it to the Dutch case remains problematic. The problem lies in Wilensky's major demographic variable, age of the population. The greater the proportion of the population above the age of 65, according to Wilensky, the greater the degree of spending. It is true that the Netherlands has a graying population. From 1948 to 1982, for example, the percentage of Dutch over the age of 65 has steadily increased from 7.74 percent to 11.73 percent; indeed, the number of elderly doubled, increasing from roughly 780,000 in 1948 to 1,680,000 in 1982 (Braakman et al. 1984, 178).

The growth in pension expenditures, however, was not as constant as population growth. Pension benefits remained steady until the late 1950s but have grown rapidly since then. To understand

9

the different pattern of expenditure on pensions, it is important to keep in mind that an entirely new pension program was adopted in 1957 (see fig. 1.2). Changes of this sort may be influenced by demographic factors, but they are ultimately political decisions, and observing changes in demographic indicators does not explain why a country adopts a new program or dramatically revises an existing one. In short, Wilensky's study helps us understand some of the reasons why the Dutch welfare state grew, but it cannot account for its late response to demographic pressures or for its relatively rapid growth.

Peter Flora and Jens Alber (1981) offer another socioeconomic explanation designed to address the influence of politics. They accept Wilensky's premise that economic development, specifically industrialization, fosters growth in the welfare state. But to increase the model's explanatory power, they add measures of political development. The assumption is that as the extension of voting rights enfranchises groups in society that favor expansion of welfare, such as the working class, governments will increase expenditures. Though this model marks an improvement over Wilensky's, the authors admit that it still does not explain the case of the Netherlands because development there was much later than the model would predict. Flora and Alber attribute this variation to a strong tradition of voluntary welfare services that reduced the demand for state intervention (Flora and Alber 1981, 43). This may explain why the Dutch case remained a laggard, but it cannot account for the transformation of the Netherlands into a welfare leader. Other states (e.g., Japan, Switzerland, and the United States) have relied on the private sector rather than developing public welfare programs, but they all remain laggards (Moseley 1983).

David Cameron (1978) offers a socioeconomic explanation that focuses specifically on the smaller European countries, including the Netherlands. He argues that countries with small, internationally open economies are likely to make substantial welfare provisions to serve as a buffer against the vagaries of the international economic system. A high degree of industrial concen-

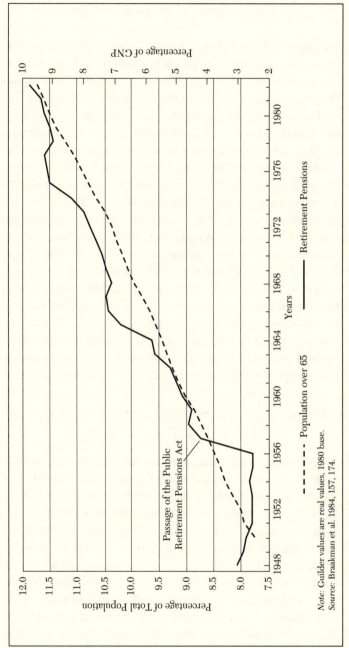

Figure 1.2 Growth in Retirement Pensions Compared with Size of Gray Population

Percentage of GNP

Percentage of Total Population

Years

Passage of the Public
Retirement Pensions Act

- - - - - Population over 65   ——— Retirement Pensions

Note: Guilder values are real values, 1980 base.
Source: Braakman et al. 1984, 157, 174.

tration, a high level of unionization, a broad scope of collective bargaining, and strong labor confederations make it possible for open economies to develop welfare programs. The difficulty with this explanation is that the periods of development of the Dutch welfare state do not correspond with increases in any of these conditions. Actually, the postwar expansion corresponds with a decline in the bargaining position of labor (Kooten 1988). Dutch workers have never been highly unionized, and the strength of labor confederations is undermined by ideological differences among unions. As with the French labor movement, these ideological divisions more often produce squabbles among unions than a unified labor voice (Windmuller 1969). Cameron's argument could explain the comparative position of the Netherlands as a welfare laggard but not the transition to leader.

In sum, none of the sociological explanations can account for the historic pattern of growth in the Dutch welfare state. The reason for this is that they deemphasize the importance of politics or reduce it to the status of an intervening variable. But, as the next section demonstrates, most of the efforts to measure political variables still fail to account for the Dutch case.

THE INCOMPLETENESS OF POLITICAL EXPLANATIONS
The Thesis of the Power of the Left

Besides the sociological explanations of the welfare state, one finds a number of political ones. Explaining divergence, or the reasons for dissimilarities, is central to accounts of this type. Growth in the welfare state is considered a product of debates in policy-making institutions and the capacity of powerful actors within them to affect the enactment of welfare provisions. In addition, the relative position of a country as a laggard or leader can be attributed to its domestic politics. Hence the focus is on cross-national differences in policy processes and political mobilization. From the multitude of studies one can distill two major variations on this theme. The first focuses on the political power of the left, while the second concentrates on institutional analysis. The work of John Stephens, Walter Korpi, and Michael Shalev is representative of the former.

Walter Korpi and Michael Shalev (Korpi and Shalev 1980; Korpi 1980) claim that the balance of political power in civic society manifests itself as a conflict between the socialist working class and bourgeois capitalist forces. They develop a "power difference" model, which tests the political mobilization of the working class according to five criteria: a high level of union organization; industrial rather than craft unionism; cooperation between blue- and white-collar unions; the existence of a strong central union that coordinates activities; and a close cooperation between the central union and the dominant party of the left (Korpi and Shalev 1980). As labor increases its power in these areas, conflict between labor and capital will manifest itself first in an increase in industrial strikes and then in a shift from the industrial to political arena. Following this, to the extent that the dominant forces of the left achieve "control over the government, they will use the government machinery for redistribution" (Korpi and Shalev 1980, 325). Control of the state is measured according to participation of socialist parties in the cabinet.

The Netherlands is one of the countries included in Korpi and Shalev's study. According to their findings, the country is characterized by a medium level of working-class mobilization (30 percent), a medium level of representation of the left in the cabinet, but a low share of cabinet positions (Korpi and Shalev 1980, 317). In terms of the model, Korpi and Shalev admit that both the Netherlands and Switzerland stand out as deviant cases. "The Netherlands and especially Switzerland have had low levels of industrial conflict since about 1920, and already had the lowest levels of strike activity in Western Europe before the First World War" (Korpi and Shalev 1980, 323). Thus both countries fail to meet the necessary conditions of conflict in the industrial arena that must precede political mobilization of the working class.

The authors offer four circumstances that may explain the Swiss deviance: religious cleavages that have hindered working-class mobilization; strong linguistic differences; a generally high standard of living despite high levels of inequality of income; and an emphasis on internal stability resulting from the external threat posed by a precarious position between two fascist regimes. While these assumptions may be post hoc and irrelevant to the theory, cumulatively they may be significant.

The Netherlands, however, has experienced none of these impediments save strong religious cleavages among the working class (it has enjoyed a high standard of living, but without dramatic income differentials). Korpi and Shalev acknowledge that if religious cleavages are the major factor in the Netherlands, it brings their whole model into question. Thus, to rescue it, they assert that the experience of both deviant cases indicates that a process of political bargaining and compromise may operate to some extent even if labor has acquired no strong and stable control over political power. After they have employed such a post hoc rationalization to explain a case as significant as the Netherlands, one wonders why the authors conclude that "nevertheless, the element of political power and behind it the collective mobilization of the working class must be central to an adequate explanation" (Korpi and Shalev 1980, 328).

To account for the possible influence of religion, John Stephens (1979) offers an alternative version of the thesis of the power of the left. Stephens also argues that the welfare state is a product of the growing strength of labor in civil society, as measured by the hegemony of the socialist movement in society and a strong role of the socialist party in government. But Stephens also states that a strong Catholic party can be powerful if it has a strong working-class base and is a center party. Catholic parties are important because of the anticapitalist aspects of Catholic ideology. According to Stephens, Catholic promotion of welfare policies comes as a result of coalitions between Catholic center parties and social democratic parties. And, when a welfare state is developed by a social democratic/Catholic coalition, public spending will not be as progressively financed as when the social democrats are dominant members of the coalition. Stephens cites the Netherlands, Austria, and Belgium as examples of this arrangement.

The major problem for Stephens's explanation stems from his assumption that stable control of the state by a socialist party or a socialist/Catholic coalition is necessary. The 1950s were the first time in the postwar period that either of these conditions were met. From 1946 until 1958 the Netherlands was ruled by "Red-Roman" coalitions of the Labor and Catholic parties. During this time some social welfare reforms were instituted; however, the coalitions were characterized by remarkable instability. Only one of these governments survived a full parliamentary term. Indeed, the parliamentary coalition between the Catholics and socialists was strained, as was manifest in long debates over the formation of governments that in one case lasted 122 days.

The evidence most devastating to Stephens's theory, however, is the fact that the bulk of social policy reform was enacted by center-right coalitions in the 1960s. In light of this, Jacques van Doorn (1978) argues that the Dutch experience confirms the contention that welfare policy is a response by weak governments that is designed to control social forces rather than a reflection of the political hegemony of a socialist labor movement.

Stephens recognizes that the Netherlands "seems to be a deviant case" because of its lower level of labor organization and shorter period of socialist rule. "It may be that the Dutch system of bargaining centralization owes more to the combination of a very heavy export dependency and the 'politics of accommodation (Lijphart 1968) than to the political and economic strength of the labor movement" (Stephens 1979, 124). Thus the major difficulty for both of these explanations based on the power of the left is that the Dutch left has not been powerful.

Another variant of the thesis of the power of the left argues that instead of a strong left, a weak right could be a factor in growth of the welfare state (Castles and McKinlay 1979; Castles 1986). This model assumes that political parties of the right constitute the main impediment to the development of welfare policies and that a strong degree of electoral support for rightist parties indicates a rejection of the welfare state. In this model the Netherlands appears to stand out as the epitome of the argument. By Castles and McKinlay's measurement, the level of welfare there is the absolute highest of all countries examined. In addition, the proportion of the vote for the major party of the right (the Liberal party) is the absolute lowest (11.8 percent). However, this explanation ignores some crucial contextual factors in the Netherlands.

Dutch politics is characterized by electoral competition of a large number of parties. Relative to multiparty systems, the percentage of the vote for the Liberal party is more significant than Castles and McKinlay's findings would indicate. Indeed, the Liberal party has usually received the fourth or fifth largest percentage of the vote in postwar elections (Daudt 1982). Also, though the Liberal party is the largest rightist party, it is not the only one. Hence the total vote for the political right cannot be based on the vote for one party.

Perhaps the greatest problem for the thesis based on the weakness of the right is the assumption that electoral support is an indication of party power. The multiparty nature of Dutch politics necessitates coalition government, and the Liberal party has participated in half of the postwar coalitions. In fact, it was a coalition partner when many of the welfare programs were enacted. Also, the Liberal party does not compare well with rightist parties in other countries. In principle, the party opposes welfare policies as an infringement on personal liberties, but the official party platform has stressed the necessity of welfare to promote social harmony (Lipschits 1969). Acceptance of welfare policies constitutes a pragmatic concession necessary to participate in the governing coalitions. Indeed, the main debate dividing the Dutch left and right has not been about the desirability of the welfare state but about the methods and timing of welfare provisions (Schendelen 1983).

The general problem in applying the thesis of the power of the left to the Dutch case is the assumption that the political center is neutral with respect to issues concerning the welfare state. This discounts the importance of Christian Democratic parties, and is especially true for the Netherlands (Becker and Kersbergen 1986), where religious parties were in power when the major expansion of the welfare state occurred. Moreover, it is an issue relevant to other countries. Giovanni Sartori (1966) has long maintained that Italian political parties cannot be reduced to a single left-right dimension but that this must be combined with a clerical-laical dimension. The observation is just as important for the Dutch case. Thus, to understand the significance of political parties for the development of a welfare state, what is needed is a more sophisticated understanding of the ideological diversity among parties and the way they develop and pursue policy issues.

State Capacities: The Untested Thesis

The party system is not the only unique contextual factor in the Netherlands. Many of the authors examined in the previous section suggested that the way Dutch political institutions operate may provide the answers to the perplexing questions about the development of its welfare state. Studies that focus on institutions as factors in the development of policy constitute the other major explanation of divergent patterns. But most of the institutionalist explanations of the welfare state have not been applied to the case of the Netherlands. Indeed, they need to be revised before they can be used to examine it.

One can only speculate as to the reason why institutionalist scholars have overlooked the Netherlands. Most likely, it is a combination of the inaccessibility of the Dutch language and the limitations of institutional analysis. Basically, institutional analysis involves studying the activities of groups and individuals — the strategies and tactics they employ to influence political decisions — and the constraints on their behavior imposed by their institutional context (Krasner 1988). Despite a few efforts to identify quantifiable variables in institutional analysis (e.g., Bates 1988), most scholars who employ this type of analysis do so from a historical perspective. It is the historical method that limits the empirical scope of the research. Unlike quantitative studies, which require statistical significance to demonstrate causal relationships, historical studies use interpretation to show causality. Since the data necessary for such studies require detailed exposition, it is virtually impossible to examine adequately more than a handful of cases. The Netherlands simply has not been included as one of the cases.

Though the Dutch case has not been examined by institutionalist scholars, there are reasons to suspect that the prevailing explanations would be of little help. Studies of this type are based on a limited set of cases and often identify significant factors that are extrapolated from those few cases. For example, because the policy-making process in the United States has been the subject of a great deal of inquiry, it is generally acknowledged that public policy develops in incremental stages over a long period (see, e.g., Lindblom 1959). Historical studies of the development of welfare states in Sweden and Britain confirm this (Ashford 1986; Heclo 1974). But the Dutch pattern differed, having developed very rapidly. An institutional approach that included the Dutch case would have to account for rapid change in policy as a theoretical possibility (see Cox 1992b).

The work of Theda Skocpol and her coauthors (Skocpol 1980; Weir and Skocpol 1983; Orloff and Skocpol 1984) represents an attempt to develop a broad theory of the development of the welfare state within the institutionalist paradigm. For Skocpol, the explanation lies in the capacity of the state to behave as an autonomous actor. Thus the more centralized state institutions are and the more autonomous that state is from its society, the more likely it is that a welfare state will develop. As evidence of this, Skocpol and her colleagues demonstrate that the relatively centralized Swedish state facilitated development of the welfare state there, while a minimalist state captured by business interests impeded it in the United States. Within this general framework, changes that do occur in public policy can be explained as products of certain "critical junctures" in the historic sequence of political development. These critical junctures are initiated by institutional changes in the state bureaucracy or by attitudinal changes of state personnel, which in turn make new policies possible. In the United States, the New Deal became possible after the institutional position of the Supreme Court and business leaders (both of which opposed the adoption of welfare) had been weakened and the power of the executive branch had been enhanced (Weir and Skocpol 1983).

To apply this approach to the Dutch case, one would have to demonstrate how a weak state accounts for the position of the Netherlands as a comparative laggard throughout most of this century. Then the model would have to identify a critical juncture in the 1960s to explain the rapid development of the Dutch welfare state. In other words, it would have to be shown that the Dutch state became centralized and/or autonomous during that decade. However, no such critical juncture occurred.

Though many have observed that Dutch society underwent dramatic upheaval at the end of the 1960s (Lijphart 1975; Schendelen 1983; Mierlo 1986), the timing of this change did not coincide with expansion of the welfare state. Nor did the state become more centralized when the welfare state expanded. Indeed, the type of state that has existed throughout this century defies characterization as either a strong or a weak state. Corporatism has characterized the structure of the Dutch state, and the greatest shortcoming of Skocpol's thesis — or any institutionalist thesis, for that matter — is that it has not focused on the way corporatism influences the development of social welfare policy. (This is an important issue in the literature on corporatism and is addressed in greater detail in chap. 2.)

RECONSIDERING THE DEVELOPMENT OF THE WELFARE STATE

The foregoing discussion points to three puzzling aspects that make it difficult to explain the development of the Dutch welfare state: the timing of that development did not coincide with socioeconomic changes; it was not a result of the political power of the left; and the corporatist structure of the state poses problems for the thesis based on the state's capacity to act autonomously. One could dismiss the problem by claiming that the Dutch case is simply different and therefore requires its own explanation. I would argue against such a quick dismissal, on the grounds that the Dutch welfare state is one of the largest and most significant. If theory cannot explain the best examples, then it is theory, and not the cases, that should be questioned.

Perhaps the most important problem in accounting for the Dutch case lies in the overreliance on quantitative measures of growth and the assumption that correlations between spending and other quantifiable variables implies causality. As Alber, Esping-Andersen, and Rainwater have noted, "Social classes and political parties never struggled over spending volumes per se; they fought over eligibility rules, coverage principles, targeting versus universalism, financial burdens, benefit levels and, perhaps most importantly, the boundaries of social citizenship rights" (1987, 463).

This is a crucial point for reconsidering the Dutch case. Though expenditures on social welfare have increased in the Netherlands, this growth resulted from a qualitative shift in the character of welfare provisions. Prior to World War II, social security provisions were of two types: workers' insurance and poor relief. Entitlement to the workers' insurance benefits was based on an individual's participation in the work force and history of premium payments. Those who paid no premiums received no benefits, and workers who did pay were entitled to benefits only for a period equal to the time they had been in the work force. The system of poor relief, which provided assistance to nonworking members of the population as well as to former workers whose insurance benefits had expired, provided minimal income assistance and was administered primarily by private charities. Following World War II, dramatic changes were instituted in these programs. In addition to the workers' insurance, public insurance programs were enacted, which instituted universal benefit entitlements for retirees, the disabled, the sick, and widows and orphans. Also, a means-tested program of public assistance, adopted in 1963, replaced the earlier reliance on private charities.

Quantitative measures cannot explain such qualitative shifts in the scope of welfare programs, and they certainly cannot explain variations in the timing and speed of these changes. Yet the correlations are significant for a number of countries. Therefore, the theoretical claims on which they are based cannot be rejected without running the risk of losing theoretical power. This means that the major theoretical concern should be readjusting the hypotheses of these models so that they may be more inclusive.

The form this reconceptualization of the development of the welfare state takes is the subject of chapter 2. For the moment, I offer a brief synopsis of my argument. Generally, I take the major explanations from the preceding discussion and recast them in a way that will encompass the Dutch case but that does not weaken their comparative utility. For the first two factors this involves replacing quantitative with contextual measures. For the third, this involves conceptualizing the impact a corporatist state has on the development of welfare programs.

The revision I offer to the first factor is to abandon the assumption that social policies automatically arise from certain changes in socioeconomic conditions. Instead, I argue that the specific development of a welfare state will result from the ways policy makers perceive the problems that arise from socioeconomic change and from the way they conceive policy responses. In focusing on the policy maker rather than structural transformation as the source of policy ideas, I put the emphasis on individual attitudes, opinions, and preferences rather than rational and systematic response to social conditions. This model opens the possibility for much cross-national diversity in policies formulated in response to the same idea. But the major goal of the sociological explanations was to explain the convergent development of welfare states.

Thus the challenge is to develop a mechanism whereby the preferences of policy makers can still account for convergent patterns. The task is made simple by the existence of such a model already: policy borrowing. This model argues that when confronted with problems they wish to address, policy makers often copy ideas from other countries. It explains the similarity of policy patterns among states in the United States, as well as the similarity of many social security programs that are variations on the schemes Otto von Bismarck introduced in imperial Germany. Indeed, policy borrowing is a simple and almost obvious explanation for the frequency, in socialist as well as liberal democratic countries, with which some form of social insurance serves as the mechanism for providing social welfare benefits to the population. It seems curious, therefore, that theorists of the development of the welfare state generally ignore the impact of borrowing (Alber et al. 1987).

To revise the theory that relies on the power of the left to explain the development of the welfare state, I retain the assumption that societal groups organized for political purposes can have a dramatic effect on final policy, but I drop the ideological association between social policy and the political left. This revision is necessary to account for the building of the Dutch welfare state by Catholics rather than socialists. A more important reason to drop this narrow association is that, when we stop reducing political contest to left-right conflict, it frees us to focus more broadly on the political dynamic of group behavior. In other words, a larger conceptualization makes it possible to examine the reasons for group organization, their political strategies and objectives, and their relative power rather than assume these a priori.

Individuals and groups all operate within an institutional context. And institutions impose constraints on the range of alternative policies that are feasible. This is the important lesson to be learned from the thesis that rests on the state's capacity to act autonomously. But when all states are placed on a weak-strong continuum, the explanation is irrelevant for the Dutch case. The corporatist state has a different structural relationship to society. Rather than being a weak state that is captured by society or a strong one that is autonomous of it, corporatism completely blurs the distinction between state and society. Furthermore, theories of corporatism suggest that in addition to possessing a different structure, corporatism performs a different type of function. It is intended to rationalize and facilitate coordination in policy decisions. To make the thesis of the state's capacity relevant to the Dutch context, it must be made to explicate the impact of a corporatist state on policy outcomes.

Indeed, perhaps corporatism properly defined and tested could provide a sufficient explanation of the Dutch welfare state, in which case the other factors would be unnecessary. I submit that this is not true and that corporatism is necessary but not sufficient for explaining the Dutch case. All three factors are crucial to understanding it. Corporatism alone does not explain why Dutch social welfare programs so closely resemble those in other countries. Borrowing helps us understand how and why policy makers looked to Germany and then to Britain for ideas. In addition, corporatism did not just appear in the Netherlands. It is an institutional structure created to fulfill the political purpose of certain groups that were important to the process of state building. To isolate corporatism from its historical context does not give a complete explanation of the real differences between the Dutch version of corporatism and those that exist in other countries.

OUTLINE OF THE STUDY

This study is an effort to explain the late but rapid growth of the Dutch welfare state. I have suggested that to focus on the politics of the welfare state, one needs to employ a perspective that analyzes the strategies and tactics of specific actors in the policy process. To do this for all the programs that comprise the Dutch welfare state would be a herculean task. Instead, I trace the development of three programs that illustrate the major factors in the development of the system. The attention is on income maintenance programs, specifically retirement pensions, public assistance, and disability. The study traces the adoption of these programs and the changes introduced during the period of welfare reform in the 1960s.

For a number of reasons these programs exhibit all the important characteristics of the growth of the Dutch welfare state. Adoption of pensions and disability and other social insurance programs at the turn of the century created the institutions of Dutch corporatism. These, along with the original poor relief program (the predecessor to public assistance), illustrate the role of religious forces in the construction of the corporatist state.

Also, these were the three most controversial programs during the postwar period of welfare reform. The controversy centered on the question of whether the insurance schemes should be expanded to become universal or remain exclusive to the working population. Public assistance was an area of great conflict between secular and laical forces over the relative autonomy of the church and the state in providing assistance to the poor. Retirement pensions were the first in the series to become universalized. The history of this program, therefore illustrates the tactics used by proponents of reform that were repeated to achieve the universalization of other programs. The public assistance program was created in the middle of the period of universalization and illustrates how changes in corporatist relations led to changes in policy outcomes. The disability program was the last to be enacted. By the time of its passage in the 1970s, politics had changed in the Netherlands, and this reform provides an indication of the new politics.

I have left out health insurance, the other major universal scheme in the Netherlands, mainly because, for understanding the process of borrowing, it is theoretically uninteresting. The three programs in this study were inspired by observations of similar ones in other countries. At the turn of the century, it was the German example that inspired the adoption of workers' insurance programs. After World War II, it was the British Beveridge Report that prompted the universalization of the schemes. Dutch health insurance, however, was different. Though based on the German model, it was initiated during World War II at the instigation of Nazi occupation forces. Therefore, it is not a good case for examining policy borrowing, since Dutch policy makers did not spontaneously seek to emulate the German program and it was enacted with disregard for the existing institutional structure (Blanpain 1978). The other programs, by contrast, illustrate a more pure form of borrowing since ideas borrowed from abroad were adjusted to the domestic situation.

The connection between borrowing and the domestic situation — specifically among borrowing, the character of group mobilization, and the structure of political institutions — in the development of the welfare state may not be readily apparent. Illuminating the connections among the three major factors of this study is the purpose of chapter 2. Indeed, the basic purpose of the chapter is to demonstrate why the three factors are so important to understanding not only the Dutch case but the development of public policy generally. There is much anecdotal evidence that suggests borrowing, corporatism, and religious mobilization are important influences on policy in countries besides the Netherlands. Nonetheless, students of public policy tend to ignore these factors. In addition, the chapter provides a comprehensive overview of the corporatist organization of Dutch political institutions. Dutch corporatism is an opaque entity comprised of numerous bodies, councils, and organs, most with cross cutting memberships.

History has produced the complexity that characterizes Dutch corporatism. Chapter 3 focuses on its historical development and connects this with the adoption of social welfare programs. The chapter demonstrates how the early programs for poor relief and social security were influenced by the power of religious political forces. In addition to influencing the content of the programs, the religious forces were instrumental in creating a corporatist institutional structure. Understanding how and why these institutions were created is necessary to explain the late development of the Dutch welfare state.

Explaining this late development is the focus of chapter 4, which it examines how corporatist institutions distributed power over policy decisions to various societal interests. The corporatist power exercised by these groups is an important consideration since, immediately following World War II, there was a great surge of support among the public as well as among political leaders for universalization of welfare programs. Despite many efforts on the part of government officials to institute change, corporatist representation allowed opponents of welfare growth to impede the reforms.

But the reforms did finally take place, and their impact was dramatic. Chapter 5 examines the rapid growth of the Dutch welfare state in the 1960s and 1970s. It focuses on how changes in corporatism restructured policy making. Part of the change was a product of new forms of political mobilization on the part of groups that pressed the government for an expansion of programs. Together these developments created a rapid shift in policy that went beyond the expectations of any actor in the process.

Today the Dutch welfare state is one of the most extensive in the world. At a time when all western countries are facing severe fiscal constraints, it is also one of the most expensive. Chapter 6 examines how Dutch governments have attempted to cope with this problem. It traces the development of a government retrenchment policy that has been frustrated by the social forces that benefit from the welfare state. At a time when the Dutch state is attempting to cut back on social expenditure, the institutional relations created by the construction of the welfare state have fostered a new type of resistance to welfare reform.

A concluding chapter summarizes the major issues that account for the growth of the Dutch welfare state and places them in a comparative perspective. It assesses the significance of borrowing as an explanation of convergence. Also, it draws attention to the themes of political mobilization and institutional structures as factors that account for divergence in the development of policy. The major conclusion to be drawn is that, while the Dutch welfare state represents a unique pattern of development, it is not the factors that are unique. Rather, it was the way they came together in the context of Ducth politics that produced the specific pattern.

2

Reconsidering the Development of the Welfare State: Suggestions from the Dutch Case

"Discovery commences with the awareness of anomaly, . . . And it closes only when the paradigm theory has been adjusted so that the anomalous has become the expected."
—Thomas Kuhn (1970, 52–53)

"The primary task of a useful teacher is to teach his students to recognize 'inconvenient' facts — I mean facts that are inconvenient for their party opinions."
— Max Weber (1958, 147)

To say that the Dutch welfare state presents a challenge to theories of development of the welfare state is to claim that it constitutes what Thomas Kuhn (1970, 52–53) calls an anomaly. Many have discovered this anomaly; some have even tried to explain it. As the previous chapter shows, these efforts have not been successful. Kuhn states that first efforts to explain anomalies usually are characterized by a reluctance to abandon basic assumptions. Instead, scientists strive to adjust the existing paradigm in ways that incorporate the anomalous case. Ultimately this effort is doomed to failure because, until basic assumptions are questioned and adjusted, reasserting the set of assumptions that produced the anomaly will never succeed in accounting for it.

Yet Kuhn also shows how a resistance to new interpretations serves a useful purpose. It prevents science from being lightly distracted. In other words, the challenging explanation must not only provide a plausible account of the anomaly, but it must also demonstrate how elements of the paradigm need to be reconsidered. The preceding chapter identified the Dutch anomaly and the overlooked factors that must constitute its explanation. The purpose of this chapter is to demonstrate how these factors should inform new ways of theorizing about the development of the welfare state. Hence the specific goal is to illustrate exactly why a rethinking of borrowing, political mobilization, and the structure of state (corporatist) institutions can not only explain the Dutch case but also broaden our understanding of the comparative development of the welfare state.

Indeed, the issues to be raised in this chapter hardly constitute a shift in the paradigm. Because I do not believe it is necessary, I am not proposing a radically new interpretation of the development of the welfare state. Rather, my intention is to articulate a way of conceptualizing it that has broader comparative utility. To do this, we need not abandon the essential components of existing explanations, but we must relieve them of some of the ideological baggage they carry. This can be achieved if the theoretical components are pitched at a higher level of abstraction. Most efforts to theorize about the welfare state share one basic shortcoming: they fail to operate at an adequately high level of abstraction. This causes them to confuse contextual facts with theoretical conditions. The point is relevant for all of the three factors that comprise an explanation of the Dutch case.

I have suggested that borrowing is one of three important overlooked elements in explaining the convergent development of the welfare state. But this line of argument stands in contrast to the approaches that emphasize large-scale socioeconomic change as the common denominator. Borrowing has been overlooked because it constitutes a challenge to the accepted methodological orthodoxy of these sociological approaches. Generally, sociological studies of the development of policy base their claims on quantitative data. Borrowing has been criticized on methodological grounds as untestable and anecdotal because it depends on psychological interpretation of individual behavior and motives. The challenge, then, is to demonstrate why the actions and motivations of policy makers are determinant factors in the formulation of policy.

The second factor in the explanation of the Dutch welfare state is the power of religious political groups to influence the timing and content of welfare policy. In comparative perspective it is curious that the Dutch welfare state was built under the aegis of a Catholic rather than a social democratic party. Here the problem lies not in a methodological bias but in an ideological one. Attempts to understand any form of collective mobilization must focus on what the group does rather than infer its activities from its ideology.

Understanding the nature of political institutions is a third crucial factor for explaining the development of the Dutch welfare state. Yet, despite the proliferation of institutional studies, they are still inappropriate for the Dutch case. For example, the relationship between the state and society is portrayed as a dichotomous variable by those who study welfare policy: the state is either autonomous or nonautonomous from society. Corporatism, which characterizes Dutch political institutions, represents a more complicated variant of state-society relations. And though many scholars have studied corporatism, most have made claims about how it operates that simply do not apply to the Netherlands. Among North American scholars corporatism is held aloft and idealized as an example of a harmonious and efficient means of reaching decisions on policy. Dutch corporatism is characterized by levels of conflict and competition that scholars usually identify with pluralism. To the extent that the Dutch pattern resembles corporatism in other countries, a more accurate understanding of corporatism is in order.

These are more than factors that need to be tested to explain the Dutch case. All are necessary components of an adequate theory of the development of the welfare state. The last theme for this chapter is to describe how they fit together as a theory. Broad theory should operate at different levels of analysis. Most of the recent studies of the welfare state isolate a particular level of analysis and explore its implications. Collectively such research has been extremely useful for identifying and elaborating the various factors in the development of the welfare state. Concern now, however, should concentrate on integrating into a broader framework factors that operate on different levels of analysis. My effort to do this begins with the assumption that broad theory should operate at three levels of analysis: it should simultaneously account for the actions of individuals, group dynamics, and the larger institutional context. Certainly any decent piece of research draws attention to these three factors, but few treat them systematically as theoretical factors.

WHY WELFARE STATES DEVELOP: THE CASE FOR POLICY BORROWING

Throughout the world, states respond to the needs of their populations in remarkably similar ways. In other words, there is a great deal of convergence in the character of welfare states. Take, for example, the case of social security. Most programs are similar in the sense that they involve a major redistribution of financial resources from a working population to a nonworking one. This is usually effected through a special tax on employers and/or employees that is distributed to members of the population unable to work. In all cases, social security involves an expanded notion of the wage contract, whereby the obligation between employer and employee transcends a specific remuneration for labor performed by recognizing an obligation to provide for the financial needs of employees when they are no longer able to work. The state either assumes the task of ensuring that employers meet this obligation or takes full responsibility for administration of the programs. Though there are variations in specifics, most countries have adopted a social security program that is similar to the ones originally established by Otto von Bismarck in imperial Germany (Briggs 1985).

There is a dispute in the academic literature about the reasons for the remarkable similarity among welfare states. The most widely held belief is that the welfare state is a response to similar types of socioeconomic problems that confront all modern societies. In other words, there are certain prerequisites that societies must meet before they have a need to develop welfare programs. Urbanization and industrialization have created housing pressures and health problems for those who live in congested cities. Industrialization in the context of a capitalist market means that economies undergo fluctuations, and unemployment becomes a consequence of economic downturn. Unemployment is also fostered by structural changes in the economy, brought on by technological developments that leave workers unable to adapt to the changes. Social modernization has broken down the traditional ties of community and kinship through which much care and support for individuals had always been organized.

But this approach does not explain all there is to explain about the similarity of welfare programs around the globe. It is not enough to say that problems exist in an objective sense and then are acted on by policy makers. Perceptions of problems differ, and it is this difference that makes for differences in how people chose to act. The nature of a problem may suggest a certain type of solution, but there are often many ways to address a single problem. The solution chosen will have much to do with how the original actors in the policy process perceive the problem and how they understand the viability of alternative solutions.

Two bits of knowledge gleaned from our understanding of the way policy is made in the United States can be useful in this context. First, policy makers are not scientists. We tend to assume that in the rationalistic modern world reasonable people will strive to find scientifically ideal solutions to policy problems. Students of public policy, however, continually remind us that this is not necessarily true. Policy makers operate under very real constraints. Some are physical, such as time limits and physical limits on resources, and require them to adopt less than ideal solutions (Lindblom 1959). A more real constraint stems from perceptions. Policy makers are human beings who possess individualized cognitive perceptions of the world they inhabit, and these perceptions influence their thought (Rein 1983). They may share with their colleagues some elements of this worldview, especially those that constitute shared values within a society, such as conceptions of justice or individual rights (Anderson 1979).

The second important lesson to be learned from the policy-making process in the United States is that most policy makers are not original thinkers. They do not sit in their offices and create solutions. More often, they look at how their counterparts in other states have attempted to solve similar problems. That is not to say that they are intellectually unsophisticated. Indeed, it is a mark of intellectual sophistication to be capable of learning from others. In the academic literature this process has been given a variety of names that I will call policy borrowing. (The various names are policy diffusion [Collier and Messick 1975], political learning [Heclo 1974], lesson drawing [Rose 1991], and policy transfer [Wolman 1992].)

Policy borrowing is not a prominent theme in the comparative study of public policy, though it has gained attention in recent years (see, e.g., Bennett 1991). Most of the studies that examine the process have focused on the transfer of policy ideas among states in the United States (see, e.g., Walker 1969). In the comparative literature on the welfare state, David Collier and Richard Messick (1975) have demonstrated that many countries in Asia and Africa began to institute social welfare long before they attained the hypothetically necessary levels of social and economic development. For example, many countries in Africa and the Middle East introduced social security programs while most of their populations were still primarily engaged in agricultural rather than industrial production. What this fact indicates is that there is a learning curve in the comparative development of welfare states. Whereas welfare innovators developed policies in response to specific problems brought on by industrialization, later states were able to develop policy before encountering such problems because they had the experience of other nations to learn from. Collier and Messick conclude that the premature adoption of programs and the similarity between programs adopted in imperial countries and in their former colonies suggest some direct lines of policy communication.

Reconsidering Welfare State Development

The biographical records of many influential figures in the development of welfare states provide further empirical evidence for the borrowing thesis. Perhaps the best-known case is that of William Beveridge, considered the major figure in the postwar development of the British welfare state. Beveridge's ideas for reform were influenced by his experience in Berlin, where he observed Bismarck's system of social security in practice (Furniss and Tilton 1977). The founder of social insurance in Japan, Goto Shimpei, provides another example of policy borrowing. The programs he developed were inspired by his observation of European social insurance while he was a medical student in Germany (Lewis 1981). Even the geographic isolation of the United States did not prevent Franklin Roosevelt from looking to other countries for ideas for social welfare legislation. Daniel Boorstin reports that Roosevelt commanded his staff to "look over the housing and social insurance schemes in England, Germany, Austria and Italy" (Boorstin 1960, 33).

While these are anecdotal examples that merely make the case for the transfer of ideas, they do not establish any etiological sequence in the development of public policy. Since the hallmark of good scientific theory is the explanation of causal linkages between phenomena, the test of the borrowing thesis would be its ability to do so. What needs to be demonstrated is that the initiators of public policy consciously borrow ideas from programs developed in other countries *and* that these ideas become realized in policy outcomes. Determining how the initiators of policy derive their ideas can be accomplished through a biographical study of the those involved. There are difficulties in this approach since the biographical records of important figures in the development of welfare policy are less complete than are the historical records of large sociological processes.

Though this problem makes the task of studying policy borrowing more difficult, it does not render it impossible. As Hugh Heclo's (1974) study of the British and Swedish welfare states demonstrates, in many instances the historical records are sufficiently complete for the examination of policy borrowing. A strong case for it must rest on identification of the specific instances of cross-national borrowing. Doing so requires two concerns for micro-level analysis: the individuals who influence the formation of policy and the history of the programs under investigation. To make the case for borrowing, the research questions then become:

Why do policy makers look to other countries?
What countries do they look at?
Which ideas do they borrow?
What use is made of the information?

Policies may be borrowed from other countries because policy makers are social theorists as much as they are problem solvers. Their decisions serve to direct a society toward the realization of certain conceptions of social justice or right that, whether implicit or explicit, underlie their proposals. To the extent that such efforts to direct society are explicit, the search of other countries may have much to do with what Reinhard Bendix (1978) calls the demonstration effect. In his study of nineteenth-century bourgeois revolutions, Bendix argued that it was the observation of economic advancement in other countries that motivated a growing intelligentsia to find a more viable mode of social organization for its own country. Perhaps, as more than social theorists, policy makers should be viewed as practitioners of comparative public policy: as individuals who, when confronted with social problems, look to the successful and failed policies of other countries in dealing with similar problems and who then try to bring the lessons home. In the recent literature, this type of transfer is labeled emulation (Bennett 1991).

From the literature, it seems reasonable to assume that policy makers look for new ideas to countries that have (or are perceived to have) problems similar to the one(s) they wish to address. The search is then an easy one of identifying nations that have similar problems and studying their solutions (Lutz 1989). Still, the search of the world for new policy ideas is not usually unlimited. Often it is restricted in geographic scope. Countries close to one another are often similar in many ways. Lines of communication are also stronger among countries where people know each other's language. Much of the trading of policy ideas in Europe, for example, is done by Europeans among themselves. And many third world nations have adopted welfare states that look similar to those of their former colonial rulers (Collier and Messick 1975). In summary, it is theoretically conceivable that any country could be the subject of an investigation by policy makers looking for innovative solutions to problems, but the practical reality is that transfer occurs when there are lines of communication among policy elites in different countries (Bennett 1991).

What is borrowed from another country is also a question with a straightforward answer. At an abstract level it may be a principle or a particular conception of entitlement. At the practical level it may be anything from an administrative technique to an entire program.

The foregoing discussion shows that policy borrowing does lend itself to rigorous investigation. Exploration of the biographical records of important policy makers can provide evidence of the extent to which they engage in the practice of learning from abroad. Examination of the history of legislation can show whether or not the ideas from abroad actually inform legislative developments and provides a way to examine the psychological dimensions of political activity. Discovering what things policy makers borrow from abroad gives clues to their perceptions of problems in their own country. Understanding the psychology of individual policy makers, then, makes it possible to understand strategies they employ to realize their preferred policies as well as their capabilities as political actors.

Yet the reasons why policy makers develop proposals and pursue them do not explain everything about policy outcomes. Eric Nordlinger (1981) has suggested that in no democratic state are policy makers entirely autonomous. Their ability to have certain preferences realized says much about their political acumen, but their proposals must also be subjected to the scrutiny of other actors in the political process. At this point the ideas may be transformed and adjusted, even scuttled. A fuller understanding of specific policy developments needs to take account of the politics of policy making, and the way in which politics may lead to revisions in ideas borrowed from abroad.

PLACING THE POWER OF THE LEFT IN CONTEXT: THE DYNAMICS OF COLLECTIVE MOBILIZATION

Regardless of whether convergence is a product of borrowing or socioeconomic conditions, welfare states exhibit sometimes subtle, sometimes pronounced differences. Accounting for these then becomes an important concern for research and theorizing. Moreover, it draws attention to the politics of policy making. Policies vary among countries because of differences in the manner of reaching decisions. How a country makes decisions on policy is a function of the individual actors involved, the nature of political mobilization in that society, and the institutional context in which individuals and groups bring influence to bear on outcomes. The discussion of borrowing outlined some important themes for understanding the influence of particular individuals in the policy-making process. This leaves the nature of political mobilization and the structure of political institutions as crucial issues to explore. Variations in these two factors contribute to produce the differences in the world's welfare states. Indeed, they are perhaps the two most important factors in accounting for divergence of policy.

It is generally acknowledged that individuals are not the only actors in the formulation of policy but that groups are also important. In other words, a number of individuals acting in unison may be capable of bringing influence to bear on the policy-making process that could transcend the impact each could have acting alone. This point is recognized by those who have studied the history of the welfare state. But the major problem for applying much of the common wisdom to the Dutch case is that it identifies the wrong group as the one that built the welfare state. It was not a social democratic party; indeed, given the structure of the Dutch state, it would have been impossible for it to do so. The type of state that has existed in the Netherlands prevented Dutch socialists from pursuing their objectives, in part because it had been built by religious political forces to do precisely that. To understand the Dutch state and the development of welfare policy in the Netherlands, therefore, it is necessary to understand the way in which religion became an important political force and the impact it had on policies.

When it becomes a mobilized political force, religion can be understood as a type of collective action, or the total of actions taken by a number of individuals more or less organized and sharing a sense of purpose. This is a broad definition but one that encompasses the variety of ways historians, sociologists, and political scientists have come to understand collective action. Researchers in each of these areas have studied how different groups organize, espouse collective concerns, and follow with actions designed to realize certain objectives.

The predominant paradigm for understanding collective action is the one espoused by rational choice (Olson 1965, 1982; Birnbaum 1988). This paradigm posits that the behavior of a collective group follows the same psychological rules that govern individual behavior. The logic of collective action, as Mancur Olson refers to the rational choice interpretation of group activity, is premised on a belief that groups mobilize for the attainment of certain collective goods that are not guaranteed by the state. People opt to join and support such groups because of special incentives that membership offers them individually.

Indeed, the rational choice paradigm provides the logical underpinnings of the dominant interpretation of state-society relations in the United States of America. Pluralism, long regarded as the most accurate model of its political system, derives from the same premise that groups are collections of individuals. But whereas the traditional pluralist model viewed all collective movements as organizations that pursue the self-interest of their membership, the logic of collective action outlines how such movements can create positive externalities for the entire population. In both cases the state is still viewed as a referee that mediates among the social groups and responds to demands that are articulated by society (Birnbaum 1988; Krasner 1984). The model of social organization suggested by these perspectives is similar to the Newtonian vision of the physical world. For Newton the way to explain the physical world was to reduce it to its smallest parts (atoms), understand how they behave, and assume that the same basic logic can be aggregated to understand how collections of atoms (molecules) move about. It is a simple and concise explanation of behavior but one imbued with two crucial errors: a logical fallacy, and an assumption of empirical relevance.

The first error made by the rational choice approach is a logical fallacy. It is not possible to assume that the operant principles that guide individual behavior apply equally to collections of individuals. That the whole is more than a sum of its parts is a trite saying but one that applies in this instance. Indeed, physicists have long ago come to recognize this. Quantum mechanics led to the discovery that atoms were not simply the building blocks of larger units. Atoms are comprised of smaller particles that behave differently. Unlike atoms, quarks are charged energy particles, unpredictable in their movement. Therefore, the logic of the atom is distinct from the logic of its constituent parts. In addition, chaos theory is a new paradigm in the physical sciences that suggests our whole basis of understanding is limited by our frames of reference. When those frames are changed, different types of discoveries and relationships among entities become clear (Gleick 1987). Despite these discoveries in the physical sciences, the social sciences have been reluctant to let go of their attachment to nineteenth-century scientific principles. Rational choice is the quintessence of this anachronism.

In addition to the logical fallacy, the second error in the rational choice paradigm is assuming that all collective action has a rational basis. This limits the empirical relevance of the approach. For example, in his seminal work on the logic of collective action, Mancur Olson (1965) asserts that the model applies only to instances of rationally based collective action. It does not, according to Olson, pretend to account for collective behavior that may have irrational origins. On these grounds, Olson dismisses religion or philanthropic organizations as candidates for analysis (Olson 1965, 6n6, 61n17, 159–62). When he does this, however, he removes most of the types of behavior that are crucial to understanding modern collective action, especially those necessary for understanding politics in comparative perspective. A paradigm that cannot help us understand nationalism, religious fundamentalism, patriotism, or other forms of affectual behavior helps us understand very little of what people do. It is indisputable that these types of behavior are prominent and pervasive and have profound impact on politics in virtually every country of the world.

Indeed, the empirical limitation applies to individual as well as collective behavior. Albert Hirschman has argued that factors such as loyalty or passions are crucial to understanding how individuals behave (1970). Decades of voting studies that strove to uncover the rational calculations individuals make when they cast their ballots have discovered that the paradigm does not fully explain how people vote. Curiously, all this research has not prompted rational choice's adherents to abandon the paradigm in favor of better forms of explanation. Indeed, the new catchword for efforts to understand individual behavior is *preference* rather than *rational self-interest* (Olson 1982, 19n). Individuals may pursue things that are not in their self-interest, giving the appearance of irrationality; however, they may prefer those things, hence there is still a rationale for their behavior. But like the theories of rational collective action, this modification fails to explain the types of behavior with the most severe consequences for policy. It is inadequate, for example, to try to develop a reasonable policy on domestic violence based on the assumption that a man beats his wife because he prefers to do so.

It is crucial from an empirical as well as a theoretical standpoint that we move beyond assumptions of rationality in collective action and employ models that do a better job of making sense of the behavior of groups and of those individuals who act on the group's behalf. Perhaps the best place to begin is with groups such as religious ones that are excluded from the rational paradigm. Thus the Dutch case becomes a good starting point since religious mobilization in Dutch politics is a fine example of the type of collective action that the paradigm of rational choice strives not to explain.

If we accept a myriad of possible reasons for people to form organizations — that is, that other things in addition to self-interest and preference may inspire people to form an association — one common denominator becomes apparent. At least for those organizations that define a public objective as part of their reason for association, the members share a goal. To assume that collective action is goal oriented does not require the assumption that it is also rational. Indeed, to understand the significance of collective action, one needs less to assume its origins and more to focus on its consequences. In other words, collective action is important in the ways it is manifest and its effect on the political order. It is this issue that determines who people subscribe to the movement or what benefits they realize from membership. For example, the rational paradigm cannot explain why a pauper upholds allegiance to a church that offers a promise of salvation in a future life but little comfort in this one. If the paradigm argues that people prefer to gamble on their eternal souls rather than their temporal existence, it has violated its basic premise and has identified a rationalization rather than a rational calculation. In contrast, an approach that examines which elements of a collective organization can have such great appeal among those who have no rational reason to support it is one that unlocks a great mystery of political study.

Indeed, such situations must be explained by a theory because they are too common to be dismissed. A better way to make sense of them is to assume that some set of expectations, or a specific perception of the world, structures how people think about their situation. And these perceptions of the world are more or less culturally bound. Societies develop unique ways of structuring reality, and therefore people in different societies understand their worlds in different ways. Perhaps it is surprising that this is not a new notion. In the comparative study of politics, the idea that perceptions of reality are culturally bound is as old as the eighteenth-century writings of Baron de Montesquieu (1949, 1973). The modern version of this thesis is built upon a more variegated vocabulary, but the idea is essentially the same. Some call this phenomenon a shared idea of state power, or state tradition (Dyson 1980); others label it ideology (Sewell 1985; Grimmer 1978); still others have called it the mobilization of bias (Schattschneider 1960; Lukes 1974). Regardless of the name given to it, the phenomenon identifies a situation in which this "social ideology" (1) is constitutive of the social order; (2) defines and determines individual consciousness; and (3) "informs the structure of institutions, the nature of social cooperation and conflict, and the attitudes and predispositions of the population" (Sewell 1985, 61; see also Badie and Birnbaum 1983).

It is within the context of this social ideology that collective action takes place. The important questions are, Where does the ideology come from and how does it structure collective behavior? Understanding the origins of the ideology of the state in a particular society demands a historical focus. States develop slowly over time, and the type of shared values their institutions embody represents an amalgam of archaic as well as contemporary concerns. The historical perspective also provides insight into what these values are and which groups propounded them. Moreover, understanding the historical evolution of values and institutions becomes useful in explaining why some groups have more trouble than others in realizing their goals.

Norbert Elias (1969) provides a useful way to understand the historical process of state building that permits the observer to focus on the role of ideology. For Elias the state is the ultimate focus of political mobilization. On one level groups mobilize to facilitate the formulation of certain policies. At another level they mobilize to challenge the structures of power. This may be necessary to realize a group's ends, but it is also an objective designed to restructure institutions in ways that will serve their interests

41

in future. The focus of such mobilization may be representative institutions, administrative institutions, or both. The choice of institutions will depend on where social interests perceive power to lie or where they perceive their activities can have some success. Upon capturing control of the state, successful groups will begin to restructure state institutions in ways that serve their vision of the proper role of the state as well as facilitate their realization of specific interests.

The major reason why mobilization is directed at controlling state institutions is that it awards long-term control of society to a dominant group. Institutions are slow to change. Though demands and expectations may fluctuate over relatively short periods, the institutionalization of certain interests and practices serves to render these more immune to challenges from other groups. Part of the consequence of state control is that the political culture of the society is affected by the new order. The values advocated by the dominant group will become those represented and replicated by the state. This theme, earlier expounded by Max Weber (1958), explains why institutions reproduce the social ideology. The group that successfully gains control of the state employs state institutions in the dissemination of its ideological values throughout society. Weber demonstrates that the modern state is predicated on an ideology of rationalism that results in the codification of institutional authority, but that the dissemination of this value in society promotes rational critique of social customs and traditions in civil society. To the extent that the reproduction of the social ideology is successful, individuals never perceive of alternatives to the accustomed ways of exercising political authority. This explains why some alternative approaches to issues of policy are never discussed (Lukes 1974), as well as why the downtrodden in some societies never challenge their oppressors (Moore 1977).

Though institutions are slow to do so, they do change, and the change can alter the ideology of the state. For Norbert Elias, institutional change results when new challengers succeed in toppling the old order and begin the process of restructuring the state to serve new goals. Such change can be slow and incremental when the status quo proves itself capable of successfully defending the old order. Rather than accept fundamental changes, controlling forces may make those adjustments necessary to appease potential challengers or even to silence opposition. Extension of the franchise to the working class is one example of the way in which liberal democracies made a small adjustment that served to avert revolutionary challenges. Small changes in state structures then allow the state to maintain ideological continuity in public activity when temporal fluctuations in societal values and expectations could foster political instability.

But on occasion states can undergo dramatic upheaval and transformation. Stephen Krasner (1988) has provided a useful framework for understanding how this can occur. He argues that though institutions are conservative forces in society, efforts to institute small changes may fail to keep pace with rapidly changing societal expectations. This could be especially true if new beliefs and values amount to a fundamental questioning or rejection of the old order. In this case state institutions can become anachronistic to the new societal environment and expose themselves as incapable of dealing with new problems and issues. Krasner borrows from biologists the concept of punctuated equilibrium to describe how new political forces, if properly mobilized, may succeed in rapidly toppling the old order. The extent to which a particular state can or cannot respond to the new politics is indicative of the degree to which its institutional structure is adaptive or anachronistic. Efforts to accommodate change within the existing structure can lead to ad hoc adjustments that, over time, render the system less flexible. At this point successive challenges could topple the whole regime and lead to its replacement by one that is more in line with new social trends.

How does this theoretical perspective answer the two questions about the Dutch case? The particular type of state existing in the Netherlands awarded bureaucratic power and influence to social forces that resisted development of the welfare state. State building at the turn of the century resulted in the creation of a "consociational corporatist" state that was dominated by religious political groups, whose ideologies articulated a limited role for the state in the provision of social welfare. In realizing the ideological imperatives, religious forces mobilized to gain control of state institutions and to use the state to reproduce the ideology. The rapid development later, by contrast, was a result of fundamental institutional change that brought down the old ideology and replaced it with a new order propounded by new types of social group. In short, the state that had functioned for most of the twentieth century became anachronistic in the context of fundamental social change and the challenges of new social groups. At this point new groups were able to press demands successfully not only for reform of social policy but also for the restructuring of the balance of power within state institutions.

RECONSIDERING STATE INSTITUTIONS: THE CONFUSION OF CORPORATISM

In the preceding section I suggested that religious forces created the state that impeded development of social welfare. In addition to understanding how the goals of social groups could influence policy development, it is useful to identify aspects of state structures that assist or impede the development of policy. The question this raises is, What type of state made all this possible?

The Dutch state is a corporatist state. Basically, corporatism refers to the institutionalized representation of private, functional interest organizations that, through monopoly relations with state officials, make public policy (Schmitter 1979). Corporatist states are distinct from both pluralist and monist states. Corporatism awards privileged representation to functional interests whereas pluralism relegates all private interests to the status of lobbying organizations that must compete with one another for influence over policy (Martin 1983). Monism, by contrast, recognizes no subnational interest, and the differentiation of the state from society results in "the systematic destruction of peripheral allegiances (languages, customs), which promotes a privileged relationship between the citizen and his state" (Birnbaum 1982, 477).

Recognizing private interests for representation in corporatist institutions amounts to the attribution of public status to them (Offe 1981). This public status is awarded to private interests that are necessary to the effective implementation of policy, which are often provided with public resources to carry out policy decisions (Cawson 1982, 38). In addition to describing a specific structural relationship between societal groups and the state, corporatism also refers to a specific style of policy making (Panitch 1980). Through a process of negotiation between bureaucratic officials and these interests, policy is developed within corporatist institutions. Hence corporatism is a type of bureaucratic policy making that allows participants in the negotiations to exercise more influence than other actors, such a parliament or government, over the development of policy (Diamant 1981).

Corporatism provides the best description of policy making in the Dutch welfare state. Policy is made by a great number of diverse corporatist bodies that have a variety of tasks including advising, implementing, and supervising welfare programs (Couwenberg 1953; Akkermans and Nobelen 1983). For example, insurance programs for workers are administered by industrial insurance boards (*bedrijfsverenigingen*). There are twenty-six of these bodies, comprised of labor and employer organizations in twenty-six different sectors of the economy. Supervision of their activities is the responsibility of the Social Insurance Council (Sociale Verzekeringsraad), a sixteen-member council with five members from employer organizations, five from labor organizations, and five plus the chair appointed by the government. Before introducing social or economic policies to parliament, the Dutch government must first ask advice of the Social-Economic Council (SER), a plenary body with one third of its members each from employer organizations, labor organizations, and the state bureaucracy.

Whereas producer groups, particularly capital and labor organizations, predominate in the Dutch social insurance system, the fields of public assistance and social work are characterized by the representation of private, particularly religious charity organizations. Private and religious charities formerly were the administrators of the lion's share of public assistance under a program of state subsidies. Though this role has changed in recent years, these groups still provide a great deal of nonfinancial social services and are still publicly funded (Breton 1982). In addition, the Dutch Council for Social Work formerly operated as an umbrella organization comprised of these charities that was designed to facilitate coordination in charity activities and advise the government on issues of policy (Kramer 1981; J. de Vries 1985). (The array of corporatist groups is even more complex than this brief summary suggests. A more complete discussion is offered in chapter 3.)

In each of these fields policy is developed in consultation between state officials and the relevant groups. Through contact with state officials, groups attempt to help formulate policy. Bureaucrats, in turn, seek the advice of the groups to draw upon their knowledge and expertise in the policy field. Therefore understanding the development of the Dutch welfare state demands focusing on the nature of policy making in these corporatist institutions.

But two problems with present theories on corporatism render the concept difficult for the study of the making of welfare policy, especially when applied to the Dutch case. First, there is much confusion over the types of group that are relevant for the study of corporatist policy making. Second, the ability of corporatist institutions to foster political consensus has been overstated. In terms of the first problem, many authors have focused on the role of producer groups in corporatist institutions. Claus Offe (1981), for example has even claimed that corporatism is an irrelevant concept for the study of welfare policy. Other recent writings have identified corporatist institutions that include professional organizations (e.g., Valentin 1978; Winkler 1981; Dejong 1984; Harrison 1984). In The Netherlands corporatist institutions also include religious groups (e.g., charity organizations).

An adequate explanation of the institutional structure of corporatism must describe how types of social interest other than purely producer groups come to be represented.

Recent corporatist studies have identified capital and labor organizations as the groups represented in corporatist institutions, and typical explanations trace the rise of such institutions either to social democratic mobilization that succeeded in establishing representation for labor interests in the policy-making process (Rothstein 1990) or to the efforts of business to accommodate rather than engage in conflict with labor (Katzenstein 1985). This explanation works well for the study of corporatism in economic and industrial policy making in countries such as West Germany or Sweden, where tripartite bodies exist that include representatives of capital, labor, and the state. Yet this focus on capital and labor groups has led to the exclusion by corporatist authors of other groups, especially religious ones, that advocate or are involved in corporatist institutions (Etzioni-Halevy 1983).

Harold Wilensky (1981) has argued that while corporatism is a theme advocated by social democratic parties, representing labor interests, it is also advocated by Catholic parties. Moreover, Catholic power has been as effective as leftist power in fostering corporatism. In fact, many of the countries where Catholic power contributed to the development of corporatism are also regarded as examples of strong and stable corporatism, for example, Austria, Belgium, and the Netherlands (Katzenstein 1985). In these countries, Catholic political forces contributed to the development of corporatism in the early part of this century. Moreover, in contrast to nations where corporatism was inspired by a social democratic mobilization of workers, the Catholic conception of corporatism represented a conservative response to the "social question" by proposing corporatist solutions in order to stave off working-class mobilization (Esping-Andersen and Korpi 1984, 180). For this reason it is instructive to focus on a longer history of religious mobilization and the reasons why religious groups advocated corporatism in order to understand the development of corporatist institutions in these countries.

Indeed, corporatism developed in this set of countries at a time when the pattern of social organization was heterogeneous, characterized by strongly competitive, isolated, and autonomous social groups. Divisions among groups were based on religious and ideological cleavages in societies characterized by patterns of vertical social segmentation, or "pillarization," rather than horizontal, class-based divisions. We can assume that patterns of corporatist mobilization will differ in societies characterized historically by pillarization than in societies where similar dominant cleavages are absent, because pillarized distinctions cut across class cleavages. Labor unions and employer organizations are subdivided by religion, which undermines their common class identity. Religious business associations are less antagonistic to labor interests, and religious trade unions compete with social democratic unions for labor support (Wilensky 1981; Kruijt 1957). Consequently the ideological orientations of groups in these societies do not correspond to a traditional left-right dimension that distinguishes an anticapitalist left from a procapitalist right.

Previously, I discussed ideology as a set of shared values in society that inform state development. Ideology can also be conceived as a characteristic of a group, and in this way it distinguishes pillar groups in the Netherlands from one another. Each group is characterized by a basic worldview, or *Weltanschauung,* of social organization that provides an epistemological interpretation of the world (Lorwin 1974). The group ideology serves as the basis of a political program that outlines the role of politics in social relations, providing a specific interpretation of legitimate state-society relations and outlining the purpose of political activity. Entrance into positions of political leadership demand advocacy of group ideology (Stuurman 1983, 309).

Such ideological complexity in a society has the potential to produce stalemate and deadlock in political decision making. When Giovanni Sartori identified numerous political dimensions in Italy, he argued that multidimensionality plus extreme polarization along the dimensions imbue Italian politics with a centrifugal drive; "a process which is one of growing radicalization"

(Sartori 1966, 139). The political systems of Europe's four pillar-ized societies are as multidimensional as in Italy (see, e.g., Lip-shits 1969; Daalder 1981) but lack the extreme polarization that threatens stability. Arend Lijphart (1975, 1984, 1985) argued that polarization is averted and political stability maintained in these countries through the adoption of mechanisms that establish a process of accommodating competing political interests. Lijphart called this consociational democracy. Political institutions in pil-larized societies provide for power sharing among pillar groups, and policy making follows rules that permit representation of all pillar interests. Corporatism in these countries has provided an institutional solution to the problem of maintaining political accommodation in the policy-making process (Lehmbruch 1979; I. Scholten 1987).

In addition to this aspect of corporatism, when applied to the Dutch case the concept suffers another major shortcoming. Many scholars suggest that corporatism represents a depoliticization of issues of policy by "promoting the concertation [*sic*] of different interests which could otherwise be expected to compete or conflict in ways detrimental to the achievement of governmental objec-tives" (Goldthorpe 1984, 324; Cawson 1982). Dutch scholars argue that corporatism in their country is not based on the absence of political conflict. Rather, the institutions hide conflict from pub-lic discussion.

One way the process of policy making under corporatism hides political conflict is by moving it out of normal representative in-stitutions. Corporatist institutions often are as powerful policy-making institutions as parliaments or governments, or more so. The locus of corporatist politics is neither in activity on the part of pressure groups nor in partisan politics, but at the bureaucratic level in negotiations between private interests and state officials who are relatively insulated from public scrutiny. In observing the development of social security in the Netherlands, J. G. Rieken claims that changes in policy are "almost impossible to carry out due to the necessity of respecting the institutionalized interest groups" (1985, 3). Indeed, in corporatist countries governments and parliaments usually are reluctant to take action on policy, or even incapable of doing so, until corporatist groups have been provided the opportunity to comment. As one Dutch member of parliament stated in 1922, corporatist bodies develop the character of preparliaments "within which important social issues are decided. The participants are more or less committed to these decisions, so that by the time the issues reach the parliament, parliament is left with a fait accompli" (G. Scholten 1968, 28–29).

This does not remove politics from the process but merely hides it, and the results appear packaged for public consumption as broad social consensus (Daalder 1985; Craig and Harrison 1984). Public pronouncements on corporatist decisions on policy are assented to by all participants out of a necessity of maintaining legitimacy with respect to other corporatist actors. Within corporatist institutions, corporatist actors will attempt to influence the specific content of outcomes in ways that favor their own interests (Bovens 1985). This point is illustrated by Arthur Wassenberg (1982), who argues that corporatist institutions do not resolve but, rather, displace political conflict. The decisions appear to reflect consensus among the actors because they are made within institutions closed to public scrutiny and are not subject to political accountability. According to Wassenberg, this type of policy making reduces political debate in representative institutions to the level of symbolic discussion; at the level of the implementation of policy, the integration of private interests with the bureaucracy renders it impossible for bureaucrats to rationalize policy decisions and fails to solve basic problems. Though I would not go as far as Wassenberg in arguing that corporatism is by definition a destructive style of policy making, his point does indicate that it must be considered a political, not a technocratic, process.

The corporatist consequences of religious mobilization are the key that unlocks the mystery of the late development of the welfare state in the Netherlands. But to stop the story at this point would be to leave it incomplete. The other major question to explore is how corporatism can be reconciled with the experience of rapid growth of the welfare state in the 1960s. From Wassenberg's critique a hypothesis can be derived to explain this rapid development. The Dutch welfare state expanded in the 1960s during a period of protest and challenge calling for more democratic participation that affected all western societies. Hypothetically, democratic protest in the Netherlands may have exposed corporatism as a structure ill suited to this new public ideology.

There is much evidence to suggest that fundamental political change could be responsible for the rapid growth of the Dutch welfare state. Beginning in the late 1960s changing social attitudes were marked by a breakdown in the pillarization of society that had existed since the beginning of the century. This breakdown has eroded the traditional practices of political decision making and facilitated the expression of new coalitions of interests. New social movements are groups that advocate issues that corporatist structures are less equipped to address, such as environmentalism and the quality of life. In the Netherlands, as elsewhere, their appearance has challenged the legitimacy of corporatist modes of representation (Kreisi 1988). Another type of societal challenge to corporatism results from the professionalization of modern societies. Professionals have become important actors in the formulation of policy as a result of what could be termed the evolution of policy fields. As the fundamental issues about the scope and objectives of policy are established, the continuing concern is with the technical problems of implementing decisions. Professionals are the ones most competent to do this, mainly because they are active in the area in question and possess information crucial to the policy maker (Valentin 1978; Heidenheimer 1989). In the Netherlands the last two decades have seen the rise of a number of such professional organizations that advise on issues of policy and have a special relationship with government officials. The proliferation of such groups and the ties they establish with bureaucrats have offered a challenge to the older institutions of corporatism (I. Scholten 1987).

This refined look at corporatism as it is manifest in the Netherlands provides useful insight into the peculiar pattern in the development of the welfare state in that nation. Though efforts to reform welfare programs were slowed by the opposition of corporatist interests, reform did come; and when it came, the rate of growth was remarkable, and not only when the Netherlands is compared with other western European countries. It also defies our understanding of policy change as an incremental process whereby successive policies represent marginal departures from previous and existing ones (Lindblom 1959). Does the Dutch case, then, represent an anomalous pattern, or can a theoretical perspective that focuses on state building account for it?

The question is important because the characterization of most policy change as incremental is one that fits well with the view of institutions as conservative forces in society that are slow to change. A theoretical approach that holds open the possibility of dramatic institutional change must also recognize that the process of policy making could also undergo similar change. This, then, would explain how outcomes of policy could change rapidly. To fit the experience of rapid growth of welfare in the Netherlands within the theoretical framework of this study, it becomes incumbent to consider the possibility that Dutch corporatism was radically transformed in the 1960s. Such change could have been structural, procedural, or a combination. In addition, to identify the causes of such change, the theory suggests that we should look for changes in political mobilization and the institutional allocation of power that would allow new political forces to redefine the state quickly and provide them the opportunity to influence policy.

With all these changes in the character of corporatist relationships, it is not difficult to see how they can establish the conditions for a rapid change in policy decisions. There is, however, one important difficulty with tracing the nonincremental growth of the Dutch welfare state to these factors. All these changes occurred at the end of the period of rapid expansion. All but one of the new welfare programs (the public disability program) were in place before the breakdown in pillarization began.

Something appears to be wrong with the causal sequence of

political change and policy reform in the Netherlands. If political change is supposed to produce policy reform, then why did the welfare state grow so fast before these political changes occurred? There are two possible answers: either the changes observed and identified in the 1970s were already well under way much earlier, at the beginning of the 1960s, or the politics that surrounded development actually brought on these later changes. Regardless of which is the case, the answer still begs investigation of the politics that underlie the development of the Dutch welfare state.

CONNECTING THE THEORETICAL FACTORS

The bulk of this chapter has been devoted to a discussion of three major factors that are crucial to understanding the peculiar development of the Dutch welfare state: (1) the beliefs and attitudes of influential individuals in the policy process; (2) the impact of political mobilization, particularly religious mobilization, in the process of state building; and (3) the impact of state structures on policy outcomes. I also submit that these are more than a list of points that account for the theoretical anomaly of the Dutch case: they are central components of a broader and more comparative theory of the development of the welfare state.

Such a broad theory should simultaneously perform two functions (Alford and Friedland 1985). First, it should isolate and identify actions occurring at different levels of analysis and describe the relationships among those levels. Perhaps the simplest way to do this is by distinguishing among the individual, organizational, and societal levels of analysis. The factors I have described achieve this goal by focusing on ways individuals strive to influence policy decisions, how they organize in the collective pursuit of goals, and how their institutional environment structures their beliefs and behavior.

Second, a comparative theory should distinguish concepts from context at each level of analysis. This is done by recognizing that concepts are abstractions of reality; hence the concepts should be explicated at a sufficient level of abstraction to afford application to a variety of societies. To do this, I focus on three basic concepts that require some clarification: policy makers, as the individuals of concern in the study; mobilized political groups, as the relevant organizations; and the corporatist state. Figure 2.1 provides a graphic representation of how these elements form such a theory.

To say that the study focuses on individuals who influence final policy, I make a claim for selection. The study is not concerned with any entity that fits the requirement of constituting an individual. Rather, it is more narrowly concerned with that category of individuals who may be called policy makers. By the term *policy maker*, I mean nothing more than "an individual who influences decisions about policy." This appears to be a simple definition, but I find scholars often perplexed by such simplicity. The usual question one hears is, "By *policy maker* do you mean a civil servant, a government official, the leaders of a lobby, or whom?" The definition I employ would answer in the affirmative for each of these on the basis of one contingency: it must be demonstrated that the individual had an effect on the course of the development of a policy. Influence could be in the form of pushing the policy through, amending it, or even halting its enactment. Sometimes a large variety of individuals will be involved, sometimes a few. But whether the policy maker is a civil servant or a cabinet official is an empirical question requiring research at a unique level of abstraction. It would be a violation of the rule of theory building to claim that a policy maker is also the holder of a specific institutional office.

Since a similar discussion could describe the relationships among organizational levels of abstraction, it does not demand a lengthy explanation. Suffice it to say that when I mention groups, I refer to those organized for a political purpose. In other words, the goal of their organization is to influence the activities of the state, either by influencing decisions on policy or by capturing control of state institutions. Scholars currently recognize a number of institutional types of mobilized group. Political par-

Figure 2.1. Theoretical Levels of Analysis and Abstraction

	Level of Abstraction		
Level of Analysis	Unique Entity	Institutional Type	Systematic Entity
Individual	Otto von Bismarck William Beveridge Ernst Wigforss Willem Drees	Cabinet minister Civil servant Union leader	Policy maker
Organizational	Labour Party Dutch Employer's Federation National Rifle Association	Political parties Functional organizations Interest groups	Mobilized political groups
Structural	Dutch consociational corporatism United States interest group liberalism French strong state	Corporatism Pluralism Monism	The state

ties mobilize to control representative institutions; interest groups lobby public officials for certain policies; and functional organizations — such as labor, capital, or professional organizations — make their concerns those of the state by being necessary to the successful implementation of policy (Heidenheimer 1989; Cox 1992a, 1992b). Hence such groups may have as their concern a single issue or many; may represent a narrow or broad sector of the public; and concentrate their efforts on influencing specific agencies or the larger context of state activity.

Finally, individuals and groups operate within a larger structural context. For the purpose of public discourse and the study of policy, the state is the basic structural concept. Like the policy maker, the state is a difficult concept for contemporary social science. Some scholars claimed to have resurrected the concept in recent years (Skocpol 1985), whereas others have insisted that it never went away (Almond 1988). The debate over whether the state needs to be "brought back in" again centers on confusion among levels of abstraction. The state is, and always was, the set of sovereign institutions that administers affairs for a given society, and it usually corresponds with a specific territory. In recent years scholars have become distracted by debates over the degree of autonomy the state exercises. As a systematic entity, autonomy is not a definitional characteristic of the state. Rather, autonomy becomes the distinguishing factor among types of state.

As I outlined in the discussion of corporatism, there are two basic concerns in identifying a type of state. One is the nature of its institutional relationship with its society, or its degree of autonomy. A strict separation between state and society is typical of the pluralist state; the monist state constitutes a subjugation of societal autonomy to the interests of the state; and the corporatist state is a hybrid type. In addition, there tends to be a relationship between the structure and process of the state. Hence, the second concern in identifying the type of state is the way it reaches closure on political decisions. Pluralist states tend to exist where the process is characterized by conflict and competition among societal interests and a distrust of majoritarian solutions to political problems. Corporatist states tend to reflect an effort to strike consensus and compromise in societies with traditions of majoritarian democracy. Monist states tend not to be democratic at all, subjugating liberty to social order and permitting little input from societal interests.

It is also important to note that this simple model lends itself to further refinement and clarification. For example, corporatism is not of a single type. As the previous discussion in this chapter demonstrates, it takes a variety of forms. It would be possible to distinguish between state and societal corporatism, or, within models of societal corporatism, between liberal and social corporatism. An equal refinement of the other factors could be attempted. Civil servants could be distinguished by whether their role is subservient to political leaders (Britain) or as partisan as government officials (the United States).

Though such refinements do much to enrich our understanding of the complexity of the world's political systems, to enter the morass of conceptual hairsplitting distracts from the effort to develop sound comparative theory (Luebbert 1991). The theoretical outline for this study is one designed to blend the Dutch case into comparative theory. I do not believe that the best way to explain the Dutch case is to say that it is different and that therefore modifiers must be tacked onto our existing concepts to explain it. Indeed, if there is to be a theoretical explanation for the Dutch case it will have to be one that divorces theoretical concepts from contextual factors. This is especially true when the contextual factors are ideological in nature. This study offers a great challenge to ideologically inspired research. It shows that the welfare state is not always built by the left and that corporatism is not necessarily a more efficient or democratic policy-making machine. The demonstration of these points comes in the following chapters.

3

The Evolution of the
Dutch Corporatist State:
The Role of Religious Forces

"Our struggle is not directed at other people, but at the
disappearance of the spirit of God in public law."
—Abraham Kuyper, Prime Minister 1901–1905
(quoted in Oud 1990, 177)

One of the accepted tenets of the
development of policy is that changes are greatly constrained by
the history of choice of policy. The adoption of a particular policy and the creation of institutions to supervise and implement
it set parameters on what can be done to reform it. This is because institutions are slow to change, and they set in place practices and procedures that affect later policy debates. Institutions
also award power to those interests that occupy strong positions
within them, and those interests strive to retain that power. But
the institutions and procedures, as well as the effects of the policy, can also set in motion new political debates. Policy creates
politics, according to Theodore Lowi (1972), and the focus of
political activity in response to a particular policy, or set of policies, can be about changing the effects of the policy. This may
require changing the institutions responsible for policy, and hence
we must admit that a struggle for institutional control can be
part of the politics of the reform of policy.

These issues are particularly relevant for understanding the development of the Dutch welfare state. Following World War II
ideas for the expansion of the Dutch social security provisions
were adopted by the Labor party, which participated in many
successive coalition governments. The original proposals for

welfare reform were designed to address specific problems in the operation and scope of existing social security provisions, but enactment of the proposed changes did not begin until the end of the 1950s, and even then changes were enacted in a slow series of incremental stages throughout the 1960s.

Why were the governments in the 1940s and 1950s unable to institute their proposals for welfare reform, and why did the programs develop so slowly? I have suggested that the reason was that corporatist institutions, rather than governments, are the primary policy-making bodies in the Netherlands and that the representation of opponents of welfare reform in corporatist institutions enabled them to stop change. Who were these corporatist actors? Which ones opposed welfare reform and how did they come to occupy powerful positions in the policy-making process? To answer these questions, it is necessary to focus on the history of state building in the Netherlands, viewing it as a product of ideological contest designed to define the state's role in society. The battle was won by religious forces, as is illustrated by the adoption of programs for income maintenance. And the history of the origins of the Dutch welfare state show how these religious forces were able to take ideas from Bismarck's model of social security and adapt them in ways that facilitated their own ideological purposes.

IDEOLOGICAL MOBILIZATION AND THE DEVELOPMENT OF THE DUTCH STATE

It is regrettable that Dutch politics has received so little attention, because it seems that every time the country is investigated, amazing things are discovered. Drafters of the Constitution in the United States derived many of their ideas of federalism from the first modern Dutch state, the United Provinces. The Netherlands is also remembered as the place where religious toleration inspired migration from England and France, where commercial opportunities gave rise to a prominent trading empire, and where intellectual freedoms spawned the writings of Erasmus as well as much of John Locke's liberalism. In the post–World War II period, attention to Dutch politics followed the publication in 1968 of a book by Arend Lijphart, who discovered a peculiar form of nonmajoritarian decision making, which he dubbed consociational democracy (Lijphart 1975).

When social scientists were busy studying state building and political mobilization in the 1960s, if they had paid more attention to the Dutch case, they would have discovered another unique feature: political mobilization takes a variety of forms. In Scandinavia it was rural and class based. In Yugoslavia ethnic nationalism was and continues to be the dominant influence. In the Netherlands its defining characteristic was ideology. The four political groups that dominated in the period of state building (Catholics, Protestants, liberals, and socialists) each had well-developed political ideologies. Ideology served as the prescription for political activity and provided the inspiration for the type of political mobilization that influenced state building. Moreover, the historical constellation of political forces in the Netherlands provides the background for the development of the peculiar corporatist patterns in Dutch social welfare.

Additionally, the ideological divisions in Dutch society corresponded with a specific pattern of social organization. In contrast to Scandinavian society, where consensus politics has succeeded because there have not been fundamentally different conceptions of how society is to be organized, Dutch society has had strong subcultural divisions. The concept of pillarization refers to a social organization based on vertical and functional separation of social groups, or vertical pluralism (Doorn 1978). In the Netherlands the four pillar groups were Protestant, Catholic, socialist, and liberal.

The political effects of pillarization in the Netherlands are especially evident in the party system. Although proportional representation has created a multiparty political system that at present boasts over a dozen different political parties, most draw only a small percentage of the vote and only four have stood out as relatively large parties. By no coincidence, these four parties represent the four pillar groups in Dutch society. Throughout the first half of this century, these parties were the Christian Historical Union (CHU), which was Protestant, the Catholic People's party (KVP), the Labor party (PvdA), and the Liberal party (VVD). Indeed, this correspondence between the four ideologies is here somewhat oversimplified. For example, different strains of Protestant thought have been represented by progressive and fundamentalist parties, while liberalism has been the rampart of three different parties in Dutch history (see, e.g., Daudt 1982).

Moreover, religious parties have been dominant centrist parties in Dutch politics. The main anchors of pillar dominance in government were the KVP and the CHU, a generally progressive Protestant party. In addition, the fundamentalist Protestant Antirevolutionary party (ARP) was a small party that exercised a disproportionate degree of influence compared with its electoral strength because it easily aligned with the dominant religious parties to form governments. The religious parties have occupied a central position in Dutch politics, which has allowed them to enjoy a virtually unencumbered tenure in government by forming center-right coalitions with the Liberal party, or center-left coalitions with the Labor party. Prior to World War II, most governing coalitions in the Netherlands were moderately conservative, comprised either entirely of religious parties or of religious-liberal coalitions. Since World War II, despite declining electoral margins, the three major religious parties (KVP, CHU, ARP) consolidated their centrist position by merging to form the Christian Democratic Appeal (CDA) in 1982.

This is a brief description of the four major pillar groups that defined Dutch politics in the twentieth century. They did not, however, all become important political forces at the same time. Indeed, the historical development of the modern Dutch state, a process that can be traced from the establishment of a constitutional monarchy in 1848, exhibits many characteristics that are common among continental European democracies. As was the case in most of continental Europe, the original challenge to the old monarchical order was a contest between liberals and conservatives. In the Netherlands the result was the creation of an elitist constitutional monarchy. At the end of the nineteenth century and beginning of the twentieth, the elitist regime was challenged by mass-based movements. The historical dynamic is similar to that in Sweden and Denmark, where liberal rebellions ushered in elitist constitutional monarchies that later were challenged by mass-based movements of workers and farmers, but the groups were different. Liberals challenged not only a conservative monarchy but also a Protestant one. Later, the mass-based pressures for democratic suffrage came first from Catholics at the end of the nineteenth century, and then from socialists at the turn of the century. Ideology played a strong role in all these phases of Dutch political mobilization, and the differences in the types of group generated differences in the impact of the mobilization on the process of state building.

The Dutch unitary state was established in 1848 under the leadership of the liberal Johan Thorbecke. Throughout Europe 1848 was a year of turmoil. Most countries in central and northern Europe experienced a wave of bourgeois rebellions directed against the arbitrary authority of monarchs. In contrast to Austria, where the bourgeois rebellions led to the destruction of the monarchy, the Netherlands and Denmark were two countries where monarchs conceded to the establishment of parliamentary government in exchange for assurances that they would not lose their thrones. Overt rebellion was averted by a peaceful transition of power. Fearing a popular uprising, King Willem II granted a constitution that restricted the powers of the king and placed liberals in control of the government (Blanken 1976).

This liberal victory, however, was not heralded throughout the country as a desirable outcome. As in other countries at the time, liberalism in the Netherlands presented a philosophy that challenged the strong conservative and confessional tradition predominant in the society. Liberalism was a typically urban merchant philosophy that placed particular emphasis on values of prosperity and freedom in social and economic activity. Conservatism represented the religious tradition of the country and placed emphasis on the values of frugality and affiliation. Religious forces, which saw the secular state as an adversary, defended themselves by organizing into smaller collectives to maintain a traditional life-style. The religious response to the establishment of the unitary state marked the beginning of pillarization in Dutch society (Doorn 1984, 29).

The liberal victory established a state based on secular democratic principles, including the possibility that control of government could change hands. While the liberal state denied religious forces their dream of full control over a Christian nation, it did allow them to partake at the national level in state affairs. Religious forces were represented in this new structure by political parties that strove to limit the meddling of the state in private affairs, thereby preserving their traditional control over social organization. Rather than *étatisme*, the development of the Dutch state represented a process of modernization of life within a pillarized social structure (Doorn 1984, 30).

One should note that the Dutch ideologies all underwent change and transformation, the character of which constituted adjustments to the concerns of competing ideologies. For example, liberalism remained a powerful ideology throughout the second half of nineteenth century. Originally this was a philosophy that derived its inspiration from British liberalism. In the 1870s, however, Dutch liberal thought underwent revisions that departed significantly from its classical roots, becoming less individualistic and laissez-faire than its British counterpart (Mannoury 1967, 46). The main character of this distinction was a more progressive social vision based on spiritual freedom of the individual, but with a more interventionist view of the role of the state in providing the conditions for individual opportunity. This social vision borrowed much from the Christian tradition of the country. Responsibility became a liberal principle borrowed from the Christian tradition that rejected the laissez-faire emphasis on competition for personal gain and tempered this with a pursuit of social harmony based on cooperation (Huysman 1986). In this way the party presented no fundamental challenge to the dominance of confessional interests, striving instead to develop an independent place in the pillarized structure and to provide a place for the pillar "homeless" in Dutch society, those who did not strictly follow Catholic or Protestant political thought (Huysman 1986).

The confessional tradition, which found itself challenged by the new liberal state, was comprised primarily of Protestant interests. Prior to 1848 the Dutch state was a fundamentalist Protestant (Calvinist) monarchy. The liberal revision created a secular monarchy. Responding to the new political situation, Calvinist thought developed a philosophy for the role this new state should assume. The new doctrine accepted a strict distinction between state and society but did not accept the sovereign legitimacy of the state. The Calvinist worldview was based on the premise that society consists of historically ununifiable social groups (Veldkamp 1949, 224). For this reason, social groups must never be subordinated to a state but should strive to coordinate activities among one another. "Sovereignty in one's own circles" is the principle that expresses the Calvinist doctrine that beside the state exist other legitimate patterns of social organization each with autonomy over its own internal affairs. The role of the state within this framework is to encourage spontaneity in private life by giving ample room for the cooperation of private groups. State intervention is permitted in the public interest to prevent a particular group from becoming dominant. And while the state's role is to regulate relations among groups, it is strictly prohibited from meddling in affairs within the private associations (Ruppert 1965, 71–77). Aside from its parochial appeal, Calvinist thought bears much resemblance to the liberal conception of a minimalist state. The basic difference is the Calvinist concern with the prevention of the state's meddling in aspects of private organization controlled by the church, a concern designed to temper the secular emphasis of liberal thought.

The competition between liberalism and Calvinism continued throughout the second half of the nineteenth century. By the turn of the century, a religious coalition of Protestants and Catholics gained control of government. In power, these confessional forces introduced the first social welfare legislation in a manner that left a decidedly confessional stamp. The arrival of Catholic power in the Netherlands began as an emancipation movement during the latter half of the nineteenth century. At the time the Catholic population constituted a minority group geographically concentrated in the southern and eastern parts of the country. In addition to its geographic marginality, it was also an economically disadvantaged group that suffered from religious discrimination (Kieve 1981). Catholic emancipation was facilitated by guarantees of religious freedom provided for in the 1848 constitution, and, by the end of the nineteenth century, Catholics were an organized political force (Bax 1985).

Catholic participation in national politics led to the development of a Catholic complement to the Calvinist philosophy of state-society relations. The Catholic doctrine was inspired by the papal encyclical *Rerum Novarum*, which also outlined a vision of relations among economic producer groups. Under Catholic doctrine, the state is the embodiment of the general interest of a population in a specified territory. As such, the state is the pinnacle of a hierarchically arranged society. State authority, however, is constrained by the principle of "subsidiarity." Subsidiarity prescribes a decentralization of tasks to lower units of authority. This includes the delegation of tasks not only to territorial units but also to functional units, or social corporations. The principle of subsidiarity demanded the state's deference to the autonomy of social organizations operated by the church, such as charities and schools (Wissen 1982).

On issues of social welfare, Catholic and Calvinist doctrines are practically indistinguishable (Mannoury 1967; Fernhout 1980). Both view welfare as the responsibility of a group to protect its disadvantaged members. Whether the defining principle is sovereignty in one's own circles or subsidiarity, social welfare is viewed as a private, church concern rather than a state concern. Moreover, a group's commitment to the welfare of its membership is sanctioned by moral duty. This defines welfare as a charitable activity and distinguishes confessional welfare from the humanitarian emphasis of socialism and liberalism. That early Dutch social legislation was influenced primarily by these religious concerns accounts for its uniqueness when compared with German social legislation. But before examining that development, it is important to understand how socialist ideology developed in the Netherlands.

The arrival of socialism as a force in Dutch politics coincided with what is known as the Compromise of 1917. On the issue of public funding for parochial education, Catholic and Calvinist interests joined forces to resist socialist and liberal efforts to create a state-supported secular education. The compromise established a dual educational system comprised of both secular and parochial schools, all with state funding, but left the parochial schools freedom over curriculum. This event established the Dutch pattern of consociational democracy, or the system of elitist politics. For the religious groups, it legitimated the idea of state support for autonomous church activities.

Although the issue brought political recognition to socialist forces, they did not become as powerful as their liberal and confessional counterparts, partly because socialism never took hold in the Netherlands as the dominant ideology of the working class. From the last decades of the nineteenth century, religious forces assumed a strong role in labor organizing, representing a self-conscious attempt on the part of Calvinist and Catholic forces to undermine the ideological appeal of socialism among the Dutch working class. Even to this day, Dutch labor organization is underscored by a pillarized division among socialist, Catholic, and Calvinist unions, often within a particular industrial sector. Without the opportunity to develop a broad, class-based appeal, early Dutch socialists developed a pragmatic orientation. As early as the 1890s, themes of class struggle and social alienation were dropped, and the Social Democratic party (forerunner of the Labor party)[1] focused instead on concrete goals,

---

1. Following World War II, the Social Democratic party and various splinter parties united to form the Labor party.

especially the development of social insurance (Mannoury 1967).

In the 1930s the platform of the Social Democratic party underwent revisions that marked a further departure from traditional socialism. Whereas most socialist thought starts with a view of the state as the initiator of social change and the object of political mobilization, Dutch socialists came to view a centralized state as a dangerous development (Schoonenburg 1930). Functional decentralization emerged as the socialist view of the role of the state. To achieve this, the socialist platform advocated the creation of quasi-public organizations, directly supervised by state officials, which would carry out lower-level state functions. These would be essentially corporatist organizations — state bodies comprised of state officials and representatives of affected private interests to coordinate the implementation of state policy. The difference between this vision of corporatism and the one presented by the confessional groups is that, for the socialists, corporatist groups were state bodies that included private concerns, while for the confessionals, the corporations represented the private religious organization for public purposes with a greater degree of autonomy from state supervision.

Nonetheless, the basic ideological differences between the socialist and confessional conceptions of corporatism were not dramatic. Both parallel Phillipe Schmitter's (1979) conception of societal corporatism. The distinction between them centered on the degree of state direction of corporatist activities within institutions that are essentially democratically legitimated (see, e.g., Albeda 1982; Beus 1984). In part, the socialist advocacy of corporatism represented a pragmatic response to organizations that already existed and had been instituted by confessional forces. Socialists argued for the inclusion of socialist trade unions in these arrangements and for a greater degree of state supervision of the tasks of corporatist agencies. Events in other countries constituted another factor that influenced socialist thinking on corporatism. State corporatism as it developed in Italy was a model Dutch socialists found undesirable; they preferred functional decentralization rather than the fascist model as the principle on which to base a corporatist society (Keizer 1979, 72).

The Development of the Dutch Welfare State

The development of political institutions in the Netherlands has been influenced by the mobilization of these four political forces, particularly the confessional forces, whose activities were informed by strong ideological pronouncements on the role of the state. Efforts to articulate a political ideology were motivated by the desire of political forces to foster change in existing institutional arrangements. In their historical development, political ideologies in the Netherlands have undergone a process of blurring: what were once clear differences among them became observable only at the margins. In overwhelming force, both socialist and liberal ideological attitudes, especially with reference to attitudes on social welfare, were dictated by confessional interests. The liberal view of the social function of the state was informed by confessional values in Dutch society. The emphasis on functional decentralization represented a socialist adaptation to the corporatist structures instituted by confessional interests. It was this ideological environment that informed the development of corporatist bodies in the Netherlands.

THE INSTITUTIONS OF DUTCH CORPORATISM

What were these corporatist institutions? That question is extremely difficult to answer, for two reasons. The first is that the institutions of Dutch corporatism are numerous. The second is that the institutions undergo constant change. The institutions of Dutch corporatism are numerous because the custom of consulting with major societal interests led to the proliferation of contacts among public officials. It seems to have become the Dutch practice to establish a new corporatist organ each time the state entered a new area of policy. Even within areas there could be a staggering number of corporatist bodies, each performing different tasks: some groups are formally policy-making bodies, others are implementating agencies, and still others are supervisory organs. The number of organs even within a particular area of policy is a result of the specialization and differentiation of corporatist tasks over time. Figure 3.1 illustrates some of this

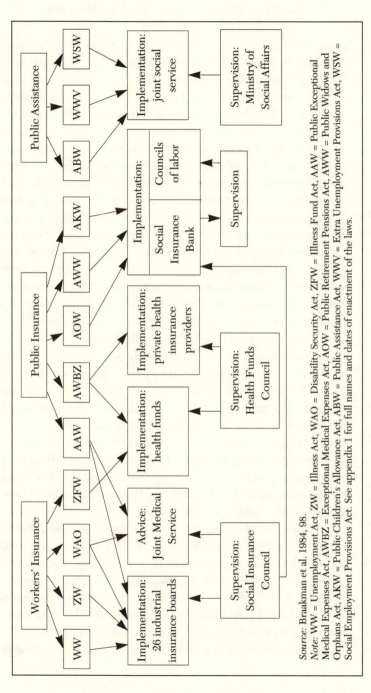

Source: Braakman et al. 1984, 98.

Note: WW = Unemployment Act, ZW = Illness Act, WAO = Disability Security Act, ZFW = Illness Fund Act, AAW = Public Exceptional Medical Expenses Act, AWBZ = Exceptional Medical Expenses Act, AOW = Public Retirement Pensions Act, AWW = Public Widows and Orphans Act, AKW = Public Children's Allowance Act, ABW = Public Assistance Act, WWV = Extra Unemployment Provisions Act, WSW = Social Employment Provisions Act. See appendix 1 for full names and dates of enactment of the laws.

Figure 3.1. Implementation of Social Security Programs

complexity, in the area of social security administration alone.

Finally, in the Netherlands the composition of the groups varies. Scholars of economic corporatism speak of tripartite arrangements staffed by representatives from labor, business, and the state. Many Dutch institutions are tripartite in this sense, but sometimes they are bipartite arrangements between business and labor. And though corporatist scholars have claimed that a country cannot be labeled corporatist without identifying formal institutions, in those countries where such institutions exist, corporatist practices permeate even the most informal of contacts. For example, many of the bipartite organizations (where there is no state participation) tend to be established under private rather than public law. While this means that they are subject to regulation rather than civil service rules, they are often important participants in discussions of policy since their membership often overlaps with that of the tripartite institutions. For this reason the voice of a body governed by private law constitutes an expression of opinion that will influence formal corporatist discussions. Furthermore, outside the realm of economic policy, the idea of bipartite or tripartite relations becomes occluded by the different constellations of interests in those areas of policy. For example, professional and university intellectuals are institutionalized advisors on policy in areas such as health care, economic matters, and education (Doorn 1984). All this produces an opaque constellation of corporatist organs. Hence one of the major problems in studying corporatism is to identify the groups involved and understand the tasks of the various bodies and their relationship to one another.

Outlining the historical development poses a second difficulty for understanding Dutch corporatism. The institutions are not static entities that, once established, never change. Indeed, over the last one hundred years, corporatist institutions have come and gone. Of those that have endured, virtually all have undergone some fundamental transformation, in terms of either their membership or their tasks. Indeed, in many cases corporatist institutions changed because of autonomous changes in society. In some areas of policy the groups that were originally represented in corporatist institutions ceased to exist, leaving the institutions empty shells. The bodies either withered, were dismantled, or were subsumed by other modes of representation that included other types of group. Many of the most notable examples of changes in Dutch corporatism are outlined in chapter 5.

This issue of change in corporatist institutions draws attention to another important characteristic of this type of system. On a scale of strongly to weakly entrenched institutions, corporatist bodies run the gamut. Some take on the status of the parliament and are just as durable features of the political system. Others, much like many bureaucratic agencies, are less prominent and more ephemeral. This fact only makes describing corporatist institutions more difficult. Nonetheless, I provide a brief description of some of the major institutions. The list is selective in that it outlines those groups that have been central to the development of social welfare policy. I focus on the tasks of the groups, their legal status, their membership, and some of the major changes they have undergone. I have divided them into two categories: those important to the development of public assistance and those important to the development of social insurance.

The opaqueness of Dutch corporatism is nowhere more evident than in the area of poor relief or public assistance. Here there are actually few formal institutions to discuss (see table 3.1). Consequently informal contacts with major organizations of private interests were more important (see table 3.2). Indeed, the general characteristic of this area is that it represented "societal corporatism" in Phillipe Schmitter's (1979) strict sense of the term. According to Schmitter, societal corporatism is that form where groups in society dictate their organization, and the state merely recognizes their legitimate right to represent a certain societal interest. Schmitter draws a contrast between this type and "state corporatism," the form in which the state decides which groups are worthy of recognition and grants them license to operate.

In Dutch poor relief the relevant corporatist groups were originally confessional and secular charities. Their internal organiza-

Table 3.1. *Major Corporatist Bodies for Poor Relief*

Name	Established	Task	Legal Status	Membership
Provincial recon-struction organi-zations (Provin-ciale Opbouw-organisaties)	1946–1963	Coordinating/Advising	Public law	Ministry officials, charities and municipal agencies
Poor councils (Armen Raden)	Variable	Coordinate im-plementation	Public law	Charities and mu-nicipal agencies
Social councils (Sociale Raden)	1963	Coordinate im-plementation	Public law	Charities and mu-nicipal agencies

Source: Kramer 1981; Valk 1986

tion was not specified in any law, hence they have always been private law organizations. They were bound only by the requirement that they register as charitable agencies. Corporatism resulted from spontaneous efforts on the part of the charities to organize themselves, the most important such effort being the Dutch Association for Social Work. I use this name for the organization even though it has undergone a number of name changes. Originally established as the Dutch Association for Poor Relief, it was an umbrella organization of private charity agencies. At the time 80 percent of its membership consisted of confessional charities (Valk 1986, 97–100).

As an umbrella organization, the association's purpose was to coordinate the way poor relief was dispensed and provide a unified voice for the charities vis-à-vis the state. Though it appears to resemble a pluralist lobby, the association's position was different in two fundamental respects. First, it was not a pressure group, but it was recognized by the Ministry of Home Affairs as the legitimate voice for charity interests. Recognizing an umbrella organization that was dominated by church charities awarded confessional interests a hegemonic position in the de-

---

Table 3.2. Major Umbrella Organizations of Private Interests

Labor Foundation (Stichting van de Arbeid)
  Peak organization comprised of the three main labor federations:
    Socialist Labor Federation (Nederlandse Verbond van Vak-
      verenigingen)
    Catholic Labor Federation (Nederlands Katholiek Vakverbond)
    Protestant Labor Federation (Christelijk Nationaal Vakverbond)

Dutch Association of Entrepreneurs (Verbond van Nederlandse Onder-
nemingen)

Netherlands Christian Employers Association (Nederlands Christelijk
Werkgeversverbond)
  Peak organizations of employers

Dutch Council for Social Work (Nederlandse Raad voor Maatschappelijk
Werk or Nederlandse Raad voor Sociale Zorg)
  Peak organization of religious and secular charity agencies

Association of Subsidized and Premium Funded Enterprises (Vereniging
Ondernemersorganisaties Gepremiërde en Gesubsideerde Sector)
  Established 1990 to foster greater coordination among social service
  agencies

Source: Guasco et al. 1979; Ministerie van Welzijn, Volksgezondheid en Cultur 1990.

---

termination of policy on poor relief. Though the secular charities were consistently outvoted within the organization, it could
not be said that they lacked voice and representation (Valk 1986,
100–111).

The second difference between the association and a pluralist
lobby was the role it performed in the implementation of policy.
Though the charities served as implementing agencies for public
policy, they were not awarded an institutional position in policy
making. No organ was established that gave charities a seat at
deliberations on policy. However, the association did exercise influence, since every piece of legislation that addressed poor relief

stated a preference for maintaining the profile of private charities in the administration of the programs.

In the post–World War II period, the association adopted an important advisory role on policy. In fact, it assumed this role when after the war a special commission was established to draft a new poor law (see chap. 5). This commission awarded representation to member organizations of the Dutch Association for Social Work. Though the commission was an ad hoc body that provided them temporary representation for the development of a specific policy, the association took upon itself to establish a more permanent policy advisory body, which it called the Dutch Council for Social Work. The council became the association's advisory organ on policy: it began to offer advice to the government and eventually was consulted on a regular basis.

In the 1960s the Dutch Association for Social Work began to lose its influence. In part, this was because the charities, which originally had been volunteer bodies, became more specialized and their staffs more professionalized, and as a result the umbrella organization began to splinter (a process that reached comic proportions in the late 1970s). In its place a number of specialized organizations developed, such as the Dutch Association for the Handicapped, a group of social work agencies. Recently, as chapter 6 points out, the government has attempted to construct a new umbrella organization by requiring that all charities join the Association of Subsidized and Premium Funded Enterprises or lose their state subsidies. It is still unclear what role the association will assume with respect to policy. Its creation was motivated perhaps more by the government's concern about retrenchment than by a desire to foster coordination in the field. Requiring membership in a national body allows the ministry to control which organizations receive subsidies, a task that historically had been delegated to municipal governments (Ministerie van Welzijn, Volksgezondheid en Cultur 1990).

Though these private umbrella organizations have been the major actors in corporatist negotiations, some public law bodies also have been important. These have undergone even more dramatic transformation over the years. The original bodies, called poor councils, involved efforts on the part of municipal governments to foster coordination in the distribution of social services and poor relief. Their legal basis was outlined in the Poor Law of 1912, under which municipal governments could establish advisory councils that included charity agencies. Since these poor councils were not mandated, their appearance was ad hoc, and the degree to which they were of influence varied among municipalities. In the larger cities that had strong municipal governments, especially Amsterdam and Rotterdam, the councils were active. In rural areas and small towns, if the councils even existed, they tended to be perfunctory.

Following World War II, the minister of social affairs, Willem Drees, attempted to formalize these consultative bodies: he mandated that they be created at the provincial level, and in all provinces. Dubbed provincial reconstruction organizations (POOs), they were again to facilitate coordination between public and private organizations. They were, however, extremely controversial, and their authority was less than Minister Drees had originally hoped.

After passage of the Public Assistance Act in 1963, the formal bodies of corporatism in the area of poor assistance were transformed. The law mandated creation of social councils in all municipalities. These were primarily designed to foster coordination between municipal officials and private social work agencies, and their establishment amounted to an imposition of uniformity on the earlier poor councils. With their creation, the POOs were dismantled.

Thus, in the area of public assistance, Dutch corporatism has had a variegated history. Over the years the institutions have changed, as has the degree to which they are involved in decisions on policy. The existence of important private law bodies alongside public law councils attests to the diversity of types of forum for negotiation. This complexity is true of corporatism not only in social work but also in social insurance.

In the area of social insurance, there are also few major corporatist institutions (see table 3.3), but they are noted for a greater degree of institutional legitimacy than are those in public assistance. Perhaps the best place to begin is with the National Insurance Bank (*Rijksverzekeringsbank*) (NIB) and the industrial insurance boards (*Bedrijfsverenigingen*). Both were outlined in the first social insurance law in the Netherlands, the Workmen's Compensation Act of 1901 (*Ongevallenwet*). The law established the NIB as a state agency for the collection of insurance taxes and distribution of benefits. In 1919 its role was expanded when parliament adopted a program that permitted the self-employed to participate in the social insurance schemes that had previously been available only to wage earners, and the task of adminis-

Table 3.3. Major Corporatist Bodies in Social Insurance

Name	Established	Task	Legal Status	Membership
Industrial Insurance Boards (Bedrijfs-verenigingen)	1901	Implementation of worker pensions	Private law	Bipartite
Social-Economic Council (SER) (Sociaal-Economische Raad)	1950	Advisory	Public law	Tripartite[a]
Social Insurance Council (Sociale Verzekerings-raad)	1952	Supervisory	Public law	Tripartite[a]
National Insurance Bank; later renamed Social Insurance Bank (Rijks-verzekeringsbank)	1901	Implementation of national insurance	Public law	Tripartite[b]
Labor Councils (Raden van Arbeid)	1913	Implementation of worker disability and illness	Public law	Bipartite

Source: Guasco et al. 1979; Rengelink 1970.
a. State appointees to these bodies are neutral "crown appointees."
b. State appointees to these bodies are politically appointed.

tering the programs was given to the NIB. Passage of this law prompted the government to draft a separate law specifying the tasks of the NIB the following year.

In 1901 the proposal to establish the NIB was extremely controversial, objected to by conservative and confessional groups who saw no reason to establish a state monopoly in social insurance administration. Later in this chapter, I describe how the political debates over this issue led to the establishment of the industrial insurance boards, the oldest forms of economic corporatism in the Netherlands. These boards were set up as bipartite, private law organizations that included representatives from labor and business. Originally this meant that they existed only in industrial sectors where business and labor were willing to organize for the purpose of administering social insurance. This situation made it possible to undermine leftist organization of the labor movement, since employers would enter into such arrangements only with confessional unions.

In 1913, as discussion progressed on other social insurance schemes, debate continued over the role of the state in the administration of the programs. Up to this point the discussion had been polarized between those who endorsed state assumption of responsibility through the NIB and those who favored leaving the issue in the hands of the private sector. The government at the time introduced legislation that led to the establishment of the councils of labor (*Raden van Arbeid*), public law, bipartite organizations of labor and business. The intention was to use these bodies as replacements for the industrial insurance boards in the administration of two new insurance schemes, illness and pensions. In their final form the councils of labor were limited to advisory tasks, and administrative tasks for the new programs were placed in the hands of industrial insurance boards.

By midcentury disputes over how to administer the insurance schemes had created a hodgepodge of organs. Often similar tasks were undertaken by entirely different bodies. Following World War II the government set out to restructure the system, eliminate redundancies, and make the lines of responsibility more clear. The result was the Social Insurance Organization Act of 1952, which introduced three major changes. First, the voluntary and spontaneous character of the industrial insurance boards changed dramatically. The new rules mandated that boards be established in twenty-five industrial sectors and that all members of the work force subscribe to their industrial board. A twenty-sixth board was created to service the remainder of the work force. This reform afforded more formality and regularity to the activities of the boards and lent greater status to the role of private interests in the development of policy.

Second, the 1952 reorganization also strove to minimize some of the confusing bureaucratic elements by establishing the Central Administration Office (Gemeenschappelijk Administratie Kantoor), whose task was to promote coordination in the administration of benefits. Previously the boards exercised a great deal of discretion in the way they distributed benefits. Indeed, the law not only charged the Central Administration Office with making benefit awards uniform but also allowed the industrial insurance boards to turn over administrative tasks to it, an option half of them made use of.

The third major reform introduced by the 1952 law was the creation of a new corporatist body. To promote more supervision of the tasks of all the administrative agencies, and to simplify the lines of communication between the administrative units and the Ministry of Social Affairs, the Social Insurance Council (Social Verzekeringsraad) was established as a public law, tripartite body. It differs from the NIB (later renamed the Social Insurance Bank) in that its task is to supervise rather than to implement. Another important difference is that the state officials on the NIB are selected by the minister of social affairs, whereas the state appointees on the Social Insurance Bank are "crown members" (*Kroonleden*), that is, independent councillors who ideally are impartial representatives of the public interest rather than representatives of the interest of the government.

The final and perhaps most noteworthy of the corporatist bodies in the area of social insurance is the Social-Economic

Council, known by its Dutch acronym, SER. The SER is undoubtedly the most prominent corporatist organ in the Netherlands. Established in 1950, it is the primary institution for corporatist negotiation. It is a tripartite body, comprised of representatives from labor unions, employer federations and crown members. The SER has a curious relationship to social policy. It was not designed to be a consulting organ in the development of social insurance policy. Its charter designates it as the primary body for consultation between the state and economic interests in all matters of economic and social policy, yet that was not originally to include social insurance. The Social Insurance Council was to be the important body for the development of legislation in that area. Indeed, the membership structure of the two bodies is very similar. Both are tripartite, with the state appointees being crown members. The big difference in membership, however, is in the character of business and labor representation. Peak organizations of business and labor, as well as the self-employed, are represented on the SER. On the Social Insurance Council, representatives are from the industrial insurance boards. In other words, the SER's membership consists of advocacy groups while the Social Insurance Council is comprised of the representatives from those groups that are exclusively involved in the implementation of insurance programs. This virtual redundancy between the two bodies would not seem so problematic were it not that the SER has come to assume a role as advisor on issues of policy that supersedes the formal role of the Social Insurance Council. How this situation came about is addressed in the following chapter.

In sum, in the area of social insurance there are a great number of corporatist bodies. Their tasks are various though often duplicate, their membership structures distinct though memberships often overlap. Table 3.2 identifies the major private interests that were represented on these bodies, as well as in the area of poor relief. This is the result of a peculiar pattern of political mobilization designed to construct state institutions that promoted certain ideological interests.

As in the area of social security, there was extensive corporatist activity in poor relief. Here the dominance of religious organizations is just as evident as in social insurance, if not more so. Whereas confessionally oriented labor unions dominated working-class mobilization, in the delivery of poor relief, religious charity agencies dominated secular ones. Moreover, until the 1950s the interests of the religious charities even dominated interests of the ministry. There is, however, one important contrast between the two areas of corporatist activity: in poor relief there were few formal institutions of corporatism, and many of the formal contacts were ad hoc, rather than institutionalized practice.

I now turn to a historical synopsis of early social welfare legislation in the Netherlands that centers on how politics informed early legislative developments and gave rise to the Dutch pattern of corporatism. The legislative history demonstrates how corporatism served as a way to grant many private interests special influence on matters of public interest.

THE POLITICS OF CORPORATISM
IN EARLY POOR RELIEF PROGRAMS

The characteristic dominance of Christian ideologies left its imprint on the development of the Dutch state and corporatist patterns in policy making. Yet the political dominance of confessional groups was tempered by a liberal democratic political system that, rather than distributing political resources, provided the opportunity for competition for them. Open political competition also allowed socialists, in the role of a vocal opposition, to force confessional interests to direct attention to issues of social welfare. Still, early social welfare policy was influenced primarily by religious forces.

In considering the original development of Dutch social policy, it is important to take the issue back to the middle of the nineteenth century. At the time the Dutch state was founded, social policy was a major concern of the liberal forces. Because this was long before any discussion of social insurance, the issue centered on whether or not the new state should assume responsibility for providing poor relief or some form of income assistance to the poor. Liberals wanted to adopt a state role, but the religious forces viewed poor relief as an area where the church should be the major provider. This early contest, and the manner in which it was resolved, set the stage for the development of corporatism in Dutch social policy. Confessional groups used their position to develop programs designed to offer an antidote to the individualistic themes in liberalism, and later they defended the programs against the collectivist emphasis of socialism. This middle-of-the-road alternative was achieved through the creation of corporatist organizations to which were delegated the tasks of administering the programs and advising the government on policy. The most significant aspect of ideological mobilization was that the religious groups were both the original advocates of corporatism and its primary beneficiaries.

Historically, as in most countries, basic assistance to the poor in the Netherlands was provided by private and religious charities. Poor assistance was never a state concern, although public councils for poor relief were established by some municipal authorities. For example, poor councils in Amsterdam date back as far as 1330 (Dam 1964). As a state concern, poor relief began with the creation of a Poor Law in 1854. Inspiration for the legislation came from the founder of the modern Dutch state, Johan Thorbecke, who proposed the establishment of a state-directed national program of public assistance. Yet, contrary to the expectations of Thorbecke and his liberal followers, parliamentary debates resulted in amendments to the law that signified a triumph for fundamentalist Protestant interests that opposed any hint of state assumption of charity activities.

In its final form, the Poor Law was designed to encourage the long-standing tradition of private charities but also provided a state guarantee of assistance only when private charities were unable to address the needs of the poor adequately. And since the preference given to private charities were intended to maintain minimal intervention of the state in social activities, in practice the Poor Law developed into a system of public subsidization of private charities whereby the state paid for poor relief but had almost no control over how the programs were administered (Couwenberg 1953). The various charity agencies were free to establish their own criteria for benefit entitlements, the only legal restriction being vaguely defined as a requirement that they operate in the public interest.

This loose definition of charity tasks led to huge disparities in the manner poor relief was administered. In addition, the domination of political institutions by religious political parties hampered effective bureaucratic oversight of the programs, since the attitude of public officials from the religious blocs was characterized by deference to their corresponding church charities. For example, in an effort to encourage better coordination in charity activities, municipal authorities in some of the larger cities attempted to establish poor councils (*Armenraden*). The councils were comprised of municipal officials as well as representatives from private charities and were given the authority to recognize charities that would receive public subsidies. In areas where religious political parties were strongly represented in local governments, however, the councils quickly became dominated by religious factions, which continued to exercise discretion in the allocation of subsidies (Nijenhuis 1978).

Because of their prominent position in the implementation of the Poor Law, private charities also were able to influence later policy decisions that affected the program. In 1912 a second Poor Law was enacted. It was originally intended to systematize the state supervision of charity activities; instead, it merely ratified many practices the charity agencies had begun on their own. One of the most important of these was the practice of "double dispensation" (*dubbelbedeling*). Under the old law, charities were subsidized on the basis of the funds necessary to make up discrepancies between funds collected through private donations and those distributed to the poor. Successive ministers of home affairs, who frequently had confessional political affiliations, utilized the loose wording in the law to justify the provision of direct subsidies to private charities, thus encouraging them to seek ways of increasing their share of state funds. Some Catholic charities made it a practice to undersupport beneficiaries, realizing that the difference would be picked up by the state. This practice allowed them to provide assistance beyond only poor Catholics, thereby enabling them to control the distribution of assistance to a greater number of individuals than would otherwise have been the case (Valk 1986, 105). Seeing this prompted Protestant leaders to adopt similar practices (Moulijn 1948, 728), and double dispensation, as it was called, made it possible for all religious charities to exercise control over individuals in the community who did not belong to their affiliated church.

Another major impact of the religious charities on the Poor Law was inclusion of a provision that guaranteed them a "right of recovery" (*verhaalsrecht*), whereby agencies could appeal to family members for financial support of an indigent. The original purpose was to prevent families from passing along the cost of caring for relatives. During the Great Depression, exercise of the right of recovery exacerbated social problems as working youth began moving away from home to avoid having their wages garnished to support unemployed fathers. In response, the charities convinced the government that the right of recovery needed to be extended beyond immediate family members so that poor relief costs could be recovered from distant relatives. The most regular use of the right of recovery was made by the religious charities, where it served as a supplement to income derived from charitable donations. In addition, many even used the right of recovery as an excuse to confiscate indigents' belongings upon their death (Valk 1986).

One thing that characterized the early stages of poor relief policy was the absence of bureaucratic supervision, but this does not mean that the religious charities dominated policy making. The second Poor Law, as well as changes in bureaucratic practice, made the ministry responsible for the poor relief program. Throughout the latter part of the nineteenth century and the first

half of the twentieth, however, religious political parties dominated governments, and confessional ministers of home affairs
shared the concerns of the religious charities. Consultation between the partners easily resulted in agreement on issues, always
to the benefit of the religious charities (Adriaansens and Zijderveld 1981; Kramer 1981).

Thus from the beginning, Dutch religious charities constituted
corporatist groups in poor relief. They served as administrative
agencies for the implementation of public policy, and this public role was even legally sanctioned. The most prominent characteristic of this type of societal corporatism was that it granted a
great deal of autonomy to private interests. Through mechanisms
such as the right of recovery and double dispensation, charities
were able to use their programs as vehicles for other forms of
religious social control. In other words, they were granted public
resources to pursue private interests. Moreover, they enjoyed the
autonomy of defining means and goals in poor relief and maintained this role as long as state intrusion could be resisted. While
this situation produced no clearly rational structure for the administration of poor relief, incongruities and inconsistencies illustrated the development of a policy whose structure was dictated by the political strength of religious forces in society rather
than by an autonomous state bureaucracy (Birnbaum 1982).

THE POLITICS OF CORPORATISM
IN SOCIAL INSURANCE, 1900–1945

For most historical observers, the modern welfare state originated
with the German social reforms established by Bismarck (Heidenheimer 1983, 5). The German reforms are cited not only as the
first comprehensive programs of social insurance, but also as a
model for their development in other countries. That claim is
true, at least for the Netherlands (Zweeden 1983). Indeed, many
sections of the original legislation for Dutch social insurance were
translated verbatim from the German (Hoogland 1940). But
though state control of the programs was a major characteristic

of Bismarck's model and was adopted by liberal Dutch proponents, confessional forces were concerned with the degree of state control over social policy. As these forces succeeded in introducing modifications to the German model, the Dutch programs took on a different form: they came to represent what Peter Katzenstein (1985) has called liberal (employer-dominated) rather than social (labor-dominated) corporatism. The reason for this is that confessional forces in business and labor desired to limit leftist groups, but confessional unions were unable to develop a strong position of power that would have allowed them to challenge business leaders.

Indeed, the reasons why Dutch unions had little voice in the early social legislation are that they did not develop until after the original legislation had been set in place and that pillarization of the union movement prevented them from offering a unified voice. The first union federation in the Netherlands was socialist, established in 1878 by a former preacher. It was a radical federation whose leader advocated class struggle as the means of garnering attention for labor interests. Concern about the potential for radical mobilization of the work force was shared not only by conservative employers and political parties but also by religious-minded union organizers, and this concern led to efforts to develop strong confessional worker federations. For example, in 1906, Protestant labor organizers participated in a conference in Zurich that brought them in contact with labor leaders in other countries. They were greatly impressed by the examples of confessional unionization in Germany that allowed Catholic and Protestant membership. They returned from the conference dedicated to establishing similar interconfessional unions in the Netherlands. These efforts failed, however, because Catholic bishops denounced the interconfessional idea (Amelink 1950). Instead, when the first confessional labor federation was established, the Dutch Christian Labor Federation, it was a Protestant organization. Catholic labor organization came later, with the creation of a federation of Catholic workers in 1925 (Oud 1990, 116). This fragmentation of the trade union movement was a product of the severe pillarization of Dutch society, and it had the effect of undermining collective labor organization.

Another matter that dates from the 1870s was the debate over whether or not an insurance program for workers should be adopted. At the time leftist mobilization of the work force raised concerns over what came to be known as the "social question" within the new economic order, or how to effect a peace in industrial relations. As in the earlier discussions on poor relief, liberals desired to address the social question by creating a strong state role in providing social insurance programs. Conservative forces (confessional and business) were also concerned with the social question but wanted to devise a response to the issue that would limit state meddling in society. These issues were first addressed by a liberal government that came to power in 1891. The following year it established a committee to investigate and propose suggestions for legislative action that would address the problems of disability and retirement among workers. The committee suggested establishment of insurance programs to be financed by premiums one-third of which would be paid by workers, one-third by employers, and one-third by the state. Participation in the programs would be voluntary and universally available (Gosker 1969). When, in 1894, a liberal government announced its intention to submit to parliament a bill based on these suggestions, a parliamentary majority raised objections. With the support of a number of renegade liberal members of parliament, confessional parties were able to pass a parliamentary resolution that acknowledged the desirability of establishing retirement pensions but demanded that the government reassess the nature of a program's entitlements. This led to the creation of a second committee, which proposed two important changes to the original plan. The first was the adoption of a mandatory pension scheme, but one that would exclusively cover workers and their dependents. The second change was in the financing, which the committee suggested be shared equally by employers and employees, an arrangement that would require state contributions only to cover shortfalls in the budget (Rengelink 1969; MvT-AOW 1955, 10).

Despite the government's conceding these points to the conservative forces in parliament, legislative action on the issue was not initiated until 1905 because of an unresolved dispute over the nature of entitlements. In the meantime, the social question remained a great concern for the liberal government, which introduced legislation designed to set a precedent for the later development of pension schemes. This effort came in the form of a workmen's compensation plan. In its first draft, the Workmen's Compensation Act (Ongevallenwet 1901) outlined a program that would be operated by a public institution, the NIB. It was to be financed by premiums paid by employers that would be directly transferred to recipients of benefits (Fernhout 1980). Confessional parties in parliament objected to both the administrative structure and the system of financing. In their view the proposed NIB would be an unnecessary centralized institution and would place too much control of fiscal affairs in the state's hands. In addition, they objected to the proposed funding scheme on the grounds that the institutionalization of direct transfer payments would open the possibility for heavy state subsidy of the program (Hoogstraten 1924).

These criticisms were brought forward by the fundamentalist ARP, which opposed the bill entirely. But, faced with its certain passage in parliament, the ARP leader, Abraham Kuyper, offered amendments to the bill that bore directly on the role of the NIB in the implementation of the programs. Kuyper argued that the program should encourage employers to organize themselves and institute insurance schemes for their own industries, as had already been done on a small scale in some industries, particularly construction (Visser 1970). The amendment proposed the creation of industrial insurance boards to operate alongside the NIB in the implementation of the programs. Modeled on the German *Berufsgenossenschaften*, these boards, as Kuyper envisioned them, would be decentralized semipublic bodies, organized in specific industrial sectors. Kuyper's amendment was a specific answer to the social question and was designed to encourage spontaneous, voluntary organization of employers and employees (Mannoury 1972, 117). Furthermore, it would also make membership in these

bodies mandatory for all workers, which would effectively undermine socialist organizations since Catholic and Protestant
unions had developed nonconfrontational attitudes toward representing workers' interests. By being able to negotiate with
Catholic and Protestant unions, the employers' federations were
able to lock out the more radical socialist unions.

Kuyper's ostensible goal in proposing the amendment was to
bring workers and employers together to bridge the differences
between the groups with an operating principle of codetermination (*medezeggenschap*). The phrasing of the amendment
appealed to confessional views of state activities because it encouraged voluntary cooperation between employers and unions
rather than mandating cooperation, and the amendment gained
the support of confessional parties. Moreover, the weaker organization of the confessional unions severely restricted labor's role
in the industrial boards. Although the amendment would grant
labor the right of codetermination, the concept of *medezeggenschap* implied the chance to express a viewpoint, not a part in
decision making. As on a ship, capital interests, as captain, would
remain at the helm of the industrial boards (Esveld 1956). In fact,
the way the amendment was developed illustrates the preference
for employers' interests. It had been drafted in secret meetings
between Kuyper and leaders of employers' groups, and the unions
were conspicuously absent from its development. While union
leaders favored the establishment of the insurance system, their
activities were of an extraparliamentary character, consisting of
protests, petitions, and demonstrations. They had no influence
on the structure set up for implementation (W. de Vries 1970,
463).

Though the amendment appealed to confessional parties, it
was finally adopted into the legislation in a different form from
that originally conceived by Kuyper. A compromise over the financing system established an insurance fund rather than direct
transfer payments but required employers to make additional contributions to maintain the constant value of the benefit against
inflation. Also, the industrial insurance boards took on a differ-

ent character from that originally suggested by Kuyper. Rather than being "neoguilds" for industrial codetermination, the boards were restricted to implementation of the program. Finally, membership of the boards was voluntary rather than mandatory. This allowed socialist unions to exist independently of the insurance boards, and the NIB was established to guarantee the availability of insurance schemes for members of socialist unions and nonunion workers in industries where industrial boards did not exist.

The compromise on the Workmen's Compensation Act created a complicated system in which the insurance schemes were administered in part by the insurance boards and in part by the NIB. The organic corporate groups envisioned by Kuyper would not be instituted until 1953, when membership of the boards became mandatory (Mannoury 1972). It was a compromise no group was satisfied with, but one that ensured passage of the law. One important point about the development of this first piece of legislation is that it represented a successful effort on the part of state and business leaders to set the terms for the organization of industrial workers, a success made possible by the fact that the legislation preceded the development of organized unions. Another important point is that this law introduced a strong religious dimension to the corporatist bodies. The premium placed on voluntary, grass-roots corporatism was one that allowed Catholic and Protestant unions to become represented on the boards because, unlike the socialist unions, the confessional ones adopted nonconfrontational attitudes concerning labor-employer relations.

The enactment of a workmen's compensation program in the Netherlands established the precedent for the corporatist involvement of producer groups in the area of social policy, and this organizational structure was to set the tone for the development of future workers' insurance programs. During debates over the issue of workmen's compensation initiative was also taken on establishing a pension system for workers who were no longer able to work because of old age or long-term disability. As I mentioned above, the question of disability and retirement pensions had reached a stalemate resulting from a dispute over the nature of entitlements.

An effort to break the stalemate came in 1905 with the introduction of a "invalidity" bill to parliament. Introduced by a coalition government led by Kuyper, the bill proposed establishment of mandatory insurance for wage earners that would include a pension for both disability and old age for workers and their dependents. However, partners in the coalition government, citing the report of the research committee, rejected the idea of a mandatory pension program (MvT-AOW 1955, 10). When a conservative government came to power in 1909, the effort was renewed. A second bill, introduced in 1911, did not differ substantially from the first except that it set no mandatory requirements for participation. The opportunity for insurance was left as a decision of the worker. The bill passed, establishing the first pension system, which went into effect in 1913 (Invaliditeitswet 1913). Like the workmen's compensation program, the pension schemes were to be administered by the industrial insurance boards and the NIB.

But the debate on social insurance did not end with the establishment of these programs. Socialists and liberals, who still favored a universal scheme, noted that the programs applied only to wage earners. The law included no provisions for participation by the self-employed. This concern led to the adoption in 1919 of the first legislation designed to cover the self-employed, the Voluntary Old Age Pensions Act (Wet op de Vrijwillige Ouderdomsverzekering 1919). Initiative for this legislation came in response to the observation that self-employed workers usually did not make adequate provision for disruptions of work, especially retirement. Like the Invalidity Act, the Voluntary Old Age Pensions Act created a state-guaranteed opportunity for subscribing to a retirement insurance on a voluntary basis. In parliament an amendment to make participation mandatory was rejected as a violation of the voluntary insurance principle. Once the act was passed, the structure for implementation was the same as for the others. The self-employed had the choice of signing on to the system through the NIB or one of the industrial insurance boards (*Vijf en Zestig* 1966).

Together these laws established the first social insurance programs in the Netherlands. While they were exclusively workers' insurance schemes, covering only workers and their immediate dependents, and only on a voluntary basis, they set a precedent for a state role in social policy. Administrative costs for the programs were borne by the state through the NIB, although the state's role was not monopolistic. Much of the implementation was left in the hands of the industrial insurance boards. The semipublic status of these boards represented the origins of tripartite corporatism in Dutch social insurance. The original proposals had been based on Bismarck's legislation in Germany. For different reasons, liberal and confessional leaders saw in the German model results that they desired to duplicate in the Netherlands. Indeed, some of the reasons for adopting and then adapting the German model were similar to those that inspired Bismarck. Social insurance was seen as a mechanism for staving off socialist organization of the work force. It also served the purpose of creating a special place for the work force within the new state. Dutch social insurance, however, unlike that in Germany, incorporated workers into an economic system governed by corporatist bodies that were divided along religious lines.

FURTHER DEVELOPMENTS PRIOR TO WORLD WAR II

The creation of programs for workers' insurance had two broad effects on social welfare programs in the Netherlands. First, they established a system of workers' benefits that outlined entitlements for assistance based on a record of productive participation in the economy. Second, the system of entitlements for workers reduced the number of individuals eligible for assistance under the Poor Law. Poverty came to reflect a notion of the truly needy — those who had no recourse to an entitlement program. This development became more pronounced in the 1920s and 1930s with the enactment of unemployment programs. The effects of World War I, especially the disruption of shipping lanes, first raised unemployment as a serious problem in the Netherlands. In 1914 a royal commission created to study the consequences of poverty and unemployment resulting from the war issued a report that concluded that there was a difference between circumstantial unemployment and simple poverty and suggested that the industrial insurance boards take measures to provide benefits for the unemployed (Berger 1936). The first policy response to unemployment took the form of a resolution (Werkloosheidsbesluit 1917) that encouraged the boards to establish unemployment funds. Initial unemployment programs were incidental and received state support at ministerial discretion (Braakman et al. 1984, 65). The Great Depression exacerbated the unemployment problem and led to the establishment of a state-guaranteed unemployment fund in 1935. World War I and the Great Depression also affected the character of poor relief services. Whereas unemployment programs might otherwise have reduced the poor rolls, the influx of war refugees from Belgium placed greater burdens on poor relief services, especially in the southern part of the country. The refugees were cared for by municipal agencies since the private charities lacked the resources to provide aid to refugees. This enhanced the position of municipal poor services as compared to charity services.

But the Dutch response to the Great Depression cannot be completely characterized as an expansion of welfare programs. The combined impact of the new programs led to concern over cost. Unlike Swedes, whose socialist governments followed Keynesian economics and used deficits to spend their way out of the depression, the Dutch were more frugal. In an attempt to cut costs of the new insurance programs, the government introduced a retrenchment bill in 1935, which proposed reducing benefits for illness, retirement, and workmen's compensation from 80 to 70 percent of the last earned wage. The government claimed that this would bring benefits in line with those in other countries, but its critics pointed out that the measures would not produce substantial savings. Disagreements over the bill prompted the Catholic party to withdraw its confidence in the government. In the new cabinet the bill was withdrawn, but the debate continued. The government insisted that the method of financing, from individual funds, combined with the low level of insurance taxes, left the insurance programs unable to operate without heavy state subsidy. A new retrenchment bill was introduced that proposed eliminating the state subsidies over a five-year period by increasing contributions from wage earners (Hoogland 1940, 184–208). This resolved the immediate budgetary problem, but the long-term implications of the decisions further illustrate the preference for business interests in early Dutch social insurance. The bulk of the social security tax increases were assessed to employees, a change that broke the parity between the relative contributions of employers and employees. This regressive component of the financing scheme was introduced at a time when labor had a limited voice in legislation, and to this day the Dutch welfare state continues to be one largely paid for by the workers.

Aside from concerns over the cost of social insurance, complaints were raised over the administration of the programs. The problems were mostly of a practical nature, arising from a discrepancy between the intention of the laws and the actual practice. The dualistic pattern of public law and private law organizations in the implementation of the legislation had proven costly and confusing. Programs were administered in part by the industrial insurance boards and in part by the NIB. The insurance boards were private law agencies often organized on the basis of pillar affiliation. For example, within a single industrial sector, Catholic, Protestant, and "independent" insurance boards provided workers' benefits to members of their group. In 1933 an effort was made to consolidate the various pillarized industrial insurance boards into a single "business council" for each industrial sector. These business councils (*Bedrijfsraden*) were to operate as public law bodies charged with the administration of all legally mandated workers' benefits. Confessional forces accepted the creation of the councils as advisory bodies, to facilitate coordination among the insurance boards, but blocked the proposal to change responsibility for administration of the programs. Consequently, while intended to streamline the administrative structure of worker's insurance, establishment of the new business councils only made the system more confusing by creating a new layer of advisory agencies, rather than replacing the plethora of pillarized private agencies (Veldkamp 1949, 243).

A larger problem existed in the operation of the voluntary pension system. The intention of the program was to provide self-employed individuals an opportunity to subscribe to a state-guaranteed retirement insurance. The confessional government that had enacted the program found the issue important enough to delay implementation of the mandatory pension program for wage earners (the Invalidity Act of 1913) until the voluntary program had been passed by parliament in 1919. The problem was that the self-employed simply failed to take advantage of the program. The NIB conducted a study of it in 1939 and discovered there were 160,000 eligible persons who had still failed to sign on and who carried no private retirement insurance. To address the problem, the Ministry of Social Affairs began drafting a bill to make retirement insurance mandatory for all self-employed individuals. With the onset of World War II, however, the initiative was dropped (*Vijf en Zestig* 1966).

Thus, by the beginning of World War II, the character of welfare services had changed in the Netherlands. The development of the insurance system found its basis in a specific response to the social question that pitted liberals against conservatives. Liberals wanted a greater degree of state control over welfare programs, while conservative religious forces strove to limit the degree of state meddling. To the extent that both succeeded in their objectives, the result was a complicated set of institutions that represented compromise between the two rather than the victory of one faction. The pattern was true in poor relief as well as in social insurance: religious charities handed out money that came from the state treasury but made their own determinations as to who was eligible for assistance.

Evolution of the Dutch Corporatist State

The basic contrast in early social welfare programs in the Netherlands, compared with other countries, is that though social reforms were written into public law, the policies were pursued by encouraging and even underwriting private law administration of welfare services. The result was a system in which public tasks were carried out in part or in whole by private bodies, bodies that under the protection of private law, continued to exercise a great deal of discretion in the implementation of public policy. The resulting administrative system of the programs possessed a confusing complexity. Four types of structure developed: (1) private bodies established under private law (e.g., the private charities and industrial insurance boards); (2) mixed government and private organizations established under private law; (3) social corporations established under public law (e.g., the NIB and municipal welfare agencies); and (4) mixed government and private bodies under public law (e.g., poor councils and labor councils) (Couwenberg 1953). This complicated configuration of organizations marked the beginning of corporatist patterns in Dutch social welfare and was fostered primarily by religious political mobilization. The development of the policies that comprise the modern Dutch welfare state occurred within the context of these corporatist institutions, and these bodies would come to play a significant role in the post–World War II development of the Dutch welfare state.

4

Reasons for Late Development: False Starts after World War II

"If the world ever comes to an end, I will go to the Netherlands, because everything there happens fifty years later."
— Heinrich Heine (quoted in Goudsblom 1967, 21)

Lateness seems to be the best word to describe the last two centuries of Dutch history. Despite its geographic location at the core of Europe, the Netherlands failed to keep pace with the developments occurring in neighboring countries. Industrialization is the best example. While just across the North Sea, England was the first country to embark on industrialization, and just to the south, Belgium was the first country on the continent to mimic the process, the Dutch failed to pay heed to this change in the mode of production. In large part, the reason was the important role the Netherlands had acquired as a commercial power in the eighteenth century. Its prowess as a trading power produced a large middle class, but one that became complacent and lacked the entrepreneurial spirit necessary for industrialization. Late industrialization also explains much of the late development of trade unions as strong political forces. Unionization made little sense in a country where the major social division was not between classes but between the cities and the countryside (Jonge 1971; Zahn 1989).

Lateness, however, does have its advantages. Alexander Gerschenkron (1962) has observed that countries that industrialized late were able to do so more quickly. They were able to draw lessons from their neighbors' experiences and avoid some of the setbacks of experimentation. Late countries were also less constrained by the existence of institutional structures that made it difficult to adopt innovations. The advantages of lateness are important for understanding the development of the welfare state. For the early industrializers, social welfare became an issue after the effects of industrialization had become apparent. Later industrializers were able to recognize the consequences of industrialization and to take corrective measures from the very beginning. Germany is a good example: Bismarck was able to introduce social security programs simultaneously with the onset of industrialization rather than waiting for its effects to create a demand for policies.

But the German experience points to another factor that helps late development succeed. Bismarck's introduction of social security worked because he was able to use the state to set the terms for industrial organization. In other words, the advantages of lateness are enhanced when there is a strong state capable of acting upon the lessons that it draws. In the Netherlands, by contrast, there was no tradition of a strong state, and the early discussions of social welfare were dictated by the political forces that characterized the preindustrial social order — forces concerned with continuing the tradition of a limited state.

To cite another example, the Beveridge Report served as an example for the expansion of welfare in postwar Europe. Countries that had strong state traditions and sought to duplicate the British model effected universalization of welfare in a short time. In Czechoslovakia, for example, this was done by 1948, before communist rule brought an end to the Czechoslovakian Republic (Rozehnal 1972). Although similar ideas for universalization of welfare were discussed in the Netherlands and they were also inspired by the Beveridge Report, it was not until 1957 that the ideas began to be realized in programs. The delay occurred even though proponents of welfare reform occupied important positions in government.

Throughout the 1950s, the Labor party was a member of governing coalitions and controlled the Ministry of Social Affairs, yet the retirement pension was the only program it managed to universalize. In part, the effort was stalled by more conservative members of the coalition governments. But the primary reason was that policy at the time was made by corporatist bodies rather than by the government. The corporatist bodies were controlled by opponents of universalization, and it was that institutionalized opposition that accounts for the delay. In this chapter attention is focused on how those corporatist institutions allowed certain interests to resist welfare reform.

THE IDEAS AND IDEALISTS
BEHIND THE MODERN DUTCH WELFARE STATE

Whereas the early part of the twentieth century was noted for pronounced cleavage among pillar groups, World War II constituted a watershed in Dutch politics. Following the invasion and occupation of the country by Nazi forces, many political leaders escaped to London and established a government in exile. Many other political leaders, unable to escape but refusing to cooperate with the occupying forces, were interned in the former Abbey of Saint Michiel, appropriated by the Nazis for use as a prison. In both places a new spirit of cooperation developed that marked a departure from the conflict-laden politics that marked the interbellum. Political leaders came to view the pillar-based conflict among political groups as a dysfunctional influence that had prevented effective governing of the country. Setting their sights on eventual liberation, both groups developed specific plans for reform that would realize this new cooperative spirit. The plans were broad and comprehensive. Attention focused on changing the ideological orientation of the political groups as well as reconstructing a war-ravaged economy. These concerns brought attention to the system of welfare provisions that had been at the core of the ideological dispute.

In Saint Michiel prison the ideas for reform took on an introspective character. Except for occasional messages smuggled in and out, the prisoners were isolated from the outside world. They did manage to keep themselves busy by developing new bridges of political cooperation, which resulted in a proposal for a new political group, the Netherlands Union (Nederlandse Unie). It was intended as a movement rather than a political party, one that would cooperate with existing parties to offer lists of candidates equally committed to fostering a "breakthrough" in the old pillar politics. Although the movement fizzled after liberation, many of its founding figures rose to positions of political influence and carried with them the ideas that inspired the movement (Keizer 1979). One of these figures was Willem Drees, a socialist leader who later became prime minister.

Drees, in conjunction with other socialist prisoners, participated not only in the Netherlands Union but also in redefining Dutch socialist thought. Class struggle was rejected in favor of functional decentralization, which took the form of a specific definition of corporatism. Dutch socialists articulated a corporatism, unlike the Italian model, based on voluntary cooperation. As it pertained to social welfare, Dutch socialist thinking on corporatism advocated mandatory membership of all workers on corporatist bodies, which would be tripartite organizations. Rather than the bipartite form of voluntary corporatism that already existed, tripartite corporatism would allow labor and capital a voice in discussions of policy, but the state would occupy a stronger role in supervising the activities of the administrative agencies. It was a vision of corporatism that found sympathy among progressive Catholics and was accepted by liberals because of the cooperative spirit that inspired it (Lehning 1984; Miedema 1957).[1]

In London the government in exile busied itself with two major tasks that had a direct bearing on future reform of social wel-

---

1. There was a third transpartisan action group comprised of political leaders in the Hague, the Nederlands Gemeenschap, which advocated a Salazarian style of corporatism to transcend the parochialism of pillarized politics and which presented its proposals to Nazi *Reichskommissar*. Dutch historians remain divided in their interpretations of the motives of this group. Some have viewed it as an attempt to maintain national autonomy in the face of foreign occupation, while others (and at the time, even the political leaders in London) have seen it as an unwitting accomplice of the occupying authorities (Smith 1988).

fare. The more important was the provision of refugee relief to Dutch civilians in hiding. Much of the relief was channeled through the underground resistance to provide food and clothing to the numerous "outlaws" of the occupation, primarily Jews and Social Democrats. The other task consisted of thoughtful studies of the issues of reconstruction of the war-ravaged country, assuming Allied victory. In contrast to the introspective activities undertaken by the Saint Michiel prisoners, the government in exile enjoyed close contact with other Allied powers, and this closeness produced much trading of ideas. A great deal of theorizing went into a report commissioned to examine possible changes in the system of social insurance to be enacted after the war. The commission was comprised of representatives of the pillar groups in London who had some expertise in the field of social insurance. Most of the members were reform minded, motivated as much by the boredom of life in exile as by their zeal for reform. A Social Democrat, A. A. Van Rhijn, chaired the commission (Tempel 1946).

The Van Rhijn Commission, as it came to be called, embarked on an exhaustive study of the extant social welfare provisions, outlining faults and offering suggestions for a restructuring of the system. In exploring potential solutions to the problems that plagued the old system, the commission studied the Beveridge Plan and the Wagner Report, which formed the basis of social security programs in Britain and the United States, respectively. The Van Rhijn Report focused on two major problems. One was a problem with the organizational structure of the existing programs. The other was a perceived inadequacy in the degree to which the public was covered by them. The general organizational problem was created by the dualistic structure of implementation that placed administrative responsibility for the programs in the hands of both private and public agencies, which had overlapping tasks but no clear demarcation of responsibilities. Moreover, the character of this administrative opaqueness varied from program to program. For some programs, such as the voluntary retirement pensions scheme, the administration was centralized, while for others, such as unemployment and disability benefits, it was decentralized. Also, in some cases the decentralization involved functional organizations (i.e., industrial insurance boards and private charities), while in others it involved local government (i.e., municipally operated poor councils). The Van Rhijn Report offered substantial but not complete proposals. At the behest of confessional members of the commission, who objected to proposing any changes in the role of private charities, references to poor relief were oblique. Instead the commission concentrated on restructuring the system of social insurance, an area where general agreement among the members could be found.

To improve the coverage of social insurance, the British Beveridge Report formed the core of inspiration for a new basis of entitlement, that of citizenship. Citing the trend in past social insurance measures toward encompassing more members of the population, the Van Rhijn Commission argued for expansion of social insurance from an exclusive system of workers' insurance to an inclusive system of public insurance. Yet the commission did not consider the creation of state-sponsored pensions a desirable means of achieving comprehensive coverage. The suggestion of a state-guaranteed pension system had already been raised and rejected in the earlier discussions of Dutch social insurance, and the sentiments of the commissioners were no different from those of their legislative predecessors. Instead the Van Rhijn Report argued that further advancements in social insurance should provide a British-style safety net for all Dutch citizens, but one that essentially would be an insurance program rather than a state pension system (*Sociale Zekerheid* 1945, 7–11).

To maintain the insurance principle, the commission borrowed ideas for financing from the U.S. Wagner Report. The plan was to finance the system through equal contributions by employers and workers. This would maintain an element of solidarity by requiring contributions from those with an ability to pay while benefits went to all citizens regardless of their record of premium payments. As in the U.S. system, the insurance principle was expressed through provisions that awarded a full pension to all individuals who had a forty-year record of premium contributions, whereas those who failed to meet the forty-year requirement would be docked 2 percent for each year short of forty. In all cases, however, the state would subsidize pension entitlements so that all citizens would receive at least 70 percent of a full pension. In the event of the death of the pensioner, the pension would continue to be paid to the surviving spouse. Thus the pension would provide a minimum to all citizens but would also retain the insurance principle by giving an earned right to members of the work force (*Sociale Zekerheid* 1945, 8–15).

Despite the large inspiration for the proposals from the U.S. and British social insurance systems, the Van Rhijn Commission did not advocate simple and complete adoption of these foreign models. In proposing changes in the administration of programs, the commission found that neither of the other systems offered useful solutions to the problems of the dualistic administration while simultaneously accommodating the array of private agencies in a restructured administrative system. In the words of the commission report:

> The time has come for a radical break from the dualistic system upon which the implementation of social insurance has until now rested . . . since soon, in our country, a more overwhelming majority than ever before will be prepared to search for that which binds rather than that which divides. It is self-evident that this cannot be imported from abroad but must build a connection between the two existing domestic types (*Sociale Zekerheid* 1945, 67).

To accommodate this duality, the commission proposed a uniform organizational format for all social insurance programs. All would be jointly administered by the NIB and the labor councils, which would supervise decentralized agencies responsible for the collection of premiums and the payment of benefits. Premiums would be paid into a single fund out of which all programs would be financed. The commission further suggested that the new agencies be decentralized on a geographic rather than functional basis. All private agencies currently involved in the administration of the program would be awarded an advisory role.

The suggestions of the commission effectively demoted the industrial insurance boards, those bipartite bodies of voluntary corporatism, from implementation to an advisory function. This presented a serious challenge to the confessional vision of social insurance, of which the insurance boards formed an integral part. In exchange for this, confessional interests appended to the report a discussion of the system of poor relief that underscored the sanctity of private charities in this field. Poor relief was to continue to form a vital part of the social welfare system as a supplementary aspect. To avoid privation, the existing system of poor relief would persist for individuals whose pension benefits were too low to meet their income needs; for those incapable of working; and for those who had denied themselves the right to a benefit of refusing to work or by being dismissed for faults of their own. Individuals who had no entitlement to social insurance would be encouraged to appeal to relatives, churches, and charities before turning to municipal poor relief agencies (*Sociale Zekerheid* 1945, 81).

The period right after World War II provided the best opportunity for action on the suggestions of the Van Rhijn Commission. The Labor party achieved its "breakthrough" of the old pattern of confessional dominance in Dutch politics by joining the Catholic party in governing coalitions. These Red-Roman coalitions, as they were known, placed power in the hands of Labor and Catholic party leaders who were advocates of welfare reform. The Van Rhijn Report was adopted as the program for social welfare reform, and some of its staunchest supporters occupied key ministerial positions. A major figure at this time was Willem Drees, a man still considered the founder of the Dutch welfare state. Drees held ministerial portfolios in every government from 1945 until 1958. The state secretary for social insurance in the Ministry of Social Affairs during much of this time was A. A. Van Rhijn. C. P. Romme was a leader of the Catholic party in parliament and of the Catholic labor movement. Romme had participated in the drafting of the Van Rhijn Report and was a major proponent of it in his party.

Nonetheless, the types of program envisioned in the Van Rhijn Report were not enacted until the 1960s, when Labor formed the opposition rather than the government. Moreover, though the programs finally adopted were more comprehensive than the original ones, the reforms fell short of the suggestions in the Van Rhijn Report. Thus the crucial question about universalization of Dutch welfare programs is not so much why it happened as why it happened so late. In other words, why was the government unable to realize the objectives outlined in the Van Rhijn Report until the 1960s? The answer lies in the nature of debates that surrounded the issue in the 1950s. Essentially, liberation of the country did not usher in the new political consensus hoped for by both the Saint Michiel prisoners and the government in exile. Not only did the old style of pillarized politics persist, but adherents to the old ways occupied important positions of power that allowed them to stave off welfare reform.

THE FIRST POSTWAR INITIATIVE

At the end of the war, the attention of Dutch political leaders centered mainly on reconstruction, but those who had been part of the new spirit of reform also sought to use the opportunity to effect long-desired changes in welfare programs. The primary mover was the Labor party, particularly its leader, Willem Drees. The initiatives taken by Drees set in motion some fundamental reforms that began to eat away at the power of the conservative forces in the corporatist bodies. His efforts pitted him not only against corporatist interests but also against more conservative religious political leaders who were part of postwar governing coalitions.

Drees's activities were made possible by the Labor party's participation in the Red-Roman governments that held power from the end of the war until 1958. Following liberation, a temporary grand coalition government was put in place. It consisted of all the major political parties, and cabinet posts were awarded to individuals who had been strong figures in the resistance. The following year, in 1946, elections were held and the Labor and the Catholic Peoples' parties were the two top vote getters. As the party that received the most votes, the Catholic party was charged with forming a government, and the task went to its leader, L. J. Beel. Beel was a figure from the old school of Dutch politics who had served in the occupation governments during the war. In forming the new government, he made a momentous decision: he could have formed a confessional coalition with the Protestant parties, but instead he broke his party's traditional pledge not to cooperate with Labor and formed the first Red-Roman coalition. Beel felt incorporation of the socialists in the government was necessary to avert the radicalization of the socialist opposition, but he also assumed the important post of minister of home affairs in the first government and used his position to temper the Labor party's attempts at reform (Bosmans 1990).

Participation in the new government marked the coming of age of the Labor party. And the opportunity to influence government was one it grasped with a vengeance. Willem Drees assumed the portfolio for social affairs and launched two important initiatives. The first, directed at the system of poor relief, was designed to undermine the dominant position of the religious charities. The second was the introduction of an emergency old age pension that constituted the first attempt to universalize social insurance programs.

Willem Drees's initiative in poor relief actually began at the close of the war. Following his release from prison, he began an informal reorganization of poor relief activities, which had been thrown into utter disarray by the war — a reorganization he would succeed in formalizing after the war. The disarray stemmed from many sources. Some of the religious charities enjoyed continued support from the government collaborating with the German occupation; however, many secular ones, especially those that provided aid to outlawed members of socialist organizations and their families, were forced underground. These underground organizations received sporadic, clandestine support from the Allies that was channeled through the Dutch government in exile in London (Nijenhuis and Schouwman 1980). Drees was responsible for supervising the support for the underground charities, and discussions between him and the organizations developed into a proposal for the Nederlands Volksherstel. This was established as a voluntary, cooperative organization for the "moral and material reconstruction of Dutch society." It was comprised of representatives from thirty-four private charities and was directly supervised by Drees (Broekman et al. 1982). Following its creation in July 1945, Nederlands Volksherstel often operated in direct conflict with many of the charities, whose activities were still subsidized and loosely supervised by the Ministry of Home Affairs.

When he became minister of social affairs in 1946, Drees used the post to continue supporting the Nederlands Volksherstel and even expand its activities. Moreover, he was successful in transforming the network of voluntary cooperation into permanent state agencies, the POOs. These were semiofficial organs consisting of religious and secular charities that would cooperate with government social services and would be affiliated with the Ministry of Social Affairs. The religious charities objected to the institutional changes, viewing them as a state intrusion into poor relief, forbidden under the Poor Law of 1912.

Creation of POOs fundamentally changed the ministerial responsibility for services and challenged the autonomy of corporatist relationships between the state and the private charities. Historically, poor relief had fallen under the Ministry of Home Affairs, which was controlled by the Catholic party and had favored perpetuation of the charity-based system. The Labor-controlled Ministry of Social Affairs, by contrast, was concerned with increasing state control of all income maintenance programs and with supplanting the charity institutions. Establishment of the POOs created a centralized program of poor assistance run by Social Affairs, which operated alongside the privatized, subsidized system run by Home Affairs. The redundancy made coordination problematic and exacerbated animosities between social democratic and confessional political forces. Tensions between these ministries increased when Drees succeeded in wresting control of another new aid program, the special War Victims' Assistance Program (Rijksgroepregeling Oorlogsslachtoffers). Hence Drees's initiatives in poor relief created conflict not only with religious charities but also within the government.

The second initiative taken by Drees was directed specifically at social insurance programs. Upon entering office, Drees and his staff took action to fulfill the Labor party's campaign promise to establish universal public insurance (*volksverzekering*). Labor's vision of public insurance included the idea of minimum income benefits, which would encompass the entire population and provide compensation for loss of income due to handicap, old age, or disability. This would be financed through contributions, the level of which would be based on a percentage of wages and salaries, which would then be distributed as a basic benefit to all eligible citizens. Such a financing scheme would reach the solidaristic goal of entitling everyone to a basic benefit, to be provided by those with the greatest capacity to pay. In addition, the Labor party's program criticized the existing situation in which state social insurance schemes were administered by private law organizations. Public insurance was to become a state responsibility and would therefore require a higher state profile in the operation of the programs (Lier 1981, 151).

Drees established a committee to review the system of social insurance, which was to use both the Labor program and the Van Rhijn Report as its points of departure. Yet, before the committee produced any comprehensive suggestions, it drew the minister's attention to some serious problems with the retirement pension. In May 1946 the NIB published a study that claimed that provisions for the elderly under both the Invalidity Act and the Voluntary Retirement Insurance Act were inadequate. Under these programs, retirement benefits had not changed since well before the war and were now inadequate to meet current living costs. Also, the many self-employed who had elected not to participate in the voluntary pension scheme had been forced by wartime inflation to dip into what funds they had saved for retirement and depreciated the value of any money that was left over. These people now faced the prospect of a meager retirement income. For Drees the situation of the elderly presented an immediate need that could not be set aside long enough for the planned review of the social insurance system.

The ministry immediately asked for suggestions from the Labor Foundation (Stichting van den Arbeid), one of the groups responsible for distribution of benefits under the Invalidity Act and Voluntary Retirement Insurance Act. The Labor Foundation is an organization of labor federations that are comprised of representatives of Catholic, Protestant, and socialist trade unions. Each of these federations, in turn, represents its respective industrial insurance board in each economic sector. The Labor Foundation responded quickly, presenting its recommendations in July 1946. In its report, the foundation suggested an increase in the level of benefits under the insurance programs from three-to-five guilders to six-to-nine guilders per week. This would require a heavy state subsidy, which the Labor Foundation suggested be enacted as an emergency measure to take immediate effect for a three-year period until a permanent review of the system of retirement pensions could be prepared for parliament. The recommendation offered no suggestions for addressing the problems of the self-employed who had no pension privileges. These individuals would have to appeal to poor relief charities.

But the suggestions of the Labor Foundation did not receive unanimous endorsement from its member organizations. The Dutch Federation of Trade Unions, Nederlands Verbond van Vakverenigingen (NVV), the federation of socialist trade unions, sent a separate letter of dissent to the ministry: though it participated in the Labor Foundation's report, it believed that action should be taken for all people over the age of 65 and not just those receiving benefits under the existing pension schemes.

The NVV's position was favorably received by the ministry officials, who saw extension of benefits to all elderly not only as necessary in light of actual conditions but also as more in line with their long-term goal of developing a program of public insurance. The ministry responded not by enacting emergency regulations to raise the benefit level but by introducing the Emergency Retirement Pensions Act (Noodwet Ouderdomsvoorziening) into parliament which was designed to replace the earlier pension programs entirely. The bill proposed that pension benefits be made available to all citizens over the age of 65 and that a new system be implemented for the delivery of old age pensions through geographical decentralization under the oversight of the NIB. The benefit levels were raised but were not set at a basic rate: three municipal classifications each had a different level of benefit designed to reflect local living costs. Additionally, as a cost-saving measure, benefits were reduced for people in higher income brackets on the grounds that they had less need of income guarantees for their retirement. Another difference between the Emergency Retirement Pensions Act and the previous system concerned the exempt status of premium payments for people who subscribed to a private or corporate retirement pension. The old system had been mandatory for all wage earners and salaried employees, but those who had alternative pension arrangements could be exempted from payments. This exemption was abolished on the grounds that the new pension was a basic benefit available to everyone that should be contributed to by everyone (MvT-Noodwet 1946, 1–5).

The Emergency Retirement Pensions Act moved quickly through a parliament sympathetic to the circumstances of the elderly. The changes in the structure of implementation were less favorably received, but anxiety was allayed by the assurance that the act was an immediate necessity and need not be viewed as a model for a permanent change in either the retirement pension system or the total system of social insurance. In parliament the Emergency Retirement Pensions Act received the support of the Labor party and the Catholic party, the other partner in the coalition government. Views on the social insurance system had formed part of the basis of coalition negotiations, and agreement between the two parties on this issue was important. From the Catholic viewpoint, a universal system of social insurance was desirable on the condition that it remain an insurance and not become a state pension (Romme 1950). In addition, the parliamentary opposition raised no major objections to the bill. Not even the controversial structure for implementation prompted debate. The bill moved quickly through the lower house, was accepted by the upper house without a vote, and went into operation in October 1947 (*Kroniek van Nederland* 1987, 952).

Drees's two initiatives constituted the first salvo in the arduous battle for welfare reform and were to have a profound impact on the further development of legislation. His inroads into the poor relief programs brought attention to problems that confessional interests could no longer ignore. In the Queen's Speech of 1946, the provisional government announced plans for a special royal commission to redraft the Poor Law of 1912. The proposed commission was less than wholeheartedly supported by the confessional parties, especially the Catholic minister of home affairs, L. J. Beel, who delayed its creation in an attempt to restrict its membership to his staff and representatives of charities subsidized by his ministry. That effort failed, however, and when it was finally established, the commission also included representatives from the POOs and the Ministry of Social Affairs (Nijenhuis and Schouwman 1980).

The Emergency Retirement Pensions Act offered a profile of the Labor party's plan for a comprehensive system of public insurance. Drees and his staff pursued the act even though they lacked the full support of the affected corporatist interests. The corporatist interests were themselves divided on the issue, and because the ministry had the endorsement of the socialist labor federation, if not the confessional federations, this minimal degree of support was enough to introduce the legislation as a temporary expedient. Yet despite assurances that the Emergency Act was a temporary measure, it instituted important changes in the program of retirement pensions. It marked a departure from the previous system by establishing a formal right to a pension for citizens and not just workers. It also created an entirely new bureaucratic structure for the implementation of the program, one that would be difficult to dismantle.

UNREST IN THE CORPORATIST RANKS

While Minister Drees had managed to take advantage of the postwar confusion to offer fundamental reforms, these reforms also offered a challenge to the prerogative of corporatist interests that did not go unnoticed by those more conservative forces. In poor relief the religious charities countered Drees's efforts to impose more state control over their activities. And this response was assisted by the Catholic party, which continued to be a governing partner and retained control of the Ministry of Home Affairs. Although the Catholic party also supported universalization of social insurance, resistance in this area came from employers' and confessional labor federations, which, from their position in corporatist advisory bodies, were able to launch a counterattack. It was the reaction from both these directions that deadlocked reform throughout the 1950s. Indeed, in comparative terms, it was the strength of conservative forces that made it impossible for the Labor party to realize fully its goal of a welfare state based on universal entitlements. Though the Labor party continued to be part of the governing coalition, policy-making power was shared with corporatist institutions that were dominated by conservative forces.

In the area of poor relief, the initiative for reform was stalled in 1952 by an ingenious maneuver executed by the minister of home affairs, Beel (ARP). Following the parliamentary elections of 1952, the queen appointed the Labor party leader, Drees, as *formateur*[2] in coalition negotiations. Slow negotiations produced an agreement among the Labor party, the Catholic party, and the two major Protestant parties (the Christian Historical Union

2. *Formateur* is the title given to the individual designated by the queen to undertake coalition negotiations. If successful, the *formateur* usually then assumes responsibility for the government as prime minister.

and ARP) on government policy. However, the agreement broke down when the ARP demanded that it receive the portfolio for economic affairs. Beel was appointed as *formateur* in the next round of negotiations, and, although he also failed to form a government, he managed to gain a coalition agreement by proposing creation of a new ministerial post to appease the fundamentalists (Ringnalda 1965).

When the new government was finally formed, the new ministry was labeled the Ministry of Social Work (Maatschappelijk Werk) and was given responsibility for all poor relief services that had previously been the province of the Ministry of Home Affairs. In addition, all noninsurance social programs, the POOs, and the War Victims' Assistance Program were taken from the Ministry of Social Affairs and placed under the auspices of the new ministry. The Labor party gained assurances that legislative tasks assigned to the new ministry would include drafting a replacement for the Poor Law. But more importantly, Beel was appointed as the first minister of social work, and consequently control of all poor relief services was now firmly in the hands of confessional forces (Peper 1972).

An important note must be made about Beel's attitude to welfare reform. He was not a reformer. Indeed, he was one of the old-guard politicians, who had not been inspired by the spirit of cooperation. that had developed in the Saint Michiel prison and in London. After the war he supported his party's commitment to reforming social insurance but objected to reforming the delivery of poor relief. During the war he was minister of home affairs under the occupation government. His position — one shared by all of the confessional parties — was that poor relief should remain a matter of charity, not entitlement (Valk 1986, 190–97).

Beel remained minister of social work for only seven months, to be succeeded by F. J. Van Thiel, another member of the Catholic party, who carried on the tradition of resistance to legislative reform. During Thiel's tenure, the royal commission that had been established in 1946 to propose legislative changes in the Poor Law issued its report. The commission took as its point of departure the premise that the freedom of private charities should be enhanced, but it suggested that the organization of these charities be strengthened to improve the quality of social care. To fulfill this goal two major suggestions were made. First, the report advocated abolition of the right of recovery (see chap. 3) and clarification of the conditions under which charities were licensed to receive state subsidies. Subsidies should be restricted to groups with poor relief as their primary task, and attention should be given to those groups that attempted cooperation with one another. Second, an increase in the oversight role of the state was needed to coordinate activities of the charities and municipal agencies. Stricter supervision of the charities would eliminate the practice of double dispensation (see chap. 3) by requiring all charities to submit yearly reports to municipal officials, who would then report to the Ministry of Home Affairs (Staatscommissie Vervanging Armenwet 1954).

The royal commission's task had been to provide the basis for a law to transform poor relief into a system of public assistance. In all, the guidelines suggested in the report did not pose any threat to the role of the religious charities but rather focused on coordination and the elimination of wasteful bureaucratic aspects of the extant system by advocating standardization of administrative practice (J. de Vries 1985). Nonetheless, proposals in the final report were challenged by some commission members, primarily representatives of the religious charities. Within the commission there was a split between humanitarian charities and municipal agencies that favored development of a public assistance program, on the one hand, and religious charities that raised fundamental opposition to state-sponsored public assistance, on the other (Waals 1975).

The differences in attitude between the religious and secular charities were expressed during proceedings of the Dutch Council for Social Work, an umbrella organization comprised of private charities. The council was designed to encourage coordination among the charities and to facilitate communication with the Ministry of Home Affairs. According to the Catholic charities, the existing system promoted solidarity in society because of the church's encouragement of philanthropy. Any changes in the role of the church would undermine the sense of charitable duty among better-off members of society, thus diminishing their sense of social solidarity. The Protestant charities were more adamant in their opposition to expanded state involvement in poor relief, arguing that church activity was protected under the legal separation of church and state (*Kerkrecht*). This protection placed religious charities in an autonomous legal position compared to the secular charities, which, according to Protestants, could be subjected to state regulation (Dam et al. 1949).

Against this position, representatives of the secular charities noted that a growing percentage of the population had left the church and demanded a status equal to that of the churches for agencies that served these people. These private charities sought equal recognition with religious charities for the growing scope of their activities and believed state supervision of all charity agencies provided the only opportunity to ensure this. For representatives from the municipal agencies, poor relief had become a massive problem that no longer could be adequately handled by private charities. Municipal officials favored abandoning the subsidization policy and creating municipal councils throughout the country to administer the program (Dam et al. 1949).

The differences in position between the religious charities, which defended the status quo, and proponents of reform were intractable. Neither coordination among private charities nor enhancement of state supervision of the administration of poor relief seemed attainable. Though the Dutch Council for Social Work was intended to promote spontaneous cooperation, disagreements among its members facilitated more debate than coordination. The influence of religious charities, which accrued from their privileged status in the field, enabled them to prevail against threats to this status. Without a firm agreement among members of the royal commission, Minister Thiel was unable to take legislative action on its suggestions. Nonetheless, Thiel did incorporate some of the suggestions into bureaucratic practice. The proposal to set conditions for the reward of subsidies, in practice, became a policy of granting subsidies to all recognized charities rather than simply to those that lacked sufficient funds. The expansion in the subsidization policy, however, merely strengthened the position of the religious charities rather than marking a step toward public assistance (Valk 1986, 115). Thiel's failure to pursue legislative reform of the Poor Law was challenged by the Labor party but supported by religious parties in parliament. Hence, by the mid-1950s, the Catholic party had succeeded in returning control of poor relief to the situation that had obtained before the war. Charities were coordinating more with one another, but they continued to operate with only loose supervision from the ministry.

And while the Labor party was forced to watch as it lost control of poor relief programs, a challenge to the Emergency Retirement Pensions Act also marked a setback for their goal of universalizing of social insurance programs. The act was very popular, and its acceptance by parliament was greeted with a public enthusiasm that catapulted Drees to the status of a national hero. Many of the older pensioners in the Netherlands still refer to "cashing Drees's checks." The Labor Foundation, however, was less than pleased with the manner in which its proposals had been ignored in the drafting of the Emergency Retirement Pensions Act and demanded a greater role in the review of a permanent retirement pension as well as the future revision of the complete system of social insurance. By 1954 negotiations between the ministry and the Labor Foundation had still failed to produce agreement on the final form of the permanent revision of the retirement insurance program. The resistance of Labor Foundation's members to proposals by the ministry prevented agreement. In the meantime, the government was forced to renew the temporary Emergency Act three times before a permanent program was enacted.

Of particular concern to the Labor Foundation was the likelihood that further revisions of social insurance programs would reflect proposals outlined in the Van Rhijn Report, especially the plan for centralization of the administrative structure. The Labor Foundation complained that it had been unable to have any input on a document produced by the government in exile, and it demanded more voice in any further legislative action. In response to these pressures, the Ministry of Social Affairs created a second commission to review the social insurance system. This commission euphemistically defined its purpose as "to seek the advice of affected parties that could not be consulted under the occupation" (i.e., the Labor Foundation) (*Rapport – Inzake de Herziening van de Sociale Verzekering* 1948, 7). This second commission was comprised of six members, three of whom represented the affiliate groups from the Labor Foundation and three of whom were staff members of the Ministry of Social Affairs; it was chaired by the ministry's state secretary for social insurance, A. A. Van Rhijn. The Second Van Rhijn Commission, as it came to be called, moved quickly and in 1948 published its report. The commission changed a number of suggestions put forward in the earlier Van Rhijn Report. It accepted the idea of expanding the availability of the insurance schemes from coverage for workers to universal coverage, but it objected to making participation mandatory, especially for the self-employed. Another difference between the first and second reports came in the form of suggestions for administrative restructuring. The second report proposed that the industrial insurance boards continue to administer the programs for their members, while the administrative duties for the rest of the population would go to the NIB.

Because the Emergency Retirement Pensions Act had already introduced a new administrative structure for retirement pensions, the commission dealt with this program apart from the other social insurance programs and suggested a number of basic changes. Most importantly, it acknowledged a desire to expand the availability of the retirement program beyond the circle of income earners. Whereas the Emergency Retirement Pensions Act had created an income-indexed benefit, the commission suggested the creation of a flat-rate benefit for all recipients regardless of

116

income. Also, the geographic indexing of the benefit would be
replaced with a uniform nationwide benefit. The former, introduced by the Emergency Retirement Pensions Act, had caused
problems. The idea had been to develop five classifications according to cost of living, which would be used to determine the
level of benefit in a particular region. The problem stemmed from
constant debates over the classification of specific municipalities.
In most cases municipalities challenged their inclusion in certain classes, and the practice had been to place disputed cases
in the higher classification.

Also, under the Emergency Retirement Pensions Act, the government had continued the prewar system of "back-service." Back-
service amounted to a subsidy of the pension program whereby
the state fulfilled the premium obligations for individuals whose
record of payments had not provided them a sufficient benefit.
The Emergency Retirement Pensions Act inaugurated a back-
service responsibility that would bring everyone up to 70 percent of a full pension, a figure chosen as the level that would provide all elderly citizens with a basic pension. A full pension was
the reward for a full lifetime's work.[3] The Second Van Rhijn Commission endorsed the back-service responsibility of the state.
Unions particularly favored the back-service provision because
it would force the state to fund pensions out of general revenues,
rather than by increasing insurance premiums.

Whereas the level of benefits and expansion of the program
did not create much strife in the commission, discussions of the
administrative structure of the system were characterized by a
split in opinion between government officials and foundation representatives. On the ministry side, commission members believed
that a system designed to include the whole population could
not be administered by the industrial insurance boards. Maintaining the role of the insurance boards would require that in-

---

3. The full pension actually was awarded only to married pensioners, since
in the 1950s most Dutch households only had one income earner. Unmarried
pensioners received a seventy percent pension regardless of work history, since
they presumably had no dependent spouse to support.

dividuals who did not belong to any board be assigned to one. Such an administration, according to the ministry staff, not only would be confusing and difficult to regulate but also would constitute a loss in freedom for the insurance boards due to the huge oversight role the state would have to assume. Furthermore, the extension of the right to the whole population shifted the responsibility for fulfillment from these private agencies to the state. Therefore ministry officials suggested the creation of a central agency to administer the whole retirement pension system, but one that was not a purely state agency. The Social Insurance Council, as this central agency was called, would be comprised of representatives of the producer groups in which the state and employer and employee associations each had one-third representation (*Rapport — Inzake de Herziening van de Sociale Verzekering* 1948, 35–37). [4]

Confessional members of the Labor Foundation disagreed with the ministry's proposal for administrative restructuring, arguing that it was the responsibility of the business community to care for workers who were no longer in a position to work because of old age, illness, or disability. Though they recognized that the division of the administrative system among a number of insurance boards would create problems, they saw this as preferable to a central agency that, despite nominal representation by corporate interests, would be fundamentally a state agency. To include nonworking citizens in the administrative apparatus, representatives of the Labor Foundation suggested the creation of a general insurance board that would operate alongside the existing boards (*Rapport — Inzake de Herziening van de Sociale Verzekering* 1948, 37–38).

The commission resolved this disagreement by proposing the creation of an administrative structure that responded to the concerns of both camps. The compromise solution proposed the establishment of the Social Insurance Council, which would rep-

4. The report noted that one member of the Labor Foundation favored this government proposal. Presumably this person was the NVV representative.

resent both state and private interests, to oversee the system. Implementation would remain in the hands of the industrial insurance boards, and under the boards would be created a permanent bureaucratic staff (dubbed the Central Administration Office) with various specific tasks, such as accounting for funds.

During deliberations of the Second Van Rhijn Commission, ministry staff had been busy preparing legislation for a permanent retirement pension program that was based essentially on the one created by the Emergency Retirement Pensions Act. The ministry's goal was to present legislation in time to meet the three-year expiration date of the Emergency Retirement Pensions Act in 1950. The drastic changes suggested by the Second Van Rhijn Commission threw these preparations far behind schedule. By May 1949 it became clear that a new law, which would accommodate the position of the Labor Foundation, could not be prepared in time. As an expedient, parliament ratified a three-year extension of the Emergency Retirement Pensions Act.

In June 1949, Van Rhijn sent a memo to A. M. Joekes (PvdA), then minister of social affairs (a position he held from August 1948 until September 1952), that shed light on the decision-making process in the Second Van Rhijn Commission. The memo stated that despite the differences of opinion over the structure for implementation, the commission chose a compromise system that it believed would find favor with the majority in parliament.[5] At the time a parliamentary majority was held by the confessional and liberal parties (KVP, CHU, VVD), which were also partners in the governing coalition. A principal issue for confessional and liberal groups was the extent to which state meddling in the social insurance system could be minimized and the role of the industrial insurance boards could be maintained. In addition, this time the ministry lacked the support of the NVV, the group of socialist trade unions that had earlier supported pas-

5. All internal memos of the Ministry of Social Affairs are on file at the Historical Archive of the ministry in files titled *Totstandkoming van de Algemene Ouderdomswet*. In this chapter all references to discussions among ministry staff come from these files.

sage of the Emergency Retirement Pensions Act. The NVV sided with the confessional federations in their desire to maintain the role of the industrial insurance boards in the administrative structure of social insurance and even suggested that participation in the insurance boards be made mandatory. In the end, the insurance boards banded together to resist the ministry's proposal to reduce their role.

The compromise developed by the commission fostered a minimum agreement among corporatist interests and alleviated concerns about parliamentary acceptance of the proposal. The compromise was introduced to parliament as a bill to reorganize the administrative structure of workers' insurance programs. The Social Insurance Organization Act (1952) established a new administrative structure for all social insurance programs that followed the outline of the Second Van Rhijn Report.[6] But the law failed to offer any means of incorporating the retirement pension schemes into the new administrative structure without abolishing some of the provisions that had been instituted by the Emergency Retirement Pensions Act, specifically the universal inclusiveness of the act. The 1952 act introduced mandatory participation in industrial insurance boards for all wage earners, but it retained the provisions for inclusion of the self-employed on a voluntary basis.

Despite this setback, the ministry continued preparations for a permanent retirement pension. Recognizing that the parliamentary strength of confessional interests endangered passage of any proposal that included mandatory participation of the self-employed, Van Rhijn suggested that the issue of the self-employed be put aside. Instead, he focused first on securing a law that adequately covered wage earners and later expanded to include the

6. The bill submitted to parliament originally proposed organization of the social insurance programs completely under the auspices of the tripartite public law councils of labor. Producer groups objected to the bill and Minister Joekes was forced to withdraw it. The second bill, submitted in 1952, followed the guidelines of the Second Van Rhijn Report and secured the position of the private law industrial insurance boards in the implementation of social insurance (Janssen and Berben 1982).

self-employed. This solution was rejected by Joekes, who saw it as a defeat for the goal of a public insurance. To pursue the creation of a public insurance, the ministry had to develop a strategy to overcome the potential parliamentary obstacle. Minister Joekes sought suggestions from the NIB on the best way of incorporating a public retirement insurance into the framework of the newly restructured social insurance. In addition, he solicited the advice of the labor councils, the public law tripartite bodies that supervised the administration of the programs.

Both of these organizations endorsed the ministry's plan for development of a public retirement pension. The labor councils suggested (1) that implementation not be left in the hands of the insurance boards because the distribution of the non–wage earners (the poor and the self-employed) over twenty-six different boards would be a monumental task; (2) that as private organizations, the insurance boards were an inappropriate body to administer entitlement programs; and (3) that a better solution would be to give jurisdiction entirely to the state agencies involved in the administration of social insurance, the NIB and themselves.

The report from the NIB was substantially the same as that from the labor councils, but it added statistical support for the ministry's position. The bank gave a detailed financial analysis of present and projected costs of the program. A number of possible scenarios were worked out showing the costs of the program at different levels of benefits and premiums, setting the retirement age at 67 or 65 years, and the administrative costs of different structures. The bank warned that, if the programs were left in the hands of the insurance boards, it would become possible for individuals to receive double pensions by signing on with two different boards. While this could be avoided by strict but expensive oversight of registration procedures, the whole system could be made much less costly by creating a single retirement pension fund managed by the NIB. It is important to note that the bank had a partisan as well as an institutional reason for supporting the ministry's proposals. The statistical advisor for the bank was a former Labor party leader, Hein Vos, a staunch proponent not only of universal insurance but also of ideological purity. He had been removed from participation in government by Drees, who viewed him as too radical and uncompromising. The financial studies that Vos conducted of social insurance always pointed to the cost-effectiveness of a state pension program.

Despite the cost-effectiveness of developing a universal, state-operated retirement pension system, the ministry's goal continued to meet political resistance. This time, Joekes was faced with opposition from other cabinet members. Inclusion of the self-employed raised the pragmatic problem of how their premiums would be collected. The easiest solution would be to collect the benefit indirectly through tax revenue. However, this was suggestive of a public dole rather than public insurance, and even Labor cabinet members were sensitive to the insinuation of a state pension. Prime Minister Drees argued that exempting the self-employed from premium payments would also require the same exemption for wage earners, and the insurance principle expressed in the program would be lost. Moreover, premium payments also put a natural brake on demands for raising benefit levels.

By the beginning of 1952, Joekes's tenure as minister of social affairs was distinguished by no notable progress on a permanent retirement pension program. The primary opposition came from corporatist interests. The minister already had the support of the governing coalition for a public retirement insurance. Catholic ministers endorsed the solidaristic goals, but they still objected to changes in the structure of implementation that would restrict the role of the industrial insurance boards. The Catholic party's position was informed by the ideological principle of subsidiarity, which prescribed that administrative tasks be delegated to private organizations in the industrial community. But this obstacle was not insurmountable. The primary opposition came from conservative Protestant interests that were not in the government. They objected to any state mandate for social insurance, on the basis of their ideological principle of sovereignty in one's own circles, that is, that social welfare should be achieved through voluntary rather than state-imposed arrangements. The dogmatic adherence of the conservative ARP to this position had isolated it from participation in government from the end of World War II until 1952 (Komdeur 1986). However, its sentiments were represented in the policy process through the Protestant representatives in the Labor Foundation, and despite their lack of governmental power, conservative Protestant interests contributed to the delaying of the legislation.

BUILDING A COALITION OF CORPORATIST SUPPORT: THE REQUEST FOR AN SER OPINION

To develop a legislative plan that would appease the "social partners" (labor and capital), it appeared that the ministry would have to abandon its goal of universalizing the pension program or give assurances that the industrial insurance boards would continue to play a substantial role in its implementation. Minister Joekes did neither. In a series of meetings between him and Finance Minister Lieftinck (PvdA), a strategy was developed to circumvent the authority of the Labor Foundation. A meeting on 6 April 1951 between these ministers and their state secretaries resulted in a decision to go ahead with drafting bill and ask the newly created SER for its advice on it.

The SER had been established in 1950 as a tripartite advisory body, and the government is required to ask its advice on all matters of economic policy. Since its inception, it has been the peak council representing labor and capital, and its opinion has come to overshadow those of other corporatist bodies. It is comprised of representatives of labor federations and employers' federations and independent councillors appointed by the government. The proposal to ask for comment from the SER on an issue of social insurance policy had been based on a broad interpretation of its purpose that extended its role from social issues concerning workers to those concerning the whole public (Dercksen et al. 1982). Joekes's proposal to ask the SER for advice on the public pension program was approved by the cabinet on 30 July 1951.

Joekes may have hoped that the SER would approve his plan

for a public retirement insurance and that the weight of such an opinion would overcome parliamentary opposition. But more important was that the request for advice constituted a public statement of plans for the new legislation. The pension system established by the Emergency Retirement Pensions Act enjoyed a huge degree of popular support, which Minister Joekes hoped to use to overcome the opposition from other corporatist bodies (G. Scholten 1968, 440). Joekes and Van Rhijn submitted a lengthy request, which amounted to a trial balloon of the plan, to include the self-employed in a system of public insurance as well as ideas for changing the administration of the system.

The request to the SER envisioned the creation of a mandatory retirement insurance system and gave two justifications for it: its administrative simplicity and the historical reality that persons who had no pension encountered financial difficulties in their retirement years. As the report stated, "One could also imagine that the risk of an uninsured retirement threatens everyone, and that society has the collective duty to ensure that no one become dependent on third parties" (Joekes and Van Rhijn 1952, 14). Retirement assistance for the whole population was to take the form of a minimum basic pension, designed to cover only basic living requirements. Individuals were left the responsibility of making their own provision for income above this level.

The request for an SER opinion on a retirement pension law marked a monumental juncture in the role the council policy would play in the development of social insurance legislation. The leadership established a special subcommittee that was given the task of preparing a draft of the SER's report. This subcommittee was chaired by a royal appointee to the council, Hein Vos, who was also statistical advisor for the NIB. Because sentiments among the council's members were unfavorable toward the proposal, Vos kept the SER report in committee for over a year in an effort to muster the necessary support.

In the meantime, a change in government produced a ministerial reshuffling. Joekes was succeeded as minister of social affairs by another Labor party leader, J. G. Suurhoff. Like his prede-

cessor, Suurhoff became impatient with the SER's slow progress
in offering its advice. The Emergency Retirement Pensions Act
had already been extended once for a three-year period, and it
now appeared inevitable that a second renewal would be required
since the delay of the SER report made it impossible to submit
the bill to parliament in time. Public and political pressure was
mounting for a swifter handling of a definite old age pension.
Responding to this pressure, Suurhoff embarked on some political maneuvering that succeeded in overcoming opposition to the
bill. Suurhoff began a public relations campaign in which he ac-
cused the SER of depriving the elderly of their due. In statements
reported by newspapers in November 1953, he announced that,
if the council did not tender its report immediately, he would
submit the bill to parliament without its advice. The parliamentary opposition viewed the minister's threat as a cheap political
stunt. However, in response to the public threat to its credibility,
as well as to its role in the future development of social legislation, the SER hurriedly acted on the proposal. It was rushed out
of committee, placed on the agenda of the next plenary meeting,
and passed at that meeting.[7]

The SER report advised that the government take measures
to establish a legal duty for *all* individuals to insure themselves
against loss of income due to old age. Moreover, the premiums
should be paid by all wage earners, self-employed, and those with
an independent income (SER-Advies 1954, 24–25). A proposal
from employers' representatives to exempt from premium payments those individuals who subscribed to a private pension plan
was voted down. The report suggested that, because of its public
rather than private character, the program not be implemented
by decentralized organs in the industrial sectors. Instead, the NIB
should be re-formed into a legally independent organization
charged with the implementation of the program. This new body
would be comprised of royal appointees, and special attention

---

7. This information is from archival files in the Historische Archiev, Ministerie van Sociale Zaken, titled "Totstandkoming van de Algemene Ouderdomswet."

should be directed toward the representation of social groups (SER-Advies 1954, 96–100).

Suurhoff's challenge had succeeded. The SER report in overwhelming proportion agreed with the original suggestions from the ministry. The precedent for asking the SER's advice on social insurance issues had been established, but at quite a cost to its role. Regardless of the SER's official status as an advisory body, the ministry had been prepared to go forward with the legislation without its advice. It had become clear that the council's position was merely pro forma and need not be taken seriously by government.

Publication of the SER's advice opened a public debate over the issue of retirement pensions. Prior to this time, public attention had taken the form of complaints over the constant delays. The SER report presented the public with the opportunity to respond to a definite proposal. The public discussion, as it was played out in newspapers and periodicals, was marked by a variety of viewpoints that corresponded with ideological groupings. For liberals, the council's advice answered the expectation for an expansion of the system beyond the circle of wage earners (Ridder 1954). Catholic leaders viewed the report as the most viable means of developing a permanent program within the present system, although strong disagreement came from conservative Catholics, who objected to the reduced role of the industrial insurance boards. This objection had also been raised in a dissenting opinion appended to the SER report that had been signed by representatives of Catholic employers' and labor federations. Aside from these differences in attitude, the report was viewed as an acceptable compromise by all parties.

The public response also put a great deal of pressure on opponents of welfare reform to back the popular plan. One consequence of the proposal was a complete about-face in the ARP's attitude toward public insurance. J. Zijlstra, the leader of the ARP, argued that his party's "sovereignty" principle was an antiquated concept that no longer provided practical political guidelines. Zijlstra's attitude became the party line in 1952, and on the basis of its turnaround on the issue of public insurance, the ARP was able to join the coalition government formed in September 1952 (Komdeur 1986). It is a matter of speculation whether the party's change in attitude was prompted by a true shift in belief or by a practical concern that it could better temper the Labor party if it were a governing rather than an opposition party.

With the SER's report in hand, the ministry began final preparations of the bill. A committee was established to bring the draft bill in line with the SER's advice and review it article by article to ensure its technical-juridical and administrative merits. The committee ended its review in November 1954, and the final version was presented to parliament in 1955. In parliament, debates centered on specific items in the bill. Most notable were complaints about the exclusion of public employees from the pension benefit even though they remained premium payers. Public employees had a separate retirement pension system, and the ministry argued that in the interest of solidarity they should also be required to make premium payments. Another issue was the designation of the benefit level for unmarried persons and the question of whether this should be set at 60 or 70 percent of a full pension. While principled objections were also expressed, they did not result in amendments to the bill. In the end, the ministry's strategy to create a bill that could be accepted by all groups succeeded. The bill passed with only two dissensions by representatives of the Staatskundige Gereformeerden, a right-wing Calvinist party (Eijk 1957).

On 1 January 1957 the Public Retirement Pensions Act went into effect. It introduced the concept of public insurance into Dutch social welfare programs. For the first time in Dutch history, an insurance program was established that entitled every citizen to old age assistance. This step, however, represented only a partial victory for Labor party leaders, for whom public insurance was the centerpiece of a plan for comprehensive welfare reform. Three factors contributed to the final enactment of the program: the initiative taken by the Labor party; the resistance of corporatist interests; and the Labor party's efforts to overcome that opposition by making appeals to the public and other corporatist bodies.

Crucial to the success of the legislation had been Labor control of the Ministry of Social Affairs throughout the entire development of the act. Though the ministry post changed hands among different members of the party, there was a consistency with which all pursued the creation of a definite retirement insurance as a program of public insurance. The initiative taken by Drees in creating an emergency program immediately after the war had encouraged public support. Joekes's strategy to overcome opposition to the program by asking the advice of the SER challenged the prerogative of the industrial insurance boards. Suurhoff's publicity campaign further garnered public support for a permanent retirement program based on the Emergency Retirement Pensions Act. Yet credit cannot be attributed entirely to the domination of the Labor party. Also instrumental was the cooperation of other political factors, the most important support coming from Liberals and moderate Catholics, who made no major objections to the legislation.

CONCLUSIONS

The decade after World War II was a period ripe for welfare reform. In many Europeans countries it was a time in which dramatic strides were made to expand programs and increase benefits on the basis of ideas found in the British Beveridge Report. The Netherlands was no exception. In London, the government in exile had produced a voluminous study of social welfare that suggested universalization of entitlement programs, drawing its inspiration from the British and American models. Following the war proponents of this new vision for social welfare occupied key positions in government that should have made it possible for them to reach their goals. Most notable on this point were the participation of the Labor party in governing coalitions from the end of the war until 1958 and Labor control of the Ministry of Social Affairs. In addition, many leaders of the other major parties, particularly the Catholic party, were adherents of the spirit of cooperation and compromise that had developed in London and in the Saint Michiel prison.

Yet during the 1950s legislation that would achieve welfare reform failed to appear. In two different policy areas, poor relief and social insurance, strong opposition to reform came from private interests that were able to block reform because of their representation on corporatist bodies. The Dutch case shows that in a country where corporatism was the rule for policy making, initiatives taken by the government cannot be realized without the support of corporatist interests. Despite the early initiatives by the Labor party's Willem Drees to challenge the prerogative of the corporatist bodies, their institutional power allowed them to resist the challenge.

The nature of the challenges and of the responses, however, varied between the two policy fields. These differences are worth noting because they say much about the way corporatism operates in a country where the nature of corporatist representation is influenced more by religion than by class. Drees first sought to break the privileged position religious charities occupied in the delivery of poor relief. That position was not a formal one, but one that had been built over the years as a result of close contact between the charity agencies and the Ministry of Home Affairs, which had been controlled by confessional parties. Drees strove to break this relationship by taking advantage of the postwar confusion to increase the role of the Ministry of Social Affairs in supervising relief activities. He found support among the secular charities, but the religious ones resisted the intrusion. Furthermore, the Ministry of Home Affairs was controlled by the Catholic party and took action that supported the status quo. Beel managed to block Drees's initiative by establishing a new Ministry of Social Work, which was placed under control of the Catholic party. That party's control of the new ministry permitted the religious charities again to enjoy their privileged relationship with a sympathetic minister and made it possible for the party to resist legislative reform.

The Development of the Dutch Welfare State

The important point about corporatism in this area is that it was characterized by informal but strongly entrenched relationships that had been built over time. The tradition of limiting state intrusion into poor relief served the interests of the religious pillars and proved to be resistant to challenges from outside. Moreover, corporatism in poor relief represented something more than the primacy of bureaucratic politics over party politics as a factor that determined policy decisions. As a feature of social organization, the religious dimension also characterized party politics. The Red-Roman coalitions precluded a coherent government position on reform in poor relief, and religious interests in government as well as society joined forces to resist the socialist initiative.

In the area of social insurance, corporatism took on a slightly different form, but the religious dimension also had a profound influence. In contrast to poor relief, in social insurance corporatist institutions had a formalized position. Unions and employers were awarded membership on the bodies, but unlike corporatism in countries where these interests are organized on a functional basis, Dutch union and employers' federations are divided along religious lines. Religious unions developed a cooperative relationship with religious employers. This dimension was more salient than class divisions between workers and employers and made the corporatist interests resistant to the Labor party's initiatives.

The Labor party's efforts to enact universal social insurance also illustrate how political leaders made use of the chaos of the postwar period. Drees was able to push through an emergency pension plan that became the model for further initiatives. Yet passage of the Emergency Retirement Pensions Act produced a backlash from corporatist interests who demanded more influence on further legislation. The influence of these groups, particularly the confessional trade federations, had two major effects: first, their incorporation in the policy-making process caused long delays in the development of the legislation that slowed Labor's plans to institute a series of public insurance programs; and second, the program retained its insurance character. Entitlement to benefits was based on the payment of premiums, and consequently it did not become a state pension.

Corporatist opposition to the retirement plan was finally overcome by the ministry's appeal to the SER. But Labor's goal of making the pension program the cornerstone of a comprehensive system of public insurance was thwarted by union involvement in the Second Van Rhijn Commission. Confessional unions gave their support to the public retirement insurance on the condition that the other insurance programs remain defined as workers' insurance, administered by the industrial insurance boards. This concession was ratified by the legislative reorganization of the social insurance system in 1952.

One of the fascinating things the history of the Public Retirement Pensions Act illustrates is the complexity of Dutch corporatism. In the 1950s corporatism in the area of social insurance had become marked by a proliferation in the number and types of institutions. There were bipartite institutions in which state officials had no representation, tripartite institutions supervised by ministries, and tripartite institutions on which independent councillors, rather than the state, served as the third party. Without a clear hierarchy among the various bodies, reform-minded ministers moved from one to the other searching for support for their proposals. Although it was a slow process, this strategy allowed them to overcome early resistance to the enactment of universal pensions.

Passage of the Public Retirement Pensions Act instituted two changes that would contribute to the growth of the Dutch welfare state. First, the inclusion of corporatist interests in the administrative structure of the program made its operation more costly because of the proliferation of redundant bureaucratic agencies that duplicated many tasks. Growth of this bureaucracy became exponential as the later insurance programs were enacted. Second, the broad popularity of the program changed the nature of debate about social welfare, as was demonstrated by the acceptance of the programs by parties of the right. This general consensus on the desirability of the Dutch welfare state translated into a greater concern with improving the level of benefits and inclusiveness that transcended objections to the potential cost. A number of later amendments to the program in the 1960s increased both its scope and its cost — specifically, raising the benefits from a basic income to a "social" level of income, and finally to the level of the minimum wage. Thus, while the politics of welfare reform delayed the development of the modern Dutch welfare state, the moderate reforms that were enacted set in place changes that would contribute to the rapid growth of the welfare state in the 1960s.

5

Reasons for Rapid Growth:
Changes in Corporatist Relationships

"Policy is not always something you're entirely sure of."
— J. Van Houwelingen, former state secretary
for defense, 18 May 1987

The 1960s were a period of so-
cial and political change. By the close of the decade, the pattern
of consociational decision making, which had typified Dutch
politics since the early part of the century, had been replaced
by open challenges to this tradition. The social relations that had
characterized Dutch pillarization began to crumble. Church at-
tendance fell off, and fewer people declared any religious affiliation at all. Secularization of the society led to a cataclysmic drop
in electoral support for the confessional political parties, prompt-
ing all of them to search for new issues to bolster their support.
Many capitalized on the popularity of welfare reform and incorporated it into their platforms. This shift in position by the religious parties generated a political consensus on welfare reform
that had been absent in the previous decade. The decline of religion as the dominant line of cleavage also affected economic relations. Unions discovered a greater degree of common ground with
one another, introducing a class dimension to Dutch politics as
they banded together against the employers. The consequent polarization between labor and capital interests produced gridlock
in corporatist decision making.

Social and political change had important effects on institutional relations, proving the old style of corporatism anachronistic in the changing political environment. The corporatist gridlock allowed the ministries to exercise more control over the policy

agenda, thereby giving the government greater freedom to pursue its new consensus on reform. As they embarked on reform efforts, ministry officials began to court professionals in the policy field for their advice, further challenging the role played by corporatist bodies in the policy process. Also, not only were the government and bureaucracy challenging the old style of corporatism, but in addition, parliament embarked on a period of political activism, and radical factions attempted to assert parliamentary authority over decisions on policy. Finally, the political pacifism in society diminished as Dutch citizens began to organize into lobbying groups. The net result was that the institutional relations that had permitted opponents of the universalization of welfare to stall efforts at reform disappeared, and into the vacuum poured a myriad of new groups each scrambling to establish itself in the new decision-making process.

Yet political consensus and institutional change were only two of the reasons for the rapid growth of the Dutch welfare state. Another was that the decisions taken went far beyond the original intentions of policy makers. That is to say, the rapid growth of the Dutch welfare state was also an unintended consequence of the development of policy. Though a political consensus had been reached on the desirability of adopting universal income support programs, the agreement among the left, as well as the right, was that they should provide a very basic level of support. Even the Labor party, the staunchest advocate, envisioned a welfare state that would provide modest incomes to keep people out of poverty. The system that was created, by contrast, granted for relatively extravagant levels of support far beyond this original objective. There are many reasons for the unintended growth. One was that ministry officials became concerned with making programs more inclusive, to ensure that there would be no holes in the safety net. These concerns overrode economic considerations. The 1960s were a period of economic growth, and programs were developed on the basis of optimistic projections of future revenues. That proved to be a mistake after the oil crises of the 1970s, when economic stagnation hit the country.

In short, the politics of social welfare in the 1960s occurred at a time when conditions were right for dramatic changes in policy. All these changes were reflected in the development of three major income maintenance programs that put the finishing touches to the Dutch welfare state. In 1963 a Public Assistance Act replaced the old system of poor relief. It made financial assistance to the poor a state responsibility rather than a matter decided at the discretion of charities. In 1967 a new Disability Security Act replaced the former accident and invalidity insurance programs. Although it was still a workers' insurance, policy makers continued to push for enactment of a Public Disability Act, and their efforts bore fruit in 1976. The influence of the changing political environment on the development of these programs and their impact on the growth of the welfare state are the themes of this chapter.

THE CATHOLIC PARTY'S TURNAROUND: THE PUBLIC ASSISTANCE ACT

The Dutch case is interesting in comparative perspective because it grew under the tutelage of the Catholic party (see Becker and Kersbergen 1986; Swaan 1988). This defies the common assumption that control of government by the left is a necessary condition for growth of the welfare state (see Stephens 1979; Korpi 1980), an assumption based on observation of the Swedish case, long considered the epitome of an advanced welfare state. But, as Giovanni Sartori (1966) has observed, left-right continua do not work well for many European countries, and confessional parties do not fit comfortably along them. Dutch observers have confirmed that Sartori's conclusions equally apply to the Netherlands (see, e.g., Jong and Pijnenburg 1986). In part, it was competition with the left that prompted the right-of-center Catholic party to become a proponent of welfare reform. Also, within the party there was no general agreement on its platform. Some of the younger members were proponents of welfare reform, and as they rose to positions of power in the party, they were able to change its position.

The changes in the Catholic party date back to the middle of the 1950s, when radical factions began to appear in it. These were on the left: some of them advocated closer cooperation with the labor party, while others advocated splitting off from the Catholic party entirely. Tensions erupted when a Dutch bishop issued a mandate in 1954 forbidding Catholics from joining socialist labor unions, voting for socialist parties, or listening to socialist radio broadcasts (I. Scholten 1980, 341n3). The bishop's mandate was publicly supported by the leader of the Catholic party, C. P. Romme, although he reportedly regretted having to do so (Bakvis 1981, 77). This created friction with the Labor party, enraged the radical factions, and even dismayed many moderate party members who viewed the mandate as an unnecessary provocation.

To keep the party from disintegrating, and to maintain peace with the Labor party, the Catholic party began to articulate a new attitude toward reform of social welfare. Whereas earlier Catholic party doctrine had advocated the principle of subsidiarity, whereby the state delegated as many tasks as possible to private agencies, the new platform advocated a lower church profile in politics and a more pragmatic attitude toward social policy. Consequently the principle of subsidiarity was dropped, and the party adopted solidarity as its primary ideological principle. The type of solidarity envisioned was derived from Catholic teachings: unlike the socialist version, which emphasized equality in status as the basis of unity among individuals, the Catholic version emphasized empathy of individuals for one another, especially empathy of the privileged for the less privileged (Beus 1983; Couwenberg 1972).

The importance of this new attitude toward social welfare was cemented in negotiations to form the coalition government in 1956. It was to be the last Red-Roman government, put in place following eight rounds of negotiations that took 122 days. One major consequence of the negotiations was that F. J. Thiel was replaced as minister of social work. Thiel's tenure had been notable for remarkably little progress on the development of a public assistance program to replace the system of poor relief. (See chap. 4 for a full discussion of Thiel's tenure as minister.) Aside from the expansion in the policy of subsidization, when Thiel left office in 1956, the delivery of poor relief was still dominated by religious charities. In fact, the expanded use of subsidization had given private charities a greater role in the delivery of poor relief services.

The Catholic party retained control of the Ministry of Social Work and put Marga Klompé in charge of it. Unlike Thiel, Klompé was committed to reform. While she had no intention of abolishing the role of religious charities, she viewed their disproportionate influence as anachronistic, and she advocated a stronger separation between church and state (Klompé 1984). Klompé's personal view led her to define two goals that she pursued as minister of social work. First, freedom from material need should be a right of all citizens. Therefore the state, rather than charities, should assume responsibility for realization of this entitlement. Second, free citizens should also be permitted to participate fully in society. This meant that the level of support for the poor should go beyond supplying basic living necessities and should also provide a minimal social existence that would be determined according to each citizen's needs (Bank 1989).

This attitude was expressed in the new approach to funding poor relief programs. In her first budget as minister, Klompé proposed an allocation of funds that, for the first time, would provide more money to the POOs than to the private charities. The POOs were semiautonomous bodies supervised by the ministry. They had been created by Minister Drees at the end of the war. Klompé's intention was slowly to make the POOs responsible for direct financial assistance, while the religious charities would continue to be supported for nonfinancial social work. In parliament the budget prevailed because of the Labor party's support, even though Klompé was criticized by members of her own party, who feared too many tasks were being taken away from church control (Broekman et al. 1982, 162).

In addition to this shift in the administrative tasks of poor relief agencies, the budget also outlined two legislative tasks that would be taken up by the Ministry of Social Work: preparation of a new bill to replace the Poor Law of 1912 and restriction of the right of recovery. Proposed revisions of the Poor Law had long been contentious. The royal commission that had been appointed to draft a new bill had produced no viable solutions, and its report merely illustrated how resistant religious charities were to legislative reform. (See chap. 4 for a discussion of the royal commission's activities.) Equally, Klompé's legislative proposal was disputed by religious groups in parliament: as one Catholic member retorted, "The time is not yet ripe for a new law and it is too late to amend the law of 1912" (*Staatsblad* 1956).

Klompé's attempt to bar private charities from exercising a right of recovery also failed. In negotiations with poor relief agencies, she was supported by municipal officials and secular charities, but objections to the proposal from religious charities prevented her from gaining the necessary consensus of all agencies in the field. While through her budgeting practices she was able to diminish the role of private charities in the administration of financial aid to the poor, her attempt to develop legislation that would make poor relief entirely a state task were slowed by the powerful opposition of the religious charities.

By the end of the decade, however, Klompé did manage to gain the support of the religious charities. But the change came about as a result of a shift of attitude on their part rather than through Klompé's efforts alone. This shift was a product of professionalization of the charities' staffs that unintentionally produced a new perception of their role. The attitude of the new professionals prompted agreement between the ministry officials and the charity agencies that led to general acceptance of the Public Assistance Act.

Professionalization of charity activities began in the mid 1950s when many religious schools began to offer courses in social work. For example, the Catholic Vocational School at Tilburg created a separate degree program for social work. The type of curriculum adopted by this and other programs was based on the burgeoning literature coming out of universities in the United States and Great Britain. Graduates of the technical schools began to enter salaried positions in the charity agencies, which had previously relied on church volunteers (Doorn 1964). These new professionals, although trained at religious schools, had a different perception of their role. Efficiency in delivery of service and coordination among agencies were higher priorities for them than serving as emissaries of a religious community.

The new professionals, moreover, adopted a different attitude toward the scope of charity activities. As trained social workers, they were primarily concerned with hands-on contact geared toward helping individuals resolve problems or cope with difficult situations. In practical terms, they were more concerned with psychological counseling, community organizing, day care, etcetera and had less patience for the sort of bureaucratic activities associated with income assistance (Institutie voor Toegepaste Sociologie 1979).

As the religious charities shifted their focus, they began to refer people who needed income assistance to municipal agencies, thereby increasing the role of municipal poor relief agencies. In addition to this shift, demographic changes in the Netherlands had diminished the significance of the religious charities. A state-sponsored program to encourage emigration was taken up by many less successful farmers who sought better fortunes in Australia, New Zealand, and the United States. Postwar reindustrialization of the country had prompted migration into urban areas. In terms of poor relief, these developments diminished the scope of religious charity services, which dominated in rural areas, and increased demands on municipal agencies in urban areas, where poverty continued to be a problem (Peper 1972).

As the attitudes of charity professionals underwent a shift in focus, so did their view of the desirability of revising the Poor Law of 1912. The new charity staff favored state assumption of all income assistance for the poor, and Klompé found them receptive to her proposals. The minister's first major legislative accomplishment came in 1960 with passage of a law that imposed restrictions on the ways in which charities could exercise their right of recovery. Meetings between the minister's staff and the Dutch Council for Social Work (Nederlandse Raad Maatschappelijk Werk), an umbrella organization representing all private charities, produced agreement on a bill to restrict the right of recovery. Specific provisions excluded exercise of the right against the elderly, who were covered by the newly enacted universal retirement pension program, and against those institutionalized for mental or physical handicaps because of the excessive costs associated with institutionalization. Most important, under the new law the right of recovery could be exercised only by civil authorities, no longer by private charity agencies (MvT-Verhaalsrecht 1960). This restriction marked the first step toward its total abolition and set a precedent for making absolutely no claims against family members and focusing instead on an individual's inability to support him- or herself. The individualized treatment of recipients of poor relief was to be the basis for an individualized means-tested program of public assistance in the planned revision of the Poor Law (Valk 1986, 202).

Formulation of a new Public Assistance Act began with a series of special ministerial conferences in 1961 and 1962, which produced a draft. Representatives of the Dutch Council for Social Work and municipal officials participated in the meetings. The draft bill marked two substantial changes over the previous system of poor relief. Most important was the uncoupling of financial from nonfinancial assistance. The new program would deal exclusively with financial assistance, and financial necessity would no longer be seen as an issue for charity but as a matter of equity and right to be guaranteed by the state.

The draft legislation was circulated to affected agencies in the field of poor relief, and advice and comment were requested of them. These agencies included the POOs religious and secular charities, and municipal social councils, as well as labor unions and employers' federations. The POOs and municipal agencies almost unanimously supported the legislation. The private charities were generally supportive, although major objections were put forward by charities that represented fundamen-

140

talist churches. For example, the Convent of Christian Social Agencies argued that under Dutch church law (*Kerkrecht*) the state's duty was to leave charitable tasks in the hands of the churches and refrain from interfering in church activity. The Central Diocese of the Dutch Reformed Church concurred, citing passages from the Bible in defense of its objection.[1] This resistance from the fundamentalist charities lost its import, however, when the fundamentalist ARP came out in support of the new legislation (College van Advies der Anti-Revolutionaire Partij 1963).

With the general if not unanimous support of the corporatist members, the minister brought the bill before the cabinet, where she was challenged on the manner of determining the benefit. The ministers of finance (J. Zijlstra, ARP), economics (J. W. de Pous, CHU) and social affairs (G. Veldkamp, KVP) all objected to the proposal to determine benefit levels on an individual basis. This, they felt, would offer too many opportunities for costs to grow and would undermine the principle of basic minimum benefits that existed for the social insurance programs. In fact, Gerhard Veldkamp's objection was so fierce that it brought Klompé to tears.[2] The result of the meeting was that Klompé was unable to sway her colleagues, and the cabinet changed the bill to provide a maximum benefit equivalent to the minimum wage (Valk 1986, 206–09). With this change, the ministry submitted the bill to parliament, where the only significant debate again focused on the levels of benefits. An amendment was offered by the Catholic party to reintroduce the individualized calculation of need. Minister Klompé offered no objection to the amendment, and it was approved by parliament (J. de Vries 1985). Following passage of this amendment, parliament ratified the bill.

The Public Assistance Act was designed to tie up the Dutch

1. The responses of these agencies are on file at the Archives of the Ministry of Health, Welfare, and Culture in a dossier titled *Voorontwerp Algemene Bijstandswet*, 'Adviezen Onvangen van Provinciale Opbouworganen, Instellingen van het Maatschappelijk Werk, diverse andere Instellingen, Overzicht en Commentaren (1961–62).'

2. This account of the meeting was given to me by Veldkamp himself.

safety net. It replaced both the Poor Law of 1912 and the special provisions for war victims (Rijksgroepregeling Oorlogsslachtoffers), thereby marking the completion of a state-guaranteed income benefit for all citizens. For Minister Klompé this marked achievement of both her goals. The law created a universal entitlement program and made calculation of needs on a case-by-case basis, But, while public assistance was to complement the system of public insurance, governmental responsibility for these two programs remained with two separate ministries. Public assistance was supervised by the Ministry of Social Work, while social security was controlled by the Ministry of Social Affairs. Not until a major reform of the entire social security system in 1986 did the two programs come under the Ministry of Social Affairs (Heuvel and Maarseveen 1986).

Still, enactment of the Public Assistance Act had a dramatic impact on the role of the private charities in Dutch social policy. It created a legal distinction between financial assistance for the poor and nonfinancial social work. Under this distinction public assistance became a legally recognized entitlement that liberated recipients from the humiliating aspects of relying on social charity. Because the law recognized the duty of the state to guarantee public assistance entitlements, it became the state's responsibility to carry out the program. The new definition of the state's responsibility resulted in the liquidation of the semiautonomous POOs, and administrative responsibility was placed in the hands of municipal social services.

The Public Assistance Act marked a significant departure from the previous system of poor relief, and its cost has grown over the years. In some ways, however, the law did little more than ratify existing bureaucratic practice. By 1963 only 15 percent of poor relief recipients were being supported by private charities. The bulk of financial assistance had much earlier shifted to municipal agencies. Thus the growth was already underway before passage of the law (see fig. 5.1). Moreover, the subsidization policy had paradoxically introduced a greater government role in the distribution of poor relief. As the charities came to rely on

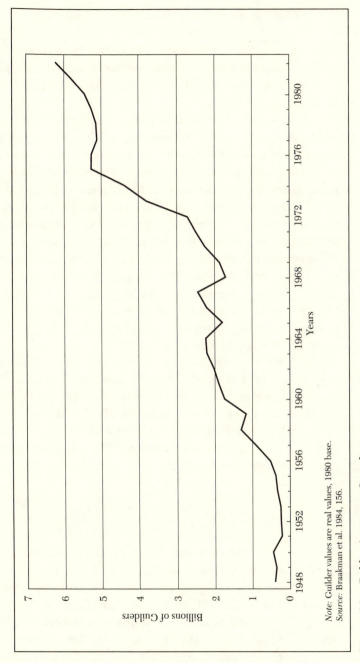

Billions of Guilders

Note: Guilder values are real values, 1980 base.
Source: Braakman et al. 1984, 156.

Figure 5.1. Public Assistance Spending

state subsidization of their work, the ministry assumed a higher profile in poor relief than had been outlined in the 1912 law; this role was simply ratified by the Public Assistance Act (Peper 1972: 324).

The few private charities that were still involved in financial assistance found ways to redefine their role in the new public assistance program. The law left open the possibility of continued involvement since it allowed municipalities to establish advisory committees on which charity agencies could be represented ("Decentralisatie" 1963). Also, many charities had already discovered new tasks they could perform, such as promoting awareness of eligibility among the poor, providing assistance in filling out forms, and acting as intermediaries in negotiations between applicants and municipal agencies. Moreover, passage of the law did not completely abolish the practice of subsidizing private charities. Though direct financial aid had been taken out of their hands, they continued to be subsidized for their new activities. The opaque network of corporatist relations that had characterized the administration of poor relief has since come to typify the field of social work. The same problems of inadequate supervision and ill-defined roles, lack of coordination among agencies, and unclear hierarchies of political responsibility characterize relations between the state and private agencies to the present (Linder 1975; Idenburg 1977; Blom and Blom-Jorna 1978, 148; Peper 1978).

UNIVERSALIZING SOCIAL INSURANCE: MORE CATHOLIC PARTY INITIATIVES

In contrast to public assistance, where reform of poor relief followed a turnabout by both the Catholic party and the religious charities, universalization of social insurance had long been a component of the Catholic party's platform. Thus, when a governing crisis brought an end to the Red-Roman coalitions in 1958 and the Catholic party took control of the Ministry of Social Affairs, progress continued on legislative action. Quick action was taken on a number of programs, but the most significant one, the disability program, proved to be a contentious issue. In part, this was because the idea of a universal entitlement for the disabled represented a challenge to the Ministry of Social Work, which provided for the handicapped under the Public Assistance Act. The initiative of the Ministry of Social Affairs on the disability issue perpetuated the interministerial battle that had been started by Minister Drees following the war. Also, reform of the disability program met with a great deal of resistance from capital and labor interests. The ministry's goal was to turn the old accident and invalidity insurance programs into a public insurance program. Both capital and labor objected to the idea of using social security taxes to provide universal disability entitlements, but they did strike an agreement that transformed the accident insurance program into a lucrative workers' disability program. Passed in 1967, the Disability Security Act led to dramatic expansion of Dutch welfare expenditures and had a number of other unanticipated consequences that eroded the position of labor and capital as corporatist interests.

The story of the development of the disability program begins with the last Red-Roman government. In 1958, after passage of the Public Retirement Pensions Act but before the minister of social affairs, J. G. Suurhoff (PvdA), could introduce further welfare legislation, the governing coalition fell apart. Friction between the parties began in 1954, following the Catholic party's endorsement of the bishop's mandate, and tensions within the coalition were exacerbated by cooperation between the confessional parties and the liberal opposition in parliament. The final straw that ended Labor's participation in government was parliament's rejection of a temporary increase in the direct surplus taxes that had been introduced by the minister of finance, H. J. Hofstra (PvdA). Together, confessional and Liberal party factions in parliament reduced the duration of the proposed tax increase from two years to one. In protest, all eight ministers from the Labor party resigned (Verkade 1965, 242). An emergency government, which took over until elections were called, was a confessional-Liberal coalition. Throughout the 1960s governments were either interconfessional, or confessional-Liberal coalitions. From 1958 until 1973, the Labor party was relegated to the opposition benches.[3]

Following Labor's departure from government, the Catholic party assumed control of the Ministry of Social Affairs. Those ministers were from the moderate faction of the party, which supported Labor's goal of instituting universal public insurance. The first explanation of the public insurance system advocated by moderate Catholics was the Public Widows and Orphans Act (1960), which provided for a flat-rate pension to all surviving dependents upon the death of the head of a household. The program was designed to be an extension of one aspect of the retirement insurance program, under which the pension continued to be paid to surviving dependents upon the death of the pensioner. However, if the head of the household died before he became eligible for a retirement pension, surviving dependents received nothing until the widow became eligible for a public retirement pension at the age of 65. The Public Widows and Orphans Act was justified on the grounds that surviving dependents should not be denied a benefit simply because the head of the household died before reaching the age of 65. Passage of the law expanded the scope of public insurance programs and introduced the principle of equal coverage for equal cases. It also provided a social security entitlement for many individuals who previously had been forced to rely on poor relief.

The minister of social affairs, J. M. A. Van Rooy (KVP) took credit for passage of the Public Widows and Orphans Act but resigned when his Family Allowance Act received weak support in parliament. Following the resignation of Van Rooy in 1961, Gerhard Veldkamp, also from the Catholic party, took over as minister of social affairs and remained in that post until 1967. Veldkamp, however, was more to the left than the other mem-

---

3. There was one exception to this. In 1965, Labor participated in a coalition government with the KVP and ARP that lasted a year and a half, but the Catholic party retained control of the Ministry of Social Affairs.

bers of the cabinet, but he had a strong relationship with the Catholic labor movement, and the support he received from the unions enabled him to retain his ministerial post.

Veldkamp's more radical attitude became apparent when he launched an initiative aimed at the development of a public disability pension. In consultation with his staff upon entering office, he identified what for him was another undesirable hole in the social security net. He claimed that the existing programs for disabled workers discriminated against two groups: the self-employed, for whom no state-guaranteed disability program was available, and the permanently handicapped who were not entitled to disability benefits because they had paid no insurance premiums prior to becoming disabled (Rossem 1962). Personal experience influenced Veldkamp's legislative proposals and led to the development of programs that are unique.[4]

In the 1940s when Veldkamp worked as a clerk in a social insurance district office, he had become dismayed by the way confusing language in the accident insurance program affected its operation. The old program provided awards to workers injured on the job, or while engaged in job-related activities, such as during travel to or from work. The issue of what constituted a job-related activity had produced a number of court decisions that Veldkamp felt violated the spirit of the law. For example, in one case the court denied a benefit to an employee who had been injured while on a social excursion organized by his employer because the excursion was not a normal job-related activity. Since such activities are useful for generating a comfortable working environment, Veldkamp felt the decision was wrong.

Another client was injured while riding his bicycle to work. The court determined that the injury was the result of carelessness on the man's part and denied him benefits. Moreover, some judges were more strict than others. Veldkamp felt that need should be an overriding concern in cases like these and that the

4. Veldkamp related these experiences to me in an interview held shortly before his death in 1990.

only logical solution was to provide benefits to anyone eligible, regardless of the cause of the injury or where it occurred: "If a man can't work, he can't work. And if he can't work, he can't earn his wage. In that case he should be assisted. It made no sense to me that of two people with injuries, one would have to starve." As it was reflected in his legislative proposals, this broad view of entitlement was called the principle of social risk. It is distinct from the principle of occupational risk, which is most commonly found in workers' compensation programs in other countries.

Veldkamp's marriage to a woman with a physical disability made him even more sensitive to the extraordinary financial demands families with modest incomes face in such a situation: "Of course it never really affected me in the same way since I always had a comfortable income. But still, I am aware of how high the costs can be, and that knowledge made me sensitive to the financial burden imposed on a family with a modest income." At the time he became minister of social affairs, there was no assistance program for disabled individuals who had not been members of the work force. This included those who had been disabled from birth, or at an early age, as well as housewives. Poor relief was the only form of assistance available to them and their families. In Veldkamp's view, forcing the disabled to rely on charity was an abomination, which, furthermore, violated his party's commitment to making entitlement programs more inclusive.

His concern with both issues led him to change the way his staff was handling reform of the workers' disability programs. The preparations that were already underway were based on the suggestions of the Second Van Rhijn Commission (see chap. 4). In its report the commission proposed merging the three existing programs that pertained to workers' disabilities: accident, invalidity, and illness.[5] This merger also would necessitate changes in the administrative structure. Under the old programs, insur-

---

5. These original programs were the Ongevallenwet 1901, the Invaliditeitswet 1913, and the Ziektewet 1930 (see chap. 3). In addition, special disability programs for sailors and agricultural workers were instituted after World War I.

ance premiums had been collected by the industrial insurance boards from all their members and by the NIB from all workers who did not belong to a board. The report suggested that membership in an industrial insurance board be made mandatory for all workers — a suggestion that had been made law by the Social Insurance Organization Act of 1952 (Linden 1980).

The commission's report also suggested unifying the three earlier programs into one workers' disability program. Eligibility for benefits would be extended to two years at 80 percent of the wage rate. For the third year of disability, the benefit would be 70 percent, and after three years, 60 percent. Aside from unifying the earlier programs, the suggestion for expanding the duration of the benefit separated the basis of the entitlement from the work history of an individual. Under the proposed plan, any worker who became disabled would never have to fall back on poor relief if he suffered from a long-term disability. Consequently, all three programs could be subsumed under one disability program, and the duration of the benefit would cease to be contingent on the history of premium payments (*Rapport — Inzake de Herziening van de Sociale Zekerheid* 1948, 20–24).

Though Veldkamp supported these reforms, he also wanted to make the disability program more inclusive. In his view, no disabled citizens should be forced to resort to poor relief, hence the disability entitlements should not be restricted to workers but should be extended to the handicapped and the self-employed. This was consistent with his belief in disability as a social risk. He argued that "a disability program should cover the disabled, otherwise you should call it a program for those who lose income when they're hurt." In 1962 he requested the SER's advice on this proposal. It was actually a broad request that asked for general comments on the expansion of all social security programs over the long term, not just the disability program. It included discussions of two new legislative proposals: a catastrophic illness insurance, to provide universal coverage for all citizens who suffered from illnesses that entail exceptionally expensive medical treatment; and a public disability insurance to cover the self-employed and permanently handicapped. Like the other public insurance schemes, the public disability program would be financed through social security taxes (*Sociale Zekerheid op Langtermijn* 1962).

The SER was slow in drafting its response because of a three-way division among its membership. Employers' organizations and Catholic and Protestant labor unions favored merger of the existing programs and also endorsed the inclusion of the self-employed, since they too would be responsible for paying insurance taxes. Representatives of the self-employed, however, objected to including their members in the new program. They argued that the existing programs had been based on the principle that disability was a responsibility of the employer, and that the self-employed therefore should provide their own coverage through the private sector. Both these factions also opposed extending entitlements to the handicapped because this would require increases in the level of insurance taxes. The only group that wholeheartedly supported Veldkamp's proposal was the leftist NVV. Royal appointees to the council were divided among these three factions.

Sentiments in the SER prompted Veldkamp to rethink his strategy for reforming disability programs. Aware that he would not receive the council's support for a single, comprehensive plan, in 1963 he submitted two bills to parliament. One was the Disability Security Act, a workers' disability bill that followed the earlier suggestions of the Second Van Rhijn Commission but also included Veldkamp suggested change in the definition of disability entitlements from an occupational to a social risk. The other was a public disability bill that would cover the self-employed and the handicapped. By submitting these bills to parliament prior to publication of the SER's service, Veldkamp was pursuing a strategy reminiscent of the one Suurhoff had used to gain passage of the Public Retirement Pensions Act. Suurhoff's challenge to the SER had been successful: the council had quickly tendered a report that basically endorsed the minister's bill. In this instance, however, the strategy was not a complete success, and Veldkamp's two bills met with different fates.

Though both were submitted in 1963, parliament did not begin discussion of them until June 1965. At that time, the lower house began discussion of the worker's disability bill but voted to table the universal disability bill pending the SER's report (*Staatsblad* 1965, 1659–78). This prompted the council to issue a report soon afterward. It endorsed the disability security bill, which was already before parliament. On the other bill, however, the report recommended that, though a program to cover the self-employed was desirable, because of the recent enactment of the Public Assistance Act, handicapped individuals were already entitled to basic income assistance and no longer needed to rely on poor relief (SER-Advies 1965). Following publication of the SER's advice, the upper house refused even to debate the public disability bill, and Veldkamp retracted it (*Staatsblad* 1966, 334–41).

Parliament's decision endorsed the SER's prerogative as an advisory body, and the council's endorsement of the bill to reform the workers' disability programs led to its passage in 1966, and the Disability Security Act went into effect in June 1967. The new law engendered two fundamental changes in the old system. The term *disability* was redefined to recognize a worker's incapacity to return to the same job or perform similar work as the basis of entitlement. This was an especially popular provision among the trade unions, which found it humiliating to expect, for example, that a construction worker who becomes disabled through no fault of his own undergo a retraining program, or accept a more menial job. While laudable for its humane focus, this principle led to huge increases in the cost of the program. As under the old program, benefits were related to earnings, and they provided complete income substitutes for workers deemed 100 percent disabled (see table 5.1). Moreover, distinctions would no longer be made with respect to the cause of the disability: a worker disabled while on vacation would have the same entitlement as one disabled on the job. This component of the program reflected Veldkamp's concern with expanding the notion of disability from an occupational risk to a social risk. Compared with other countries, this is the most unusual component of Dutch disability programs and also contributed to the dramatic increase

Table 5.1.   Benefit Levels under the Disability Security Act

Extent of Disability	Earnings-Related Entitlement
15–25 %	10 %
25–35	20
35–45	30
45–55	40
55–65	50
65–80	65
80–99	80
100	100

Source: Kleine Gids voor de Nederlandse Sociale Zekerheid (1986).

in the number of beneficiaries, as well as the cost of the programs (see figs. 5.2 and 5.3).

In addition to changes in levels of disability benefits, the law also significantly altered the program's administrative structure. The new law instituted the Joint Medical Service (JMS), a permanent staff of medical professionals responsible for evaluating levels of disability and assessing changes in the status of an individual's disability that would affect the entitlement to benefits (Scheyde 1967). Establishment of the JMS was deemed necessary to end the costly redundancy in the old programs whereby each industrial insurance board that administered the program hired its own staff of doctors. The JMS's role was merely advisory, however, and was further limited by the fact that many insurance boards opted to retain their own staffs of doctors rather than utilize JMS services (Fortanier and Veraart 1975, 120). Yet even in this limited capacity, creation of the JMS did make doctors important actors in the implementation of the policy.

By 1967 the only progress Veldkamp had made on expanding disability programs was the Disability Security Act. This law expanded the coverage awarded to workers, who continued to enjoy access to a state-guaranteed disability insurance while the

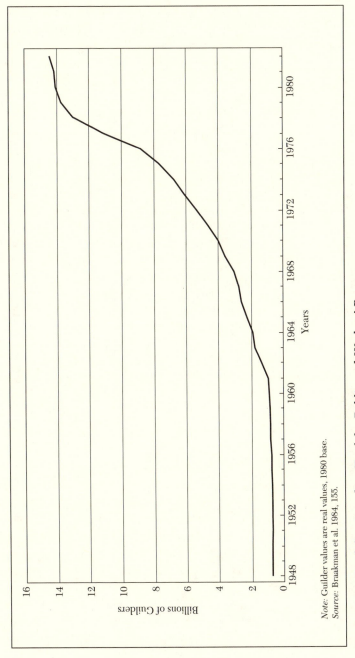

Note: Guilder values are real values, 1980 base.
Source: Braakman et al. 1984, 155.

Figure 5.2. Disability Spending Total for Public and Workers' Programs

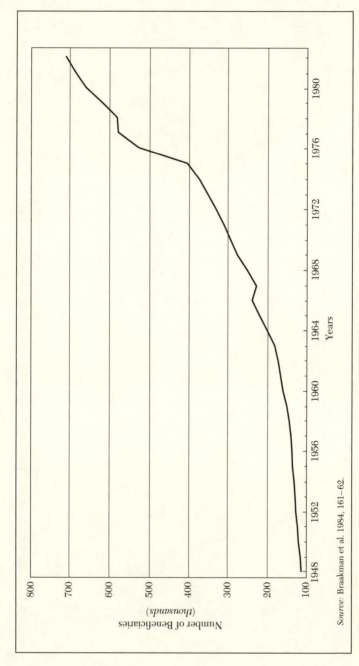

Number of Beneficiaries
(thousands)

Years

Source: Braakman et al. 1984, 161–62.

Figure 5.3.   Disability Beneficiaries Total for Public and Workers' Programs

self-employed had to buy their own insurance through private carriers and the handicapped were forced to rely on public assistance. The power of the SER as an advisory body marked a setback for Veldkamp's efforts to create a public disability program. Undaunted, however, he continued with his plans.

NEW POLICY COALITIONS AND THE DEVELOPMENT OF THE PUBLIC DISABILITY ACT

Despite the general consensus, reflected in the SER report, that a disability program for the self-employed was desirable, Veldkamp remained unwilling to offer a bill that did not also include the handicapped. Although he did not stay in office long enough to see the Public Disability Act passed, his unwillingness to compromise on the issue delayed action long enough for changes in the old style of politics to foster the development of new policy coalitions that supported his position. Two factors contributed to the creation of these new policy coalitions. First, various lobby organizations generated broad-based political support for the public disability bill. Second, assuming that the program was to become a public insurance, the ministry began consulting with the newly created JMS on the best way to implement the legislation. Both the public pressure and the consultation with the medical professionals provoked conflict with the industrial insurance boards, which assumed that they were the major bodies for advising the ministry on administrative matters.

The new policy coalitions developed at a time of crisis for the traditional political groups. Beginning in the mid 1960s, all confessional parties in the Netherlands began to experience electoral decline. In part this was brought on by the secularizing trends that were part of the breakdown of the pillarization of Dutch society. This decline had its greatest impact on the Catholic party, whose stable 30 percent share of the vote throughout the postwar period plummeted to a mere 17 percent by 1977. Moreover, the general trend was exacerbated by radicalization of the Catholic unions. In 1967 the Catholic party pulled out of a seven-month-old coalition with Labor that was supported by the Catholic Federation of Labor Unions. In the ensuing election voters punished the party for bringing down a popular government. The new government was a minority coalition led by the ARP, Veldkamp declined to serve as minister of social affairs, and the ARP took control of the ministry. The departure of Veldkamp, the labor movement's major supporter in government, contributed to the tensions between the Catholic party and the Catholic Federation of Labor Unions, which threatened to withdraw its support for the party and even entertained the possibility of a merger with the leftist NVV, although this idea received weak support from the rank and file (Bakvis 1981).

The increased radicalism of the Catholic unions also affected relations within the SER. In 1970 the council finally published its full response to Minister Veldkamp's 1962 request for advice on social security reform. In the interlude it had produced only two interim reports, one that led to passage of the Disability Security Act and another that advocated adoption of a program for exceptional medical expenses. In the report issued in 1970, the SER restated its support for the suggestions in the interim report on the disability program. It endorsed establishment of a special disability scheme for the self-employed but again rejected expansion of the program into a public insurance scheme. Moreover, the SER argued that any provision for the self-employed should be restricted to cases where the disability resulted in loss of income. In rejecting not only the expansion of coverage to the handicapped but also provision of coverage to self-employed individuals with independent means, the SER thus effectively retreated from the principle expressed in the Disability Security Act that existence of a disability, rather than loss of income, should serve as the basis of entitlement. Dissensions to the SER's report were again offered by the socialist union federation, and this time it was joined by the Catholic union federation, both of which desired to retain the more generous definition of entitlement.

This disagreement between unions and employers on the disability issue contributed to the general breakdown in consensus between employers and unions within the SER (Wolinetz 1989). And the stalemate was exacerbated when it became apparent that similar problems existed in organizations of the self-employed. Leaders of organizations of the self-employed also sit on the SER and had originally opposed creation of a separate disability program for those they represented. But interviews with dozens of shopkeepers and other entrepreneurs, made public in a dissertation published in 1968, showed that the leadership did not accurately reflect the interests of its rank and file. That study showed that only 26 percent of self-employed individuals, primarily agricultural workers, failed to carry their own disability insurance, and there was much support among them for the SER's suggestion (Vaandrager 1968).

Armed with the increased support of the unions and citing the Vaandrager dissertation as evidence that the self-employed could potentially be counted on for support, in September 1970, the minister of social affairs, B. Roolvink asked parliament for a show of support for a public disability program that would cover both the self-employed and the handicapped. Although he was from the ARP, as minister he remained faithful to Veldkamp's commitment to enact a disability bill that would include the handicapped, a commitment that led him to circumvent the SER by appealing directly to parliament. The Catholic fraction in parliament endorsed the minister's initiative, which passed with the additional support of the leftist parties. Parliament's willingness to entertain discussion of a legislative proposal that departed from the suggestions of the SER offered a substantial challenge to the council's prerogative as an advisory body on policy. With the support of parliament, the ministry submitted a second public disability insurance bill in January 1971, but it failed when the government fell a few months later.[6]

Failure of the second public disability bill was not well received by one particular group that felt slighted by the government. The

6. Unless otherwise cited, information on the development of the Public Disability Act is from the archival files of the Ministry of Social Affairs in dossiers titled *Totstandkoming van de Algemene Arbeidsongeschiktheidswet.*

Action Group for the Self-Employed, arguing that since the SER had already shown its support for extending disability entitlement to the self-employed, became angry with the Ministry of Social Affairs for what it perceived as unwarranted delays. In the context of Dutch politics, this organization constituted a prototypical political lobby. It represented farmers, truck gardeners, and small shop owners who "felt forgotten as a political force."[7] Its specific complaints were that in contrast to other groups in the work force, the self-employed lacked the type of income guarantees against unemployment, disability, and illness that were available to wage and salaried employees. The action group sent letters to the minister of social affairs and the leaders of all parliamentary parties stating its "desire for a change in this situation."

The interests of the self-employed found that the heartiest reception from the ARP, a conservative Protestant party and one that drew a large degree of electoral support from the self-employed. In its platform for the 1971 elections, the party pledged to support immediate action on a disability program for the self-employed and set this as a condition for participation in a governing coalition. The significance of this demand became evident when the ARP was again given control of the Ministry of Social Affairs. This time, however, Roolvink was replaced by another party leader, J. Boersma. The ARP's parliamentary fraction also underscored the demand. In 1972, during a question-and-answer period, the state secretary for social affairs, J. G. Rietkerk, was taken to task by the ARP members of parliament, who demanded to know why the ministry had not developed any special regulations for the self-employed. They further demanded that he confirm or deny rumors that the delay was caused by the ministry's obsession with creating disability benefits for the handicapped. The state secretary replied that disability insurance for the self-employed was a high priority but that legis-

7. The quotations are from a letter dated 8 February 1971 from the Aktie-groep Zelfstandigen to the minister of social affairs (see n. 6).

lative proposals were being held up by technical difficulties (*Staatsblad* 1972, 2339).

As a result of the parliamentary pressure, however, ministry staff began meeting with the two umbrella organizations representing the self-employed — the Central Small Business Organization and the Central Agricultural Organization — to seek their input on the disability bill. Minutes of these meetings indicate that the "technical difficulties" in drafting the legislation stemmed from the continued commitment of the ministry's staff to the development of a universal insurance that would also cover the handicapped. The umbrella organizations wrote letters of protest to the ARP. Under pressure from that party, Prime Minister Biescheuvel issued a directive to Boersma to pursue immediate enactment of a disability program for the self-employed, drop the issue of the handicapped, and ignore any other technical difficulties that had been holding up drafting of the law. However, the directive came too late. The government fell after the Democrat-Socialists '70, one of the partners in the coalition, withdrew. A rump parliament continued in office until elections in November 1972, but it took no action on the disability program.

Developments during this stage in the drafting of the public disability bill confirm Steven Wolinetz's assertion that changing corporatist relations led to the establishment of new policy coalitions (Wolinetz 1989). Parliament was becoming increasingly assertive in the policy-making process, even challenging the SER's prerogative as an advisory body. Also, the self-employed became dissatisfied with the attitude of their leaders, who, they felt, did not represent their interests in the SER's discussions. Consequently they took direct action by lobbying parliament and the ministry rather than the SER for attention to their concerns.

The Ministry of Social Affairs remained steadfast in its desire to enact no disability program for the self-employed that did not encompass the handicapped, and instead it continued to work on the development of a universal disability program. As further debates over the legislation unfolded, both parliament and the ministry were lobbied by a new set of interest groups representing the handicapped and housewives. This campaign engendered support for including the handicapped in the legislation. Furthermore, within the ministry, drafters of the legislation sought the input of the medical professionals in adding the final touches. Discussions between the ministry and these other groups created new networks of contact that further alienated capital and labor interests from the policy-making process.

What also had become clear up to this point was that the minister of social affairs had little control over his staff. Boersma was unable to follow the prime minister's directive to initiate a program for the self-employed because his staff was still committed to developing a program that would include the handicapped. The reason for this is that Dutch civil servants generally are more autonomous than are, for example, their British counterparts. In the early 1970s this autonomy was enhanced by the political situation. Following the 1972 elections it took almost six months to form a new government, the longest such process ever in Dutch history (Bosmans 1990). Alfred Diamant (1981) has argued that during times of governing stalemate the bureaucracy governs by default. The activities of civil servants in the ministry during 1972 are a prime example of this postulate. Petitions and letters from many lobbying organizations were received by G. H. Jansen, the general director for social insurance, who was receptive to the initiatives of many of these advocacy groups. He incorporated provisions into the draft legislation that reflected their concerns and significantly altered the successive development of the public disability bill. When a left-center coalition agreement was reached in 1973, the government took seriously the provisions that had been added by the civil servants.

This new lobbying campaign was conducted by a number of umbrella organizations that represented social work agencies, which were the main providers of social services and the cornerstones of their delivery to the handicapped. These agencies had evolved from the old system of poor relief as professionalization in the charities led them to redefine their tasks. Moreover, they continued to be subsidized by the Ministry of Social Work (Dejong 1984). The Dutch Family Council, one of the first of these umbrella agencies to lobby the ministry, drew attention to another handicapped group that had been left out of previous discussion of the public disability program: disabled housewives. The council argued that under the proposed bill a single disabled woman would be entitled to a benefit and that equal consideration should be given to a married woman unable to continue doing household chores because of disability. The sentiments of the Dutch Family Council were reinforced by further lobbying by the Dutch Association of Housewives and Aktiegroep Man Vrouw Maatschappij (a gender equality lobby).

The effect of the lobbying for housewives was substantial enough to prompt Jansen to request advice from the SER on the possibility of incorporating them as a category of entitlement under the disability program. The council rejected the idea, claiming that it would require a 1.4 percent increase in the insurance tax, which was unacceptable to both employers' and employees' groups. Moreover, the SER argued that in the case of disabled housewives, there was no question of lost income as a result of the disability and, therefore, no basis for entitlement. Nonetheless, Jansen argued that the SER's exclusion of housewives was inappropriate because it violated the entitlement principle that underlay public insurance. Jansen circulated an internal memo in which he argued that since the existence of a physical disability was to serve as the right that would entitle a person to public disability insurance irrespective of whether the disability resulted in a loss of income, the ministry needed to include housewives in the draft legislation. The collective concerns of the advocacy groups found their way into the third draft, and by 1973 the bill had gone far beyond the type of program originally envisioned by Veldkamp in 1962.

During further drafting of the bill Jansen asked the JMS to outline its position on the proposal for a public disability insurance and to detail any problems it could foresee in its capacity to implement the scheme. Traditionally the ministry had sought the advice of the industrial insurance boards on issues of administration; in seeking that of the JMS, Jansen had circumvented the normal corporatist practice of seeking consultation with labor and capital organizations that administered the program. In part, his reason for consulting the JMS stemmed from the technical expertise it had acquired in the administration of the Disability Security Act. The doctors had come to play a strong role in the program's administration because they were the only people capable of making assessments of degrees of disability (Scheyde 1967, 97). Consequently effective control of the operation of the disability program was exercised by these medical advisors rather than by the industrial insurance boards. In its response to the ministry, the JMS endorsed the proposed insurance, suggesting that the public insurance scheme should use the same categories of disability as those used in determining the level of benefit under the workers' disability program. Furthermore, the JMS suggested that its role be expanded from being an advisory body to being responsible for administration of the program. If the proposal was accepted by the government, the JMS would replace the industrial insurance boards, which administered all the public insurance programs.

The control of the disability program was a contentious issue for the industrial insurance boards. Rumors that the ministry was asking the advice of the JMS angered leaders of the boards, who saw it as a challenge to their prerogative for first consultation with the ministry on issues of policy. G. Immanuels, director of the Social Insurance Council, a tripartite body that represented the industrial insurance boards, contacted the Ministry of Social Affairs by telephone and voiced his concerns about the alleged consultation with the JMS. In Immanuels's opinion it was an ineffective and inefficient agency, comprised of a "huge, huge gaggle of overpaid doctors who do not even bother to keep their mandatory office hours."[8] He claimed it would be better to liquidate the JMS than to incorporate it into the public disability program.

---

8. Quoted from State Secretary Rietkerk's handwritten note about the conversation. For the source see note in bibliography on archival sources.

In his opinion the new scheme should continue to be administered by the industrial insurance boards. The council's protest was effective. The administrative structure of the programs remained in the hands of the industrial insurance boards to preserve the parallel, according to the ministry, with the other public insurance programs (Winter 1972).

In short, the interregnum had produced changes in the way policy was made. The rise of lobbying organizations for the self-employed and the handicapped created new modes for voicing concerns that limited the influence of the SER. And the ministry's concern with working out technical details in the law led it to ask advice of the medical professionals rather than the bi-partite industrial insurance boards, which had historically operated the programs. These new coalitions involved groups that were more directly affected by the programs, whose input was deemed more important than that of labor and capital because the ministry assumed that the law should express a specific conception of entitlement and consulted only with groups that shared or refrained from challenging that assumption.

In May 1973 the governing crisis was resolved. The coalition government that was finally formed represented a victory for the left. Under Prime Minister den Uyl (PvdA), the government's program advocated a turnaround (*keerpunt*) in its approach to social policy, calling for further redistributive measures and further extension of the welfare state (Wolinetz 1983, 16–17). Boersma returned as minister of social affairs and accepted the provisions to include housewives in the scheme on the grounds that similar treatment for similar cases was to form the basis of entitlement. Therefore, any disabled person would be entitled to a benefit, regardless of whether the disability resulted in a loss of income. He offered the bill to the cabinet in March 1974, where the confessional partners in the government supported the provisions for inclusion of housewives. Their support derived from the claim that the wife of a self-employed man often contributed to her husband's business, although her work was not monetarily compensated. In such circumstances, a wife's disability could constitute a loss of income for the household and therefore necessitated an entitlement to a disability benefit. The concern of the confessional parties was also motivated by the fact that many of their supporters lived in traditional families, where the woman stayed at home, and thus this provision would benefit their potential voters.

The mid 1970s, however, were also a time when economic crisis began to cause anxiety about the growing costs of the Dutch welfare state. Hence, despite the Den Uyl government's coalition pledge to expand welfare, ministers from the Labor party began to initiate a series of cutbacks that effectively reneged on the promise (Roebroek and Therborn, forthcoming). As this affected the public disability bill, these ministers expressed concerns about the cost of including housewives in the program. They won a vote to remove the provision, against the protests of some ministers from the confessional parties. After this change the cabinet approved the bill and sent it to parliament.

Thereupon many groups attempted to lobby members of parliament. Groups representing private insurance companies complained about the potential loss of revenue to them if the bill passed, but their arguments did not sway members of parliament. The housewife lobby was a more vocal group and managed to gain parliamentary support. Though Labor party leaders and the Liberal party supported the cabinet's decision to exclude housewives, the "Red Woman's" caucus of the Labor party, arguing that failure to include all women in the plan would be a blow for women's liberation, introduced an amendment to include housewives. The amendment was supported by the confessional parties, which had earlier argued at least for the inclusion of those who worked part time in their husband's business. The amendment passed after being modified to provide an entitlement only to housewives who worked outside the home and who paid insurance premiums.

The Public Disability Act was passed in 1976 and went into effect the next year. It introduced a flat-rate benefit for income assistance to most permanently disabled citizens. It covered individuals who had acquired their disability at birth or in their youth and adults who had at some point paid insurance premiums. Permanently disabled workers continued to receive an earnings-related supplement under the Disability Security Act. The debates that surrounded the development of the public assistance bill highlight the issues that contributed to the expansion of the Dutch welfare state. The law was dogmatically pursued first by Minister Veldkamp, of the Catholic party, and later by the staff of the Ministry of Social Affairs. These efforts had the effect of dramatically expanding the scope of the disability program and of diminishing the power of opponents of the law.

One of the most easily overlooked yet crucial factors in the development of both disability programs was the role of religious parties. They were responsible not only for their passage but also for their relative extensiveness. Though the Labor party generally supported the expansion of welfare, Labor members of government actually tried to slow the expansion, often citing the potential cost as a reason to adopt more limited programs than those suggested by the confessional interests. Why the more centrist confessional parties became advocates of a more extensive welfare state than the left is a question that can be understood only as a function of their pragmatic concern to bolster sagging electoral fortunes. They viewed the disability programs as a type of pork barrel legislation that would do this. In addition, at the individual level Veldkamp's personal conviction that just disability programs were necessary was based on personal experience and went beyond his party's official position.

UNINTENDED EFFECTS AND GROWTH
OF THE WELFARE STATE

Enactment of new laws was one reason for the rapid growth of the Dutch welfare state. Another important reason was that a number of unintentional consequences increased costs. The principle of inclusiveness had been pursued without consideration of the final costs of the programs, as was reflected in discussions of all the legislation, and some of the major themes are worth noting. For example, prior to submission of the Public Retirement Pensions Act to parliament in 1956, it was subjected to review by a ministerial committee that addressed two major issues: the provision for married women and the manner of calculating the reduction in benefit for years of nonwork. Though these were minor issues that merely required working out technical details, every solution raised the potential problem that some individuals would fail to be covered or that, if all were covered, some would receive a greater benefit than they were entitled to. Minister Suurhoff became impatient with the committee's delays. He implored it to consider the public demands for a permanent retirement pension and to solve the legal problems by making sure that no one was excluded.

Hence the committee finally solved the problems by making the program more inclusive. For example, rather than requiring a documented work record to determine the level of entitlement, the program would, for all cases where work records were missing, consider all undocumented years as full work years. Also, all women were considered entitled to a full pension, which meant that all married couples would receive a full pension regardless of their entitlement. These details were designed to guarantee that all citizens would be covered, and this inclusive approach place the burden of proof on the state to determine that someone was not entitled rather than on the beneficiary to provide proof of entitlement. While this solution indeed increased the potential costs, it was incorporated as the only way to maintain the right to benefits as the basis of the program.

Similar concerns with inclusiveness were reflected in the other laws. Sometimes they even took on absurd proportions. For example, in discussions of the public disability bill, consideration was given to covering not only housewives but also hippies. This was at the beginning of the 1970s when the hippie movement was big in the Netherlands. Many young people, in rebellion against the establishment, lived by the American slogan "Tune in, turn on, and drop out." Ministry officials deemed that these people should receive full disability benefits if they qualified. Although the cabinet was less tolerant and the provision was removed from the legislation, the concern was reflected in the development of the Special Assistance Programs for Artists (1969). This program set few conditions on its awards, and virtually anyone who claimed involvement in an artistic endeavor received assistance, regardless of training or qualifications.

Another major reason for increases in expenditure was the introduction of the new Catholic vision of solidarity in welfare programs, according to which the types of benefit available to the work force should also be made available to the general public. The principle had first been reflected in the Public Assistance Act of 1963 when Marga Klompé succeeded in replacing the flat-rate benefit with a floating one to be calculated on the basis of individual need. Veldkamp incorporated a similar idea into the public insurance programs. For example, workers received a vacation allowance as a primary labor benefit; in 1964, Veldkamp added a vacation allowance to the public insurance and public assistance benefits. In 1970 he also raised the minimum benefits by coupling them to the minimum wage, and in 1974, Boersma introduced automatic inflation adjustments to the minimum wage (this was ratified by parliament in 1979), thus further raising benefits. These provisions expanded the costs of the programs as wages rose.

Unions and employers raised little objection to the increases in benefits. Indeed, political resistance to expansion of the welfare state had virtually disappeared by the mid-1970s. In part, this was because unions and employers saw advantages for themselves in the new welfare programs. Following passage of the Disability Security Act in 1967, the number of workers receiving benefits skyrocketed, a phenomenon that cannot be explained by any deterioration in the health of the Dutch work force (Haveman, Halberstadt, and Burkhauser 1984). Rather, the Disability Security Act provided benefits that were far more lucrative than those available under the unemployment program. As the oil crises of the 1970s forced employers to consider massive layoffs, they began to refer employees to their doctors. Use of the disability program as a substitute for unemployment was compounded by the generous criteria for eligibility. Because of the philosophy of inclusiveness, the entitlement was available for not only physical but also psychological disabilities. Especially in the construction industry, many older workers were granted benefits simply because they claimed fatigue. Doctors, in turn, were unwilling to assume the task of policing the program and were lenient in their assessments of patients (Tex and Verhey 1987). Cynical action on the part of labor and capital, combined with inadequate control of the disability program, contributed to the overall increases in the cost of the welfare state.

CONCLUSIONS

In terms of the theoretical issues that guide this study, the rapid growth of the Dutch welfare state in the 1960s was not a direct product of policies borrowed from abroad. The impact of policy borrowing had already been evident in the immediate postwar period, when the ideas for universalizing welfare programs were articulated by the government in exile and the governing coalitions. The original plan was to provide universal entitlements that would offer modest income support. Once the ideas from abroad had been introduced, it was the domestic political situation that shaped the development of programs. Strong resistance to welfare reform had characterized the first fifteen years of the discussion, but in the 1960s the situation changed, and programs were not only enacted but went beyond the notion of providing basic income support.

More important in terms of the theoretical issues that guide this study is the role of confessional political forces. Indeed, it must be kept in mind that it was the confessional center that created the expansive Dutch welfare state. Throughout the postwar period, the Labor party had been mindful of the cost of programs. Its intent was to universalize benefits, not to make them the world's most generous. It was the centrist parties that conducted a purely populist campaign by making welfare programs generous as well as inclusive. And, while the Labor party was concerned with creating modest income supports for all Dutch citizens, the Catholic party viewed benefits as pork barrel for constituents. Declining electoral margins prompted the party to embrace reforms that appealed to potential supporters, such as housewives. Nowhere was this utilization of social welfare more evident than in the ranks of the ARP, which, though it had always been a vehement opponent of expansion of welfare, suddenly became the most strident advocate of programs that affected one of its strongest constituencies, the self-employed. Together these confessional parties became the advocates of the adoption of universal programs that provide more generous benefits than anything the Labor party strove to realize. To understand why this situation obtained it becomes critical to abandon a priori assumptions about what positions left, right, and center parties take on welfare reform and examine the actual positions they advocate and the reasons why they do so (Scharpf 1991). The confessional parties embraced popular issues to bolster electoral support and thereby were forced to compromise or adjust ideology, though the pragmatic rationale for these choices is clear.

Finally, institutional structures had a substantial impact on the outcomes of the policy. But whereas in the 1950s corporatism explains much of the late development of the Dutch welfare state, in the 1960s it was institutional change that explains its rapid development. Beleaguered by challenges from the government and rendered impotent by internal divisiveness, corporatist institutions entered a period of deadlock. The vacuum in decision making was filled by a greater parliamentary assertiveness and especially by challenges from new groups in society that demanded more voice in decisions on policy.

The changing political climate allowed welfare reformers to realize their goals, but political change was not the only reason for the dramatic growth of the Dutch welfare state. Discussions of policy had taken on a logic all their own and produced consequences unanticipated by policy makers. The epigraph at the beginning of this chapter epitomizes how the decisions reached can sometimes defy the expectations of all participants. Although Van Houwelingen's comment was not about the Dutch welfare state, it might well have been. The series of decisions that led to the growth of the welfare state introduced changes that went beyond the original intentions of policy makers. Perhaps because the Dutch economy was doing well, the net effect of these changes was not immediately felt. When economic stagnation hit in the mid-1970s, cost became a central concern of policy makers. Once set in place, however, the programs have proven difficult to dismantle, and Dutch policy makers have come to learn that the politics of retrenchment is an equally thorny issue.

6

The Politics of Retrenchment

"The state is crucial. To reduce it to a condition of an-
orexia or to fragment it is an effort in self-castigation."
— Roel in 't Veld (1989, 31)

Modern welfare states are in
crisis. Since the world recessions of the 1970s, all advanced industrial societies have found it difficult to maintain expensive entitlement programs in a period of declining public revenues. The
attention of political leaders now centers on the need to make
cuts in public expenditures, or retrenchment. However, efforts
in this direction have proven difficult to realize. The problem is
deciding where to make the cuts. Welfare programs are expensive, but they have instituted a system of entitlements that no
one desires to lose. Hence, when governments try to make cuts
in them, the result is usually an outcry from the affected groups,
and sometimes even the general public.

This dilemma of retrenchment in the welfare state is one that
has gained the attention of scholars and has taken on various
themes in the literature. The most alarmist have dubbed the problem a crisis of legitimacy resulting from the inherent contradic-
tion between capitalism and democracy that makes it impossible
to accommodate both within the same political system (see Wolfe
1977; Bowles and Gintis 1987; Offe 1984). Other, less radical ver-
sions of the thesis divide into two camps. One calls it a problem
of overload emanating from a fundamental shortcoming in the
liberal philosophies that underpin modern democracies. Liberalism grants the greedy desires of individuals a superior position
to the collective good, compelling individuals to pursue their own
greedy desires at the expense of the interest of society (Lindblom

1982). The second thesis labels the problem one of ungovernability, brought on by democratic mechanisms that force politicians to sacrifice economic well-being to popular pressures. Indeed, the difference in conceptions of the crisis has ideological roots (see Birch 1984).

Regardless of the differences in theoretical perspective, there are some common strands in this body of research. The major problem is that governments have a difficult time balancing the conflicting demands of cutting public expenditure and assisting those most affected by economic downturn. Also, sustained economic stagnation has discredited the Keynesian approach to reconciling these contradictory tendencies. Deficit spending, the epitome of Keynesian economics, was the short-term approach to dealing with temporary economic downturns while simultaneously maintaining welfare entitlements. This has proven to be an inadequate solution for long-term economic stagnation, but policy makers have yet to come up with an alternative approach. Hence they walk a tightwire that not only has been raised higher from the ground, but also appears to lack any safety net. For fear of falling, policy makers cling more tightly and more timidly.

The Dutch experience over the last two decades is a good example of the problem of retrenchment. When recession hit, the government was faced with declining revenues at the same time as it was carrying out the last expansions of welfare programs. It responded to the crisis with a set of ad hoc and incoherent measures that ultimately failed to relieve some underlying structural tensions in the welfare state. By the late 1980s, a more coherent approach to retrenchment in welfare was articulated. This time, though, the difficulties in carrying it out were produced not by conflicting governmental goals but by resistance from forces in society. As in all countries, in the Netherlands the welfare state has created a clientele that now has a stake in the programs and is willing to defend them against government retrenchment.

This chapter addresses these issues. In doing so, it tells two stories about the politics of retrenchment in Dutch welfare. The first story is about the arduous process of developing a coherent retrenchment policy — a tale of failed efforts to maintain entitlements that finally gave way to a policy that substantially undermined those entitlements. But even after chipping away at the entitlements, the desired budgetary benefits have been elusive. The second story demonstrates how the new welfare clientele has stymied efforts at retrenchment. Here attention focuses on reforms that have been attempted in the public assistance and disability programs, two of the areas of policy that have been the major focus of this book and are the most controversial in the Netherlands. Running through both stories is one common theme: attempts to make fundamental shifts in public policy are circumscribed by politics and the history of past choice of policy.

And though the dynamic of retrenchment differs from the dynamic of growth in welfare, the theoretical approach that so effectively explained the expansion in the Dutch case offers much to explain its contraction. Again, group mobilization explains much about the difficulties individual public officials face in effecting change. The institutional practice of consultation, introduced with the establishment of corporatism, continues to add more voices to the process of forming policy. Yet because retrenchment is a different issue from expansion, and because Dutch politics has changed over the last thirty years, many aspects of the present discussion are different. Religion is no longer a dominant political force. Into its place have stepped many more single-issue, clientelistic groups. Corporatism in its old sense of tripartite negotiation between the state and the social partners is on the skids. The social partners have been superseded by welfare and medical professionals. And in general, politics in the Netherlands has become more open and pluralistic than previously.

THE TRIAL AND ERROR OF GOVERNMENT POLICY

The world economic recession of the 1970s hit the Netherlands particularly hard. It is a country with a small, open economy subject to fluctuations in the international economy. While in the bigger countries the existence of a large domestic economy can cushion some of the effects of international economic crisis, in the countries with small and open economies greater demands are placed on the state to alleviate the consequences of international economic downturn (Katzenstein 1985, 104). Like most European countries, the Netherlands is largely dependent on foreign oil. And because the recessions of the 1970s were exacerbated by dramatic increases in the world price of oil, the Dutch government had very little room to maneuver. Unemployment rose, inflation rose, and economic growth dropped.

A left-center government was in office when the crisis hit. Its incoherent response was produced by its efforts to continue expansion of the welfare state in the midst of the crisis. Under the stewardship of the Labor party, the Den Uyl government had come to office with a pledge of developing postindustrial policies that included calls for codetermination and profit-sharing on the part of workers. The ambitious project was tempered by Catholic and ARP partners in the governing coalition, who agreed to further expansion of the welfare state but rejected the larger reforms in economic relations. The former were to be achieved by coupling social benefits to the average wage rather than the minimum wage and through passage of the Public Disability Act (1976). These were not simply concessions made by the confessional partners in the government; as I described in chapter 5, both changes were carried through by the momentum of the expansion of the welfare state that had preceded the Den Uyl government. Also, enhancement of benefits and passage of the Public Disability Act were supported by the confessional parties as part of the coalition agreement.

It was while these changes were being put in place that the oil crisis hit. Initially, Dutch policy makers viewed it as temporary and increased public expenditure to ease the effects of unemployment and inflation. This Keynesian approach to the problem was initially funded through increasing taxes and kept in check through freezing social security benefits. In 1975, for example, the government adopted a program that would allow benefits to rise only at the rate of 1 percent per year. Though the plan effectively uncoupled the levels of benefits from the average wage, it did not challenge the basic entitlements. Consequently, it failed to produced the intended cutbacks.

With the entitlements intact, demands on welfare services began to increase. By the end of the seventies, unemployment not only continued to rise but proved to be structural and permanent. To make matters worse, a graying population made greater demands on the pension program. As economic growth began to slow, total government outlays reached an unprecedented 96 billion guilders in 1976 and broke the 100 billion mark in 1979 (Bosmans 1990, 105). From the time it entered office in 1973 until it left in 1977, the Den Uyl government presided over the transformation of a budget surplus of 555 million guilders into a deficit of 8.4 billion guilders (Braakman et al. 1984, 173).

The budget deficit resulted from a misperception of the depth of the crisis. It was not a short-term problem that could be alleviated by more public spending. Also, this was not only the fault of Labor participation in the government. One of the truisms of retrenchment policy is that the response of leftist governments differs very little from that of rightist governments, especially in the Netherlands (Vliet 1986). It was not only the Labor party ministers who advocated more public spending. Ministers from the confessional parties, even the more conservative ARP advocated Keynesian solutions. For the confessional parties, moreover, defending the welfare state had become an issue that helped them maintain popular support at a time when their electoral fortunes were in decline. Thus the policies devised to respond to the crisis were influenced more by political considerations than by sober economic reflection.

The growing budget deficit was a major issue in the 1977 election. The election was also notable for an important change in Dutch politics. The major confessional parties (the Catholic party, the ARP, and the CHU) offered a joint list of candidates called the Christian Democratic Appeal (CDA), a precursor of formal merger of the parties in 1980. But even this failed to stave off the decline in support by voters. Labor received the highest vote tally and therefore got the first chance to form a government. The expectation was that Den Uyl would again lead a left-center government. But coalition negotiations were held up by disagreement over how to handle the economic crisis, as well as the issue of abortion, and took 208 days, a new record. After Den Uyl's efforts to form a coalition failed, the CDA leader, A. A. Van Agt was able to come to an agreement with the VVD. The new government was a center-right coalition that took up the issue of welfare retrenchment with more vigor. At the behest of the Liberals, the CDA retreated from its Keynesian position and agreed to a program designed to cut the budget deficit.

What was noticeable about the Van Agt government's attempt at retrenchment was that it was a boon for business and industry and a bane for households. Cuts were made in employers' contributions to social security, while the contributions of households were raised (see fig. 6.1). Indeed, this negative redistribution has long been a trend in Dutch social security funding. Since 1948 state subsidy for total social welfare expenditures has hovered around 10 percent of total revenues. The contribution by employers had actually fallen from 59 percent in 1948 to 41 percent in 1970. At the same time, revenue generated by households for social welfare grew from 18 to 51 percent (see fig. 6.1). Increasing the tax burden for funding social welfare was undertaken in conjunction with further cutbacks. Successive retrenchment programs advocated trimming a total of 9.7 billion guilders from the public budget, and 59 percent of these cuts were realized (Roebroek, and Therborn, forthcoming). In the area of social welfare, the cuts were primarily in benefit levels to compensate for the growing demand.

The center-right Van Agt government survived a full parliamentary term. But the outcome of the 1981 elections left the CDA and Liberals two seats short of a majority. Van Agt managed to negotiate a left-center agreement with the Labor party and a smaller left-wing party, the Democrats '66. It was a tense coalition, however, strained by differences among the parties over how

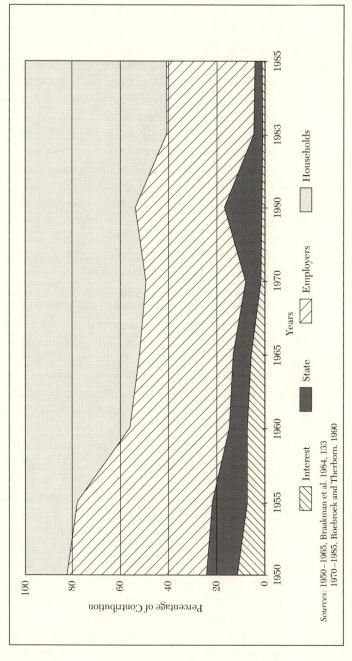

Figure 6.1. Financing for Social Security

Sources: 1950–1965, Braakman et al. 1984, 133
1970–1985, Roebroek and Therborn. 1990

to handle economic problems. Labor wanted programs to maintain household spending power and enhance employment, while the Democrats '66 joined the CDA in their call to roll back the budget deficit. After seven months of feuding, Labor pulled out of the coalition. The remaining partners attempted to preside over a minority government that received the parliamentary support from the Liberals for further retrenchment. But this government lasted only four months, after which early elections were called. Unlike Van Agt's first government, the second and third under his leadership were less successful in carrying out further retrenchment.

This situation changed following the 1982 elections. The electoral results represented a basic shift to the right among Dutch voters. The Democrats '66 lost eleven seats while the Liberal party picked up twelve. Although the Labor party received the largest number of seats, it was unable to form a left-of-center coalition with the Democrats '66, and the CDA refused to enter a coalition with Labor. On the other hand, the CDA and Liberal party together held a majority of seats, and when Labor's efforts to form a government failed, a center-right agreement was reached between the CDA and Liberals. Under the leadership of Ruud Lubbers, the new government embarked on a more ambitious program of retrenchment.

Most noticeable about the Lubbers government was its ability to develop a more coherent retrenchment policy. This was facilitated by general agreement between the CDA and the Liberal party on the issue of cutting the public deficit. In large part, the ability of the Lubbers government to develop a coherent retrenchment policy was a product of an institutional change in the way governments are formed, a change that allowed the Liberal party to exercise a greater degree of control over policy even though it was a junior governing partner. In the Netherlands there are two stages in the formation of a government. In the first stage, the parliamentary fractions that form the governing majority arrive at a governing agreement (*Regeerakkoord*), which outlines the issues the parliamentary fractions wish the government to address. In the second stage, the new government outlines its program (*Regeringsprogram*), which, along with the set of policies derived from it, would then be discussed by parliament.

Traditionally in the Netherlands the government program has had a more important status than the governing agreement, which has enabled the cabinet to exercise a great deal of autonomy in policy, that is, autonomy with respect to parliament. Primacy of the government program affords the government the freedom to place greater emphasis on the negotiations conducted in corporatist bodies than those conducted in parliament. Since the early sixties, however, parliament has increasingly tried to exercise more control over government policy by making the governing agreement more detailed and specific. The first effort in this direction came in 1963, and since that time governing agreements have taken on the status of contractual obligations between parliament and government (Bovend'Eert 1988). The consequence of this institutional shift is that relations with parliament are becoming increasingly more important than relations with corporatist councils.

In 1982 the Liberal party succeeded in negotiating a retrenchment package as part of the governing agreement. Part of the incoherence of past retrenchment policy was a result of the CDA's waffling between retrenchment and benefit increases to placate middle-of-the-road voters. It was, indeed, a conscious strategy, pursued by the party to maintain and enhance its centrist position. While CDA ministers defended one set of policies in cabinet meetings, the party's parliamentary contingent advocated the opposite position. By forcing the CDA members of parliament to agree to a retrenchment package, the Liberal party was able prevent its coalition partners from sitting on the fence any longer.

The governing agreement set reduction of the budget deficit as the primary goal of the new cabinet, and the minister of finance, H. Ruding (CDA), offered budget-cutting plans that came down hardest in the area of social security. Though Ruding's budgets were supported by Liberal ministers, they brought him into conflict with ministers from his own party. Ministers De

Koning (Social Affairs) and Brinkman (Health and Social Work) objected to the attack on welfare benefits, since the government agreement said nothing about making cutbacks in entitlement programs. Instead, they argued, attention should be paid to increasing employment before cutting the deficit. The disagreement was resolved through compromise. Ruding gave up some of his cutbacks in benefits in exchange for a commitment to reorganize the administration of social security and reduce the number of beneficiaries. The cuts in benefits, nonetheless, were substantial. In 1984, 1985, and 1986 pensions and family allowances were frozen. In 1984 unemployment and disability benefits were cut by 3 percent, and in the following year the maximum award for these programs was reduced from 80 to 70 percent of last earned income. As a result of the compromise, the total savings amounted to around two-thirds of Ruding's goal (Toirkens 1988, 106–42).

The plan to reorganize the administration of social security was intended as a way to shave administrative expenses. When a formal plan was finally put into effect in 1986, it introduced two changes. One was a reshuffling of ministerial responsibility for income maintenance programs. Responsibility for public assistance was taken from the Ministry of Health and Social Work and placed in the hands of the Ministry of Social Affairs. This change finally brought all income maintenance programs under the direction of a single ministry, a reform that had been advocated by various ministers of social affairs since the end of World War II. But this reshuffling of ministerial portfolios had a negligible impact on administrative costs.

The second change was to impose more uniformity on levels of benefits. Prior to the 1986 reorganization these varied among different pension programs, as well as among the various income-related programs (unemployment and disability). Uniformity was achieved partly by reducing entitlements in programs that provided the most lucrative benefits. For example, the length of time one could receive disability or unemployment benefits was curtailed. This amounted to a de-entitlement, since those benefits were earnings related. When an earnings-related benefit is allowed to expire, it no longer represents the belief that support for an accustomed standard of living should be the program's goal. After expiration of the benefits, the same individuals, if still disabled or unemployed, must rely on public assistance, which is a basic income, rather than earnings-related support. De-entitlement has generated some savings, but since demand for the programs continued to increase, the net result has been less dramatic than anticipated.

In addition to the restructuring of programs, another element of the retrenchment compromise struck between Liberal and CDA ministers was reduction of the number of welfare beneficiaries. There are two ways to do this. One is to eliminate entitlement programs, in the Netherlands not a politically viable solution. The Dutch public is generally supportive of the system of income support, and there are many vocal lobbies that defend the interests of beneficiaries. The other way is to scrutinize the programs more diligently to weed out fraud and misuse. It is the latter approach that was a major preoccupation of the Lubbers government. The attempts to combat fraud and misuse focused directly on the public assistance and disability programs. Unlike the other social security programs, these two have the most opaque criteria for eligibility and, therefore, are the most easily abused.

For retirement pensions, it is easy to determine when a person reaches the age of eligibility. Public assistance and disability benefits, by contrast, are based on more complicated calculations. Public assistance is an income supplement of those unable to earn what is considered to be a basic income. The benefit is calculated on the basis of an individual's income and the supplement brings one up to this minimum level of support. This allows a potential for misuse if people attempt to hide or fail to disclose additional sources of income. Disability benefits are based on a doctor's determination of the extent to which the disability renders one incapable of earning an income. If doctors are lenient, the levels of benefits are exaggerated.

Efforts to impose more control on these programs began in

1985, when a 10 percent reduction in public assistance benefits was introduced for individuals who share a household. The idea behind the reduction was that sharing household expenses reduces level of need. Again, the reform amounts to a de-entitlement in the sense that the program was originally designed to make calculations on an individual basis, without regard to a person's choice of life-style. In the area of disability, concentration has been on enhancing state control of the medical profession as a way of limiting access to disability benefits. It is these attempts to reduce the number of beneficiaries that have led to organized resistance from the affected groups. More will be said on this issue later in this chapter.

The relative coherence of the Lubbers retrenchment policy, combined with its success at meeting goals, carried the center-right coalition through the 1986 elections. Lubbers returned as prime minister, the government stayed the course, and by the latter part of the 1980s, government policy appeared to have had the desired effect. Although unemployment remained high, significant reductions were made in the budget deficit, and the economy began to grow (Wolinetz 1990). Paradoxically, however, economic growth lessened public support for further retrenchment. Indeed, the CDA members of parliament began to challenge the government on its dogged adherence to further retrenchment (*NRC Handelsblad* 1988, 25 March 1988). Though the dispute pitted the senior governing party against the government, the tension became moot a few months later when the Liberal party failed to support the government's environmental plan and the government resigned.

The ensuing election campaign was characterized by a debate over whether an end to retrenchment was now in order. Labor indicated a desire to participate in a government that would direct attention to boosting employment. The Liberals became sensitive to the public's desire to roll back retrenchment and even advocated increasing social security benefits (*NRC Handelsblad* 1988, 25 March). Consistent with its earlier strategy, the CDA failed to clarify the issue, leaving voters uncertain over whether a vote for it was a show of support for its members of parliament, who wanted to enhance benefits, or for the Lubbers government, which desired to continue retrenchment. This uncertainty also enhanced the centrist position of the CDA. Lubbers advocated continuation of the successful economic policies in an effort to push the Liberals farther to the right. At the same time his party's pledge to maintain benefits undermined Labor support (Bik 1988).

The outcome of the election confirmed another truism of Dutch politics: voters punish any party deemed responsible for bringing down a sitting government. As a result, the Liberals were the big losers. Yet neither the CDA nor Labor profited from the Liberal defeat. Instead, the major beneficiaries were Democrats '66 and a far-left Green alliance. Rejection of the Liberals paved the way for a left-center coalition between Labor and the CDA, again under the leadership of Ruud Lubbers. Though this cabinet has deemphasized retrenchment — indeed, has increased social security benefits — it has continued the effort to crack down on welfare fraud and misuse. This continued effort has prompted a mobilization of clientele interests and at the same time generated a more fundamental discussion of welfare reform.

RETRENCHMENT AND SOCIAL MOBILIZATION

Through a long and arduous process, Dutch retrenchment policy has gained a level of coherence. The era of expansion of the welfare state is at an end, and the attempt to address the problems created by it have shifted from stopgap measures toward a more considered discussion of fundamental reform. But, just as political leaders have taken a harder look at the welfare state, societal interests that have a stake in it have begun to demand a voice in the process. The types of group in this new wave of mobilization, however, are different from the ones that typified the period of growth. The new welfare programs have engendered a sense of identity among groups that previously had not existed. These groups, moreover, exist alongside the corporatist interests that

183

have always been central to the making of welfare policy. What this means is that the welfare state has prompted a change in the nature of state-society relations, but it is still too early to identify a new style of policy making. In the context of a policy-making process that has broken wide open, the new and the old societal interests compete with one another for influence, and the state is trying desperately to develop a more commanding role.

Differences in state-society relations between the era of growth and the era of retrenchment are striking. Throughout the historical development of the welfare state, state-society relations were characterized by the corporatist involvement of societal interests in the policy-making process. Initially, the Dutch corporatist solution served as a means of limiting the role of the state in providing social welfare. Religious charities dominated the field of poor relief, and employers and unions exercised a great deal of control over the workers' insurance programs. It was, therefore, a unique type of corporatism, one in which the state was a junior partner in the process of developing policy. Though the rapid growth of the welfare state in the 1960s and 1970s has enhanced the state's role, corporatist representation of societal interests has persisted.

As was noted in the preceding chapter, disability and public assistance are the two areas where changes in the old style of corporatism are most evident. In public assistance, private charities have been replaced by municipal social services as the main providers of financial assistance to the poor. The charity agencies, in turn, have evolved into professional social work agencies that continue to receive state subsidies for nonfinancial services such as day-care, community organizing, and counseling. These new agencies are even more numerous and even less organized than were the private charities. In the area of disability, unions and employers are still important corporatist actors in the policy-making process. Most of the insurance programs are still administered by the bipartite industrial insurance boards. And labor and capital organizations, to which the Dutch refer as the social partners, still wield great influence through the SER. But the influence of the social partners has been diluted somewhat by the rising prominence of medical professionals in the area of disability. Also, some of the social work agencies that deal with the handicapped have come to serve also as lobbying organizations for their clientele.

One of the consequences of the declining voice of the social partners has been an increasing assertiveness on the part of government. Many studies of postwar Dutch corporatism agree that, though the sixties were a period of bargaining and compromise among corporatist partners, this began to change in the seventies, and the eighties were marked by a greater degree of governmental assertiveness (Keman and Woldendorp 1985). Though the government was less constrained by business and labor, as the preceding section pointed out it was under attack from a more activist parliament. The groups that had traditionally been important political forces were waning in influence, but the new ones were not yet firmly established.

Much of the Lubbers government's attempt to restructure income maintenance programs centered on public assistance and disability. The effort was ostensibly directed at limiting access to cut down on the number of beneficiaries. In addition, the reforms challenged the autonomy of the providers of services. In public assistance, the government has tried to exercise more control over the social work agencies. In the disability program, the government has tried to circumscribe the autonomy of medical professionals who screen applicants. Because of differences in the programs, as well as the types of societal interests involved in each, the focus of reforms has been different, so that the politics that surround the reforms has been different. But one common theme persists: even during times of retrenchment, the habit of corporatist negotiation still affects state-society relations.

In public assistance the effort to combat fraud and misuse has been controversial from the very beginning. In 1985, when the government reduced benefits for those who shared a household, the policy made it necessary to send officials into the field to determine who was or was not living alone. The need for diligent inspection was enhanced the next year when the government introduced a change that allows public assistance agents to make a more comprehensive assessment of an individual's resources and needs by, for example, considering the income of a beneficiaries' living partner as part of household income — a move that was a tacit recognition that common law partnerships were becoming more common than marriages (*NRC Handelsblad* 1986, 30 January).

In addition, penalties for fraudulent or inappropriate receipt of benefits have been increased, and more resources have been committed to sending staffers into the field to verify the status of beneficiaries. While the preliminary report is that these "toothbrush inspectors" (so dubbed because counting toothbrushes in the bathroom is a means of determining how many individuals are part of a household) have succeeded in weeding out more fraud than it costs to fund their positions, the net savings have not been dramatic. Moreover, although such scrutiny of choice of life-style is common in the United States, where there is a prevailing belief that beneficiaries of public assistance are lazy or fraudulent (Leibfried 1978), in the Netherlands much criticism has been leveled against the practice of state officials acting on the assumption that people are cheating (*NRC Handelsblad* 1986, 31 January).

The controversy over retrenchment in public assistance has also provoked tensions between the ministry and municipal governments. The reforms were introduced shortly after the research department of the Rotterdam Municipal Social Services published a study that found that most recipients of public assistance and public insurance still lived in impoverished conditions. The study found a high incidence of indebtedness, especially among unemployed youth. It also found that many beneficiaries are unable to cover basic costs, such as electricity. Or, if they are, they do so by forgoing amenities such as fresh fruit or public transportation. The study criticized government policy for leaving these individuals able just to survive but not to participate in society (Oude Engberink 1984).

The cutbacks in benefits only exacerbated the problem of the new poor. In 1987, after the reforms had been introduced, the Rotterdam Municipal Social Services conducted a follow-up of its 1984 study that discovered an increase in indebtedness among the poor that had been compounded by a 15 percent drop in spending power. The impact has been most severe on elderly citizens who have little more than their retirement pensions to support themselves, and on youth from ethnic minorities who suffer discrimination in their search for employment.

The plight of the worst off in Dutch society produced a type of public outcry that would be virtually inconceivable in the United States. The minister of social work appeared on a television talk show, where she was barraged with the angry complaints of welfare beneficiaries. The socialist radio network devoted call-in programs to discussions of the impact of cutbacks on beneficiaries. The general tenor of these discussions was an expression of concern over the fact that public assistance beneficiaries would no longer possess the means to participate in normal social activities, such as going to the movies with friends. Public outcry prompted a rethinking of government strategy. Although the government remained committed to its position on the levels of benefits, it advocated devoting more attention to programs that would allow beneficiaries of public assistance to escape the cycle of poverty. Dubbed "social renewal," the new policy recognizes that simply giving more money to the needy will not improve their position. At the same time it rejects the idea that the state should assume the responsibility for providing the type of care desired. Instead, what is needed, according to the government, is self-help and community help programs that will give individuals the skills and opportunities to find employment, programs that should be organized and operated by private organizations rather than the state. Thus the policy is consistent with the government's general commitment to decentralization and privatization of public tasks.

The policy of social renewal has drawn attention to the role of social work agencies in the Dutch welfare state. These agencies are the ones called upon to make the policy work. But the government has recognized a need to impose more uniformity and coherence. Since the 1960s, when social work agencies underwent their transformation from voluntary charities to mobilizing organizers, the number of agencies has mushroomed, and their activities have often been directed at confrontation rather than cooperation with policy makers. Governmental efforts to impose structure in this field have been directed at rewarding agencies that move away from being mobilizing activists and become responsible managers.

The most significant component of the restructuring has been the creation of the Association of Subsidized and Premium Funded Enterprises. This body was set up by the Ministry of Health and Social Work as an organization of all private agencies that handle activities in health and social work. In contrast to the previous proliferation of agencies and umbrella organizations, creation of this association was intended to simplify contact between the ministry and the agencies. It has also allowed the ministry to exercise more control over which agencies will be recognized. This aspect of the reform has minimized the significance of mobilizing agencies in favor of those with a more managerial focus. The establishment of a peak organization also appears to constitute a return to some form of corporatism, but, unlike the earlier form, the new one would award the state a more commanding role in the process. By the end of the 1980s, it was too early to determine if the reforms would work. Social work agencies remained skeptical about their participation in the Association of Subsidized and Premium Funded Enterprises, and the body failed to become the forum for corporatist discussion that it was intended to be.

At the same time a plan for governmental decentralization has made municipal social services more responsible for deciding how to implement government policy. But from the standpoint of the municipal authorities, decentralization has put them in a difficult position. One of the problems stems from the fact that 90 percent of the funding for public assistance benefits comes from the national government and 10 percent from municipal general revenues. Yet municipal councils are not allowed to institute special taxes to support welfare programs, so that maintaining benefits for the poor forces councils to make cuts in other projects. The result has been one not usually typical of a unitary state. The level of assistance an individual receives in the city of Rotterdam compared to The Hague, for example, may vary depending on how their respective municipal councils decide to allocate general revenues.

Municipal councils are also upset about another component of the decentralization policy that has given them more responsibility for controlling subsidized social work agencies. The formal procedure for the award of the subsidy is that the agency must request support from the municipal council, which then seeks reimbursement from the Ministry of Health and Social Work. In 1990 the ministry demanded a 10 percent cutback in subsidies in an effort to eliminate the ideological and mobilizing agencies. The decision, however, forced the municipal governments to decide which agencies would have their subsidies cut.

The net sum of all these reforms in public assistance is that the position of the worst off has deteriorated, the government has attempted to impose more order over the social work agencies, and municipal councils have been burdened with tasks they lack the resources to perform. While this has led to savings in the public budget, it has also severely undermined the principles upon which the Dutch welfare state was founded. Gone is the idea that the state should provide the means for all citizens to enjoy a meaningful social existence. Also, individualizing the assessment of need was originally intended to bring an end to the social control that marked the former poor relief program. Now, public officials are scrutinizing the life-styles of those who receive public assistance. Corporatism is again a topic for discussion, but this time with the state in charge.

Attempts to reform the disability program have met with a different set of problems. Attention to this area, particularly the occupational disability program, have been at the center of the general discussions on reforming social security. The universal insurance programs (retirement pensions and public disability benefits) have suffered little more than freezes on benefits. The burgeoning occupational disability program, however, has come under direct attack. The problem is that the lucrative benefits provided for under the Disability Security Act (1967) have created a population of beneficiaries that makes the Dutch work force among the most disabled in the world. Attempts to cut back on the number of beneficiaries have focused on making the programs a less attractive alternative to unemployment insurance and on imposing more control over the program's gatekeepers — medical professionals — as well as unions and employers. Efforts at reform, however, have provoked a stream of controversy.

For example, in 1984 the SER published its advice on retrenchment that exposed a great deal of disagreement among the participants on the council. Employers came out in favor of reducing the benefit levels of all social security to subsistence level. The unions objected to this radical suggestion. And though the suggestion was never taken up by the government, that was because it was listening to other groups in society, not the SER (Social-Economic Council 1984). Following the SER report, the Dutch Scientific Council for Government Policy published its own assessment of the situation. This body is comprised primarily of university researchers, and it periodically commissions studies on issues of government policy. Its proposals were less drastic, but it did advocate substantial cuts and suggested that private insurance could still serve as an important alternative for workers who feared a loss of income from disability (Wetenschappelijk Raad voor het Regeringsbeleid 1985).

The government's own plan was more modest. Implemented in 1987, it was intended to result in savings of 4.2 billion guilders, most of which, 3 billion of the total, was expected to come from the disability program. This goal was primarily to be achieved by imposing more stringent evaluation criteria on disability beneficiaries in an effort to eliminate loopholes in the program that allowed people with only minor physical afflictions to receive benefits. Often beneficiaries not only were able to work but also, in many cases, worked at jobs where they were paid "under the table." The mechanism for achieving the retrenchment goal was to hold the doctors of the JMS accountable for lenient assessments of disabilities.

These changes were effected in three ways. First, in the new law a distinction was made between not having a job because of a disability and not having a job because of conditions in the labor market. This has been an important issue because, unlike recipients of unemployment insurance benefits, beneficiaries of disability insurance who might otherwise be capable of working had no obligation to seek substitute employment. The program is now designed to encourage reemployment of the partially disabled by requiring them to look for work or enter retraining programs, and it requires doctors to identify those who are capable of seeking work.

Second, a reevaluation is required of all disability applicants according to standardized benefit criteria. Until the recent budget crisis, little attention was devoted to the possibility of improvement in a patient's condition, and the determination of disability was entirely at the doctors' discretion. If one was determined to have a permanent disability, that assessment went unchallenged. Now all patients are being reexamined for improvements.

Third, there have been across-the-board reductions in the levels of benefits. These cuts, introduced in 1985, were dramatic. Now individuals deemed fully disabled receive 70 rather than 100 percent of the last earned wage. These cuts, however, have not resulted in substantial immediate savings. In part, this is because for low income earners cuts in benefits have merely led to an increased burden on the public assistance roles. Also, the new percentages apply only to new beneficiaries. Those that entered the program under the old system have been "grandfathered in" according to the entitlements in existence at the time they acquired their disability.

The burden of implementing such cutbacks has fallen on the

doctors, who complain that the reforms have severely circumscribed their autonomy. They are now expected to assess whether
beneficiaries are capable of working at any job instead of determining to what extent they are prevented by their disability from
returning to their previous job. The doctors argue that rather
than saving money, the changes only shift the costs to either the
public assistance or the unemployment roles and in the process
burden doctors with the thankless task of denying applicants'
claims. Doctors further complain that the reforms, by turning
them into policing agents, limit their capacity to act in the interests of their patients (Kranenburg 1986; Tex and Verhey 1987).

Indeed, the medical profession is only partly to blame for the
growth of the disability program. Unions and employers have
viewed disability as a more benign way than layoffs of culling
their work force. Much of the recent growth in the number of
disabled workers has consisted of older ones who are less productive and more costly than younger ones. The very lax criteria of
eligibility, particularly for psychological disabilities, has encouraged older workers to make claims based on stress or fatigue. To
assert that such instances are cases of abuse is a touchy accusa-
tion. No one wishes to suggest that the applicants are insincere
or that their employers are systematically sending older workers
to see the doctors. Yet in the aggregate some patterns are evident. The percentage of workers not participating in the work
force as a result of a disability varies among economic sectors.
Public employees have the lowest percentage, while sectors such
as construction have high percentages. This difference can be attributed to the greater risk of physical injury that manual labor
entails in comparison with sitting at a desk. But it cannot account for the rapid growth in the number of disabled workers,
since it is not true that the Dutch workplace has become more
dangerous than in the past.[1]

The suggestions that employers and unions are taking advan-

1. The information in this paragraph is a composite of data collected from
interviews with Nico van Niekerk of the Social Insurance Council, Professor Dik
Wolfson of the SER, and the former minister of social affairs, Gerhard Veld-

tage of the disability policy has prompted a discussion of means
to impose more control over them. Yet, in contrast to its handling
of the medical professionals or the social work agencies, the government has been timid about directly challenging the employers and unions. The result is that the hand of the social partners
has been strengthened. In September 1989 the government asked
the SER for advice on a proposal to reorganize the structure of
implementation of social insurance programs. The major reform
suggested in the government's proposal was to reduce the autonomous status of the JMS by placing it under the direct supervision
of the Ministry of Social Affairs. The proposal failed to offer any
suggestions for making the social partners more accountable for
the growth in the number of disabled workers. This has left the
social partners free reign to discuss their own solutions. Even so,
agreement on the issue is difficult to reach. As the SER began
discussions on the problem in the first part of 1990, unions and
employers' organizations put forward their own suggestions. The
solutions they came up with, however, seem self-interested attempts to wrest further profit from the program more than sin-
cere efforts to correct the problems.

The unions have cynical reasons to resist reform. Disability,
like all social security programs, is still operated primarily by the
industrial insurance boards. This decentralized character of administration has always given great control to the unions, which
serve on the insurance boards. In addition to operating programs
that benefit their membership, the industrial insurance boards
are a great boon to union leadership. A salaried position on an
industrial insurance board provides a substantial income supplement to the otherwise modestly paid union leaders. Allowing the
state to exercise more control over administration of the program
would come at the expense of the interests of union leaders. For
this reason the unions have adopted the government's call for

kamp. No one was able to provide me with specific figures, but all shared the
same perception of the causes for the high numbers of beneficiaries of disability
insurance.

general decentralization of state activities and used it to claim that they should be permitted more autonomy in the administration of social security. Thus their position with respect to the medical professionals is to agree with the government that doctors do need more supervision but that it should be achieved by placing them under the direct control of the insurance boards rather than the Ministry of Social Affairs.

Employers have supported the unions on the issue of decentralization and have even offered further suggestions that appear self-serving. It may seem paradoxical, but employers benefit from the existing disability program as much as any group. One of the most significant characteristics of the Dutch economy is its high level of labor productivity, which serves as a great attraction for foreign investment. The disability program, which allows employers to cull their work force without excessive hardship to the employees, is largely responsible for maintaining this high level of productivity. Moreover, it is a program that serves business interests at relatively little cost to employers, since high taxes on wages and salaries account for the largest portion of the financing of the program. Workers pay, but employers benefit. Consequently employers have found little reason to advocate fundamental reform.

But because the government is demanding attention to the problems of the disability program, employers' federations have offered a set of suggestions. A major one has been to revamp the classification scheme for disability. Employers' organizations have suggested reducing the number of classifications from seven to three and changing the level of benefit that would accrue to each. Under the proposal, those deemed under 33 percent disabled would receive no benefit, those 34–67 percent disabled would receive a half-benefit, and those more than 67 percent disabled would receive the full benefit. The proposal would thus amount to a de-entitlement for those with a limited disability, but employers argue that individuals in the least disabled category should be capable of finding alternative employment. It is a suggestion that maintains the program, which is good for employers, and forces beneficiaries to bear the burden of cutbacks, which is also good for employers.

The other major suggestion that has come from employers is to institute an incentive and penalty program. The incentive would amount to social security tax rebates for employers who hire the partially disabled. The penalty would set quotas for the percentage of the work force that could be considered disabled and would impose fines on employers who exceeded their quota. While most employers agree in principle, they still disagree over what percentages should be applied to each industrial sector. Small businesses and the self-employed, moreover, have argued for exemption from the quotas because of the small size of their work force. The debate, however, is spurious: the only potential winner would be employers, who would receive compensation for employing disabled workers.

When the SER finished its discussion of the issue in June 1990, the advice it sent to the government followed the interests of the social partners. It endorsed the union plan for decentralization of administration. In internal discussions some of the independent (state-appointed) councillors expressed doubt over whether this suggestion would provide enough of an incentive to bring down the volume of beneficiaries. And though the independent councillors echoed the government's concern, they failed to press its position. Instead they waited for the social partners to reach a consensus.

The government recognized that the SER's advice would not result in substantial reductions of the number of disability beneficiaries and refused to take action on it. Had it done so, the implications would have been enormous. It essentially would have revived the older pattern of postwar corporatism: the central role of the SER in discussions of policy would have been reestablished, and the government would again be placed in a reactionary position. The government, however, wanted an agreement that would truly address the problem of the number of beneficiaries. It requested a second report, a delay that allowed critics of the SER more time to mobilize and voice their concerns.

Dik Wolfson, one of the independent councillors on the SER, was a vocal critic of the council's first report, arguing that decentralization of governmment tasks to the social partners is a slap in the face to democratic accountability. It places responsibility for performing public functions in the hands of unelected organizations and grants them too much discretion over the disbursement of public funds (*SER-Bulletin* 1990). By the summer of 1991, more independent councillors had become openly critical of the corporatist solutions. As it began to formulate a second report, members of the SER found their differences of opinion more intractable.

Indeed, the criticisms of corporatism had begun to engender a shift in opinion among some parliamentary fractions. The Liberal party began advocating a restructuring of the SER. According to its leader in parliament, the corporatist representation of employers and employees creates a conflict of interest. Instead, the SER should be entirely made up of independent councillors, appointed on the basis of their knowledge of policy. This would make the council truly an advisory body rather than a vehicle for societal interests to exercise influence over policy. (*NRC Handelsblad* 1991). It is an argument that is winning support within the Lubbers government, which finds its efforts to develop sound policy constrained by the self-interested concerns of the social partners.

As in the area of public assistance, retrenchment in the disability program has been stalled by the mobilization of societal interests, and the ability of the social partners to do so is enhanced by their institutional position. Although the government is now attempting to exercise more autonomy over policy, the institutions of corporatism continue to provide vested interests with a vehicle for influencing the content of policy. And as long as the government is willing to wait for advisory bodies such as the SER to reach a consensus, fundamental retrenchment is not likely.

The strong influence of the social partners is in sharp contrast with that of the medical professionals. The government has operated virtually unhindered in imposing controls on doctors, in part because of the support of the social partners. Perhaps most important, however, is that doctors do not enjoy the institutional position in the policy-making process. As experts, the doctor offer advice that can be useful to policy makers, but without a formalized channel of influence they are easily ignored.

CONCLUSIONS

Taken together, the two stories of Dutch retrenchment illustrate some important points about the making of welfare policy in an era of economic crisis. One of these is that governments have a difficult time making the transition from expansion to contraction of the welfare state. This is perhaps even more true for the Netherlands since the later development of the welfare state there forced it to shift gears relatively quickly. The welfare state was still in its period of expansion when the economic crisis struck, and consequently the government was forced to plan a strategy of retrenchment before the country became accustomed to the system that was in place.

In part, the reason the politics of retrenchment in welfare is so different from the politics of expansion lies in the fundamentally different circumstances from which the two originate. Anxiety about certain growing and apparently endemic social problems was the inspiration for the original development of social policy, development that can best be described as relatively slow and deliberate. In almost every country, by contrast, retrenchment can best be described as an issue prompted by crisis. It was not the slow decline in economic productivity that raised concern over the costs of social programs but the rapid onset of a worldwide recession that thrust the problems of social spending under the noses of policy makers. Hence welfare states cannot be dismantled in the same manner as they are constructed.

Yet the contrast between growth and contraction of the welfare state offers some fundamental challenges to a very basic, long-held belief about policy making. To cast the above discussion in other terms, the development of the welfare state (in most countries) as an incremental process, whereas retrenchment is non-incremental, brought on by crisis. This conceptualization of the problem conforms with our understanding of incrementalism and nonincrementalism. The former is the normal mode of policy making, whereas the latter prevails during times of crisis. Yet in virtually every country, the actual history of retrenchment in the welfare state is one of incrementalism, and sometimes policy stagnation, rather than dramatic response to crisis. Few countries are able to pursue an effective retrenchment strategy even where there is general agreement among the political forces as to the depth of the crisis and the need for a solution. Consequently, something deeper than incrementalism is the important consideration for understanding public policy, and the manifestations and impacts of politics on outcomes express too much variance to be reduced to considerations of normal versus crisis circumstances.

Not only did Dutch policy makers have to grope and crawl in their efforts to find a solution to the crisis. Also, in making the shift from expansion to contraction, there were few foreign examples to learn from — or this is what the Dutch themselves believed. Though there is evidence that the Lubbers governments looked intently to Britain and the United States for lessons on how to privatize state enterprises and decentralize many of the remaining public activities, those active in the area of social policy believed the Dutch case was unique. This uniqueness is best expressed by the introduction to the study published by the Scientific Council for Government Policy:

> Above all, the burden on the social insurance has been dramatically increased by a number of sociological factors that could not have been anticipated, such as graying of the population, the breakdown of traditional family structures, the increased participation of married women in the labor market, *and the increase in disability* (Wetenschappelijke Raad voor het Regeringsbeleid 1985; emphasis added).

Whereas the first three of these factors are experienced by all developed countries, the fourth is unique to the Netherlands. To identify them as conditions with a sociological cause is to claim that human action cannot correct them but can only address the consequences. But, as was demonstrated in chapter 5, the increase in Dutch disability was a result of choice of policy, not sociological factors. If we assume that change in policy can correct problems caused by past choice of policy, it would have to be admitted that the burgeoning disability problem could be addressed. The way the Dutch define the problem leaves policy makers without foreign examples to observe. No other country, save perhaps Italy, has such a peculiar disability policy. And in Italy policy makers have similarly been unable to come up with a workable solution (Ferrera 1990). If, however, Dutch policy makers decided to define the problem as one brought on by the way the entitlements are defined, they would be able to look around and find numerous alternative ways of conceptualizing a right to disability benefits.

Without a foreign example, the Dutch attempted to improvise. As in other countries, dealing with the crisis forced them to experiment, to try a number of approaches. The failure of early attempts to cut back on public expenditures taught them a lesson that all western countries quickly learned. Keynesian spending provides no solution to long-term economic downturn. On the positive side, they learned this lesson quickly and set out to develop a more balanced approach to cutting public expenditures. Yet the major focus of recent retrenchment efforts has undermined some of the principles of the Dutch welfare state. The system was built on the solidaristic principle that the working population should support those unable to work. More and more, the cuts in benefits have undermined this, and the system now places greater emphasis on individual responsibility. This shift has generated a great deal of political debate and discussion, which only slows the process. The public seems much more reluctant to accept the types of cut the government claims are necessary.

Furthermore, even after a more coherent retrenchment policy was articulated, some of the problems that are peculiar to the Dutch case left them on their own to devise solutions. As unemployment rose, they strove to borrow some of the Swedish retraining programs to reintroduce workers into a more mechanized economy, but the increased reliance on disability kept much of the unemployed work force from undergoing this transition.

The difficulties in reforming the disability program illustrate a deeper problem. It is difficult to institute an effective retrenchment policy when the state is unable to overcome the opposition of well-entrenched vested interests. While this is true of all western countries, for the Dutch it is compounded by the history of corporatism in social welfare policy. The historical prominence of corporatism has left the state with a limited degree of autonomy. In fact, corporatist actors have contributed to the present fiscal crisis. Occupational disability is the fastest growing of all Dutch welfare programs. Blame is placed on employers and unions for using the program to avoid laying off workers and on doctors for making lenient assessments of applicants. In public assistance, the charity agencies had little reason to exercise budgetary restraint under a program of state subsidization, which to some extent encouraged them to broaden their activities, with a consequent increase in demand on state revenues.

At present the Dutch government is attempting to increase the state's autonomy by placing more control in the hands of ministries, but the mechanism for doing so consists of streamlining and formalizing informal networks of corporatist negotiation rather than disincorporating those groups. Nonetheless, professionals cry foul at the reforms. Unions and employers' federations have taken advantage of the opportunity to demand that they regain their former status in corporatist policy making. Moreover, as the government and ministries succeed in wresting control from the corporatist interests, they find themselves constrained by a more watchful parliament.

These are important developments. It appears that the specific history of corporatism in the Netherlands structures the way discussions of policy are framed. Efforts to enact difficult decisions, such as welfare retrenchment, are made through painstaking corporatist discussions. In addition, since the early part of this century, the Dutch style of corporatism has been intended as a means of restricting the role of the state. It seems that, although the policy networks may become more complex, there is still a great deal of resistance to granting the state more autonomy.

Though the definitive history of Dutch retrenchment is yet to be written, one can reach an initial conclusion that a waxing of corporatism remains a viable possibility. That this theme is important for understanding the retrenchment debates indicates a certain continuity in the history of Dutch welfare policy making. Politics and history explain the unique growth of the Dutch welfare state. Likewise, the institutional relationships created by the welfare state set the stage for the debates on how to roll back its growth.

7

Conclusions:
Lessons from the Dutch Case

The development of the welfare state epitomizes the dramatic transformations all advanced democratic societies have undergone in the twentieth century. New forms of support and protection allow citizens to enjoy a more secure life, one less preoccupied with basic living necessities. The state has taken on a larger role in providing these forms of support. Public programs for income maintenance, health, housing, and so on have expanded the state's activities. And where the state does not directly provide the services, a myriad of regulations encourages the private sector to fill in the gaps.

How are we to make sense of the phenomenon of the welfare state? This question has provoked a wealth of scholarship. Yet, for all that is known about the welfare state, there is still much that remains unexamined, such as its development in the smaller European countries. The purpose of this study is to remedy this situation by giving an account of the development of the Dutch welfare state. Indeed, the Dutch case is more than a neglected case. It is an example of one of the most extensive welfare states in the world. Also, its pattern of development stands apart. In no other European country did the welfare state develop so late, and then so quickly. Hence it is a case that deserves more attention.

A major purpose of this study has been to place the Dutch experience within the comparative study of development of the welfare state. At a theoretical level the theses of convergence and divergence in development have guided this study. On the surface, welfare states appear remarkably similar. They seem to have developed during roughly the same period and to encompass similar types of program. There are several ways to explain this apparent convergence. The one that is central to this study holds that the similarity of welfare programs is a product of the borrowing of policy. Channels of communication make it possible for policy makers to learn from the experiences of counterparts in other countries and bring the lessons home. Diffusion accounts for much of the effort on the part of Dutch policy makers to borrow welfare programs first from Germany and later from Britain.

Still, the borrowing thesis cannot account for the vast differences that exist among welfare states. Though one can make general comparisons, closer inspection reveals that each country has developed its own type of welfare state. Accounting for such divergences poses another theoretical problem. How do ideas borrowed from abroad give rise to different policies? The question draws attention to the way decisions about policy are made in a particular country. The argument in this study is that differences in decisions about policy are a product of different politics. And politics in a particular country is structured by the institutions that offer the means for political forces to bring influence to bear on the policy-making process. The peculiarities of Dutch politics account for the unique development of its welfare state.

Dutch scholars describe their welfare state as one that fits "between Bismarck and Beveridge." It is a phrase that describes not only the geographic location and historical sequence of the development of the Dutch welfare state, but it also describes the influence of German and British models on its early development. At the same time, the phrase suggests that the Dutch case is different from either of its neighbors. Like the Bismarck system, the early Dutch welfare state was based on the concept of earned entitlements. Social security was an insurance system available to members of the work force. It distinguished between individuals who earned social benefits by paying insurance premiums and the unentitled, who were left to rely on the generosity of state-subsidized charity agencies. After World War II, policy makers attempted to introduce a system of universal entitlements based on the Beveridge model, but the insurance idea continued to influence policy. Rather than offering cradle-to-grave state support, Dutch social welfare is based on the idea of universal insurance. Members of the work force pay for their insurance, and the state underwrites insurance for those unable to work.

Postwar welfare reforms in the Netherlands were not as extensive as the Beveridge model because the welfare state there was built by confessional political forces, not by the socialist left, which had been the advocate of a Beveridge style system. In terms of the comparative literature on the development of the welfare state, the fact that centrist, confessional political forces were responsible offers a strong challenge to the prevailing assumption that welfare states are built by the political left. I take this situation to be evidence that further underscores the need for scholars of the welfare state to stop making assumptions about the political forces that promote the welfare state and to focus instead on the dynamics of policy debate and political mobilization around issues. Indeed, this is not a bold new discovery on my part. Fritz Scharpf (1991) has already demonstrated the need to focus on the actual policy strategies political parties pursue rather than assuming their behavior from their ideology.

Furthermore, focusing on the dynamics of political mobilization draws attention to the institutional context in which policy develops. Dutch political institutions are characterized by corporatism, and though much attention has been paid to corporatism and how it operates, little of that research is applicable to the Dutch case or to the examination of social policy. The Dutch case shows that corporatism can include religious rather than economic groups in discussions of policy. Though there are many institutions of economic corporatism in the Netherlands, historically the unions and employers represented on these councils have been divided by religious affiliation. The important comparative implication is that one cannot assume that the conditions that gave rise to corporatism in Germany, for example, were the same ones that fostered it in the Netherlands. Therefore, though the institutions are similar, we cannot assume that they are identical.

In this study these theoretical considerations have been employed in an effort to answer two perplexing empirical questions that set the development of the Dutch welfare state apart. Why did it develop so late, and why did it develop so quickly? Much of the following discussion summarizes the way this study has answered these questions. Then I examine the lessons that can be drawn for broader comparative study of the development of welfare states.

LATE DEVELOPMENT: THE LEGACY OF CONSOCIATIONAL CORPORATISM

Throughout most of the twentieth century, the Netherlands has lagged behind most other western European countries in developing its welfare state. At the turn of the century, when most countries began to institute social security, the Dutch only began to talk about the issues. Across Europe, social security was adopted in two phases (1883–92 and 1892–1908). The Dutch adopted a workmen's compensation program during the second phase (1901), but it was not until 1913 that retirement and disability programs were instituted. Similarly, when most countries began to universalize social welfare programs, it was a trend that bypassed the Netherlands. Whereas most countries made these changes before or shortly after World War II, the Netherlands did not do so until the 1960s.

Was it the structure of the Dutch state that impeded the development of social welfare policy? This study suggests that the question must be answered in the affirmative. From the time of the first discussions about social welfare, the Dutch state was corporatist in its structure. Any institution can be distinguished by its structure and the way it functions. The general understanding of corporatism is that it is a structure for the representation of select private interests in the policy-making process. That process, in turn, promotes compromise and consensus building among partners in the negotiations.

The Dutch case represents a slight deviation from this type. Dutch corporatism has provided representation to important societal interests. Contrary to the situation in other countries, however, in the Netherlands corporatist interests parallel the religiously defined cleavages in society. This is slightly different from economic corporatism, the more pervasive variety, which awards representation to labor and capital in societies where class cleavages are more salient. In addition, the functioning of Dutch corporatism varies somewhat from that of other corporatist models. Dutch corporatism was designed to foster a conservative policy-making process. Religious forces in Dutch society historically were not concerned with the creation of a welfare state. Their position was that the welfare needs of citizens should be supplied by nonstate organizations. Representation of these interests on corporatist bodies offered an influential position for their attitudes to be reflected in policy. Corporatism effectively locked out of the policy-making process those interests that favored a more extensive welfare state. Thus the bargaining and compromise occurred not among antagonistic interests but among groups that already shared a common objective. Indeed, the correspondence between the structure and functioning of Dutch corporatism was more than mere coincidence. The institutions were a product of confessional efforts in the early part of this century to create political institutions that would grant predominance to their interests over those of the more socialist left, or even of the more liberal right.

My argument is that the pattern of political mobilization in a country has institutional consequences. This study shows that corporatism was a type of state outlined in confessional political ideology, advocated by confessional leaders, and created through successful mobilization of confessional forces. The object of confessional forces was to resist what they perceived as state encroachment on private activities. For this reason the operation of Dutch corporatism successfully halted the calls for more extensive state intervention to provide social welfare. In the Dutch context corporatism was a way to limit the degree of state meddling, whereas in other countries corporatism is often perceived as a way to manage state intervention.

Beginning in the middle of the nineteenth century, discussions

Conclusions

of welfare policy in the Netherlands were conducted in a society where religion was the defining characteristic of social and political organization and mobilization. Contest between religious and secular political forces marked the early development of democratic political institutions. Social welfare, or the provision of poor relief, was one of the battlegrounds. Liberals, paradoxically, advocated greater state involvement, an attitude prompted by a desire to restrict the degree of social control that religious forces exercised through church-operated charities. Both Catholic and Protestant forces were antagonistic to the idea of the state assuming a greater role in the provision of social welfare and sought to devise ways of maintaining their position. The outcome was the creation of a state program of poor relief that was administered by the church charities. When industrialization came to the country, religious forces mobilized to exert their influence in economic relations. Leftist mobilization of the working class was almost undermined by the creation of confessional labor organizations. And tensions between labor and capital interests were averted through the creation of confessional employers' associations that cooperated with confessional unions. This guildlike arrangement in industrial relations was entrenched in early social security legislation.

A type of corporatism that limited the role of the state in policy making explains much of the long delay in the development of the modern Dutch welfare state. In many countries, including the Netherlands, the idea of extending social welfare entitlements to the entire population was inspired by the British example, on principles set out in the Beveridge Report. Universalization of entitlement programs, that characteristic of modern welfare states, occurred in most western European countries shortly before or after World War II. In the Netherlands, similar ideas for universalization of welfare received a great deal of attention from prominent politicians. Indeed, throughout the 1950s the governing Labor party adopted universalization as one of its principal goals. Yet this expansion of the Dutch welfare state did not begin until the 1960s, after the Labor party was out of power. The Labor party's reform efforts were frustrated by corporatist policy-making bodies. In the area of social security reform, Labor politicians found it impossible to gain the agreement of confessional labor and business interests, which were represented on corporatist councils.

These were the origins of corporatist relations in the Netherlands. What sets the Dutch case apart from many other corporatist countries is the prominent role played by religious forces. In contrast to Scandinavian countries, where corporatism is defined by the representation of labor and capital interests, in the Netherlands religion was a more important line of cleavage in economic relations. Another element that sets it apart is that Dutch corporatism existed in many areas of policy. The confessional political ideologies advocated corporatism in all state-society relations, not just in economic and industrial policy. This is why religious charities were important actors in the poor relief program. Also, while corporatism is often understood as a partnership between the state and societal interests to facilitate coordination of policy, the determination of religious forces to keep the state out of society led to the creation of corporatist institutions that are dominated by societal rather than state interests. In this respect the historical concerns in the Netherlands bear more resemblance to those in the United States. The drafters of that country's constitution created an institutional structure that was consciously intended to prevent the state from taking dramatic decisions and acting upon them. In the United States the mechanism was the separation of powers whereas in the Netherlands it was capture of the state by certain private interests, but the consequence for policy was the same.

Actually, the history of Dutch corporatism should not be surprising. The Dutch experience fits with some of the unfortunately often overlooked literature on the role of religion in the development of corporatism. Harold Wilensky (1981) has argued that Catholic power has been as effective as leftist power in promoting corporatism. In fact, many of the countries where Catholic power contributed to the development of corporatism are also regarded as examples of strong and stable corporatism, for example, Austria, Belgium, and the Netherlands (Katzenstein 1985). In these countries, Catholic political forces contributed to the development of corporatism when industrialization was either not yet underway or only beginning. The constellation of interests that typify corporatism in a specific country will depend on the historical position of those interests in the process of state building. And variations in the process of state building will produce variations in the ways policy making occurs. In the Netherlands religious forces resisted reform of the welfare state, and their representation on corporatist councils allowed them to block attempts to expand welfare programs throughout much of this century. It is this history of institutional development, and the attitudes of the groups represented in these institutions, that explains the late development of the Dutch welfare state.

RAPID GROWTH: THE IMPLICATIONS
OF SOCIAL AND INSTITUTIONAL CHANGE

Though efforts to reform welfare programs in the Netherlands were slowed by the opposition of corporatist interests, reform did come during the 1960s. And when it came, the rate of growth was remarkable, not only when compared with other western European countries. The rate of growth also defies our understanding of change in policy as an incremental process whereby successive policies represent marginal departures from previous policies. Nonincremental policy making tends to be viewed as something that happens under special conditions, such as war, revolution, or crisis (Lindblom 1959). Is the Dutch case, then, an anomalous pattern of growth of the welfare state, or can a theoretical perspective that focuses on state building also account for it?

The question is an important one because the characterization of most change in policy as incremental is one that fits well with the view of institutions as conservative, slow-to-change forces in society. A theoretical approach that holds open the possibility of dramatic institutional change must also recognize that the process of policy making could also undergo similar change. This, then, would explain how the outcomes of policy making could change rapidly. To fit the experience of rapid welfare growth in the Netherlands within the theoretical framework of this study, it becomes essential to consider the possibility that Dutch corporatism was radically transformed in the 1960s. Identifying the causes of such change, therefore, must focus on changes in political mobilization and the institutional allocation of power that would allow new political forces quickly to redefine the state in their own interests. Such a study then has to demonstrate how this would alter the resulting policies.

What were the characteristics of rapid welfare state development in the Netherlands? In terms of spending alone, the Dutch welfare state has come to rival Sweden's as the most extensive in the world. Yet there was more to the growth of the Dutch welfare state than simply an increase in spending on it. In addition, growth resulted from a qualitative shift in welfare provisions. Prior to World War II the Dutch welfare state consisted of some rather limited income assistance programs. These were of two types: workers' insurance and poor relief. The workers' insurance system was established around the turn of the century. Beginning in the late 1950s, a spate of legislation was passed that dramatically expanded welfare programs. One important feature of this legislation was not that it increased benefits (although it did) but that it instituted dramatic changes in the existing programs. In the area of workers' insurance, two fundamental changes were introduced. The first was an increase in the level of benefits awarded to insured workers to guarantee them a "social minimum" income. For example, retirement benefits originally designed as income supplements were increased to provide a livable income, and disability benefits, which had the same original purpose, were pegged to the last earned wage to maintain an accustomed standard of living. The second important change was the extension of these programs to the population at large. Successive legislation created new public insurance programs that instituted universal entitlement to benefits for retirement, disability, illness, and widows and orphans. Likewise, the poor relief program was replaced by a system of means-tested public assistance to ensure that all needy citizens would receive support not as an act of charity but as a right.

It is this qualitative shift from workers' insurance and poor relief to universal insurance and public assistance that is the real source of Dutch growth in the welfare state. Decisions were taken not only to alter the spending on social welfare dramatically but also to transform the definition of the state's responsibility to provide income assistance for its citizens. Taken together, these changes and the speed with which they were enacted are responsible for the rapid growth of the Dutch welfare state.

But what factors account for this rapid shift in policy? Many observers of the Dutch case have pointed to a change in the institutions that make social policy. Dutch corporatism has undergone a transformation that reflects a general trend among corporatist countries. One factor is that the legitimacy of corporatist institutions to make policy decisions has come under attack from other institutions, such as parliament and government. According to corporatist theory, governments and parliaments will be reluctant to of take action on policy, or even incapable of doing so, until corporatist groups have been given the opportunity to comment on it.

But in many western European countries, governments have become dissatisfied with playing a secondary role to such institutions. The most dramatic case of governmental challenge to corporatism has occurred in Britain, where Margaret Thatcher's government consciously set out to dismantle corporatism. Similar challenges have occurred in other countries, and in the Netherlands parliament has endeavored to strengthen its role in policy making by increasing its scrutiny of government-proposed legislation and by initiating more legislation on its own (Gladdish 1990).

A second factor that has changed the nature of corporatism is an increasing inability of participants in the institutions to reach closure on issues. This can be partly attributed to a general downturn in economic performance during the late 1970s and 1980s that polarized labor and capital interests. When economic prospects are rosy, it is easy for corporatist actors to reach agreement on how to direct economic production. As economies enter periods of stagnation, or even decline, the different concerns of labor and capital become more pronounced. In the Netherlands this factor, combined with decline in the power of labor as an mobilizing force, has led to stalemate in corporatist institutions (Wolinetz 1989).

A third factor that has fostered changes in corporatism is a change in the nature of social mobilization. Corporatism allows some interests to monopolize the decision-making process while other (potential) interests are denied similar representation. The concerns of other social groups, if heard, are likely to go unheeded. Also, corporatist institutions have a specific influence on the perception of legitimate political activity in a country, and they consequently determine what means groups and individuals employ to influence specific outcomes of the policy-making process. Corporatist policy making reinforces the perception that to exercise effective influence, actors must be represented in corporatist institutions. Corporatism further creates the perception that other channels of political influence are not likely to be successful.

But new patterns of political mobilization are emerging in the Netherlands. New interests are demanding more voice in policy decisions and bring a variety of challenges to corporatism. One type of challenge is pluralist, directed at changing public attitudes and at lobbying many different state institutions. Beginning in the late 1960s, such changing social attitudes illustrated a breakdown in the pillarization of Dutch society that had existed since the beginning of the century. This breakdown has eroded the traditional practices of political decision making and facilitated the formation of new coalitions of interests. As Arthur Wassenberg (1982) has noted, the Dutch public is becoming increasingly dissatisfied with accepting the legitimacy of decisions made in ways that are immune to public scrutiny. With this the Netherlands has experienced a surge in the activity of new social movements and other lobbying interests.

The other type of societal challenge to corporatism stems from the professionalization of modern society. Professionals have become important actors, in policy making as a result of what could be termed the evolution of policy fields. As the fundamental issues about the scope and objectives of policy are settled, more attention comes to focus on the technical problems of implementing decisions. Professionals are the most competent people to do this, mainly because they are active in the area concerned and possess information crucial to the policy maker. In the Netherlands the last two decades have seen the rise of a number of professional organizations that advise on issues of policy and have a special relationship with government officials. The proliferation of such groups and the ties they establish with bureaucrats have offered a challenge to the older institutions of corporatism (I. Scholten 1987).

With all these changes in corporatist relationships, it is not difficult to see that they can establish the conditions for a rapid change in decisions on policy. There is, however, one important difficulty with tracing the nonincremental growth of the Dutch welfare state to these factors. All the changes that have been observed occurred at the end of the period of rapid growth. All but one of the new welfare programs (public disability) were in place by 1967. It was at this time that the breakdown of pillarization began. Parliamentary assertiveness did not begin until the 1970s. Also, it was not until after the oil crises of the 1970s that disagreement among the social partners led to stalemate in corporatist decision making.

Something appears to be wrong with the causal sequence of political change and change in policy in the Netherlands. In contrast to the claims of the many scholars in the 1970s who asserted that a silent social revolution had caused a change in Dutch politics, the evidence in this study makes a strong case that the breakdown of pillarization began much earlier. Indeed, much of the new thinking can be traced to the exile groups that were in Lon-

don during World War II. And, contrary to the prevailing explanation of the breakdown, the desire for change was expressed
by an elite before it became a grass-roots upsurge of discontent
in society. Thus, in this context of dramatic political change,
which was brought on by a number of factors and became manifest in a number of ways, a window of opportunity was opened
in the normal institutional procedures that allowed welfare reformers to push through dramatic reforms.

LESSONS FOR COMPARATIVE RESEARCH

Though this study has striven to give a comprehensive account
of the history of welfare policy in the Netherlands, its purpose
has been broader. It has also endeavored to place the explanation of the Dutch case within the comparative theories of the
development of the welfare state. The importance of this second
goal is that the Dutch case represents a curious anomaly for virtually all comparative theories. I have asserted that three omissions or errors in the way the development of the welfare state
is currently conceptualized produced the Dutch anomaly. This
means that the Dutch case really is not unusual but that theory
must be improved in order to accommodate it properly. What,
then, are the theoretical lessons to be gleaned from examination
of the Dutch case?

I have maintained that the pattern of development of the welfare state in the Netherlands is peculiar, but those who study the
welfare state as a convergent phenomenon will still be able to
demonstrate that the Dutch have instituted social security programs that are generally similar to those in neighboring countries. The first lesson from the Dutch case is that this apparent
convergence can be traced to ideational as well as material causes.
Indeed, in defiance of the socioeconomic explanations, the enactment of welfare programs did not coincide with the society's
reaching certain thresholds of development or modernization.
Quite to the contrary, the reason why Dutch welfare programs
are similar to those in neighboring countries is that policy makers

searched around and sought to borrow ideas from abroad. When the discussions of social security were initiated at the turn of the century, confessional forces looked to the programs established by Bismarck in Germany. What they liked about the German model was that it lessened the appeal of socialism among the work force. But rather than achieve this by creating a bond of loyalty between workers and the state, confessional forces in the Netherlands still desired to minimize the state's role. Consequently they developed a system of social insurance operated by bipartite institutions representing employers and unions.

Following World War II, a different concern dominated debates over social policy. The ideals of the British cradle-to-grave system of universal entitlements, outlined in the Beveridge Report, had a substantial impact on the thinking of many prominent policy officials. These ideals were adopted by some bureaucratic reformers and were incorporated into the Labor party's political platform, becoming crucial components of the postwar debate on welfare reform. It even led reformers in the 1960s to place a greater emphasis on formulating programs that would encompass every citizen than on containing the potential costs of the programs.

As a lesson for comparative research, one of the important findings from the Dutch case is that empirical study of the process of policy borrowing is indeed possible, the evidence being obtainable when the historical record is complete. For example, the impact of the British Beveridge Report is documented in the studies that were commissioned by the government both during and after the war (the two Van Rhijn commissions). Moreover, when the biographical records of influential officials are complete, we can determine if their policy ideas were influenced by their observations of foreign countries. Biographers of Abram Kuyper confirm that at the early part of this century his ideas were inspired by Bismarck's programs, and, since Kuyper was a major author of legislation, his ideas came to be reflected in the policy. Following the war, the commitment of the Labor party leader, Willem Drees, to the goal of universal entitlements inaugurated a new discussion. And though it was the Catholic party that finally enacted most Dutch welfare legislation, the influence of the socialists' early efforts to emulate the British welfare state set the terms of the debate.

The identification of an occurrence of policy borrowing also offers the occasion to make note of its mechanisms. There are a number of ways that policy borrowing may take place. The one cited most often in the literature is that it occurs through elite channels of interaction. In his study of bourgeois revolutions in Europe, Reinhard Bendix (1978) showed that it was an educated elite in central Europe that became aware of the progressive economic changes occurring in western Europe and then pressed for reforms that would make such progress possible in their own countries. In the study of the welfare state, virtually every case of an official who was strongly influenced by examples from abroad occurred as a result of travel and observation in a foreign country. For William Beveridge it was his experience in Germany. For Goto Shimpei, architect of the Japanese welfare state, it was his student years in Germany. For Dutch political leaders, especially in the postwar period, it was close contact with the other Allied powers that introduced them to alternative ways of creating a welfare state.

The study of policy borrowing draws attention to individuals in the policy-making process and the ways they strive to have their ideals realized in public policy. Consequently research at such a close level of analysis sheds light on the importance of individuals in determining policy. In other words, the impact of borrowing is affirmed not only by the discovery of new ideas by policy makers but also by their diligence in striving to turn these into real policy reform. Some important aspects of this process are worth noting.

Policy makers borrow ideas that are viable as well as desirable: they try to adopt foreign examples that can easily be adapted to the domestic situation. Moreover, they strive to make the appropriate adjustments. Abram Kuyper sought to emulate the decentralized components of the German social security programs but adapted them to the confessional principles of corporatism, rather than duplicating the components that stemmed from Bismarck's concerns of *realpolitik*. For the postwar expansion of the welfare state, Dutch leaders found inspiration for the new entitlement principles in the Beveridge Report but deemed the British administrative structure inappropriate for their purpose. Instead, they looked to the American case for an example of an administrative structure that was more to their liking.

Another important lesson is that ideas borrowed from abroad make a difference when their advocates are willing to pursue their objectives steadfastly. In part, the reason the Labor party was unable to expand welfare provisions when it controlled the government during the 1950s was that its leaders were unwilling to accept programs that only partially met their goals. In addition, one can identify innovative strategies as factors that produced success. In 1953, minister of social affairs, J. G. Suurhoff (PvdA) departed from the traditional practice of consulting corporatist councils and openly challenged them. He threatened to ignore the advice of the SER and tried to stir up public opinion. In the 1960s major welfare reformers exhibited a similar conviction about their policy ideas. Gerhard Veldkamp continually courted ostracization from his own Catholic party when he advocated the Labor party's welfare reform platform. He and his staff challenged corporatist practice by consulting new social groups that were not part of the traditional policy-making process. Marga Klompé, as minister of social work, prevailed in creating a state-operated public assistance program by simply outlasting the charity agencies that opposed her. Then, when other factors had rendered them impotent in policy making, she was able to enact her reforms.

In addition to making a case for further examination of policy borrowing, another crucial lesson from this examination of the Dutch welfare state is that much of the thinking on the way political groups influence the outcomes of the policy-making process should be reconsidered. I have argued that the conviction of many scholars of the welfare state that bigger welfare states happen in countries where the left is powerful is simply wrong because the Dutch welfare state, one of the world's largest, was built by centrist, confessional forces. Instead, what needs to be done is to release the comparative examination of welfare states from the inductive logic that so far has dominated. Claims about what causes the general phenomenon should be stated in generally applicable terms, not induced from observation of the Swedish experience. Indeed, for empirical reasons the Dutch case needs a new model. That is why I argue that it would be more useful to examine the dynamics of collective mobilization and the ways in which groups develop and pursue policy strategies, rather than to assume these strategies from the ideological position of a group. This continues to affirm the importance of mobilized groups as forces in the policy-making process. On this count the research that has examined mobilization of workers or control of government by socialist parties has been useful. What needs to be added to the discussion is a recognition that the stated ideology of a group can be misleading.

It is more useful to distinguish between the ideological position a group represents and its political program. The two cannot always be assumed to correspond. This is no news to those who have studied other policies, or politics in other regions of the world. It is commonly understood that the ideological principles espoused by the Communist party of the Soviet Union were not consistently acted upon. In western countries the 1970s and 1980s demonstrated that parties of the left do not always pursue their ideological goals of nationalization or socialization of production once they are in office. Mark Kesselman's (1982) study of France during the Mitterrand presidency reveals that once in power, French socialists behave less radically than their ideology would indicate and are perhaps not clearly distinguishable from the right.

In the Netherlands this issue is crucial to understanding why the confessional forces, whose ideology espouses a parochial version of the limited state, could come to be responsible for one of the biggest welfare expansions in the world. Though they had marginal differences, both Catholic and Protestant ideologies argue that welfare should be left to society rather than assumed by the state. Why, then, were coalition governments of Catholics and Protestants the ones that expanded entitlements, assumed public assistance as a state task — in short, the ones that built the Dutch welfare state. These reforms violated their ideological principles. Furthermore, in the late 1960s it was the Labor party that attempted to slow the expansion, citing the potential cost of the programs.

The only satisfactory explanation is that the behavior of confessional forces was inconsistent with their ideological principles. It was a complex set of circumstances that prompted this programmatic shift in position. In general, fundamental social change rendered religion a less important force in Dutch social life. Various aspects of the phenomenon had direct bearing on the programmatic concerns of the confessional groups. Secularization in society led to a decline in the vote for confessional parties. In response, the parties downplayed many of their less popular principles and even adopted some popular causes, such as universalization of welfare, in a effort to bolster support. Rationalization of life in a modern industrial society exposed Catholic and Protestant ideologies as anachronistic, more appropriate to a preindustrial age. Charity agencies became more involved in professional rather than missionary aspects of their activities. Labor unions, at least the Catholic ones, discovered common cause with leftist unions, and they banded together to oppose employers. The traditionally passive population became more vocal and politically active. The new activism was expressed in the development of single-interest groups and direct lobbying campaigns that would have forced a government of any ideological color to acknowledge the interests of these newly mobilized groups. The implications for the comparative examination of welfare states is that scholars should study group dynamics at a more abstract theoretical level, emphasizing the dynamics of collective mobilization and its consequences. This type of theorizing lends itself to broader comparative analysis than extrapolating universal claims from the experiences of a few northern European countries.

Finally, this study has attempted to make a relatively radical statement about the role institutions play in the development of policy. Two claims have been of concern. First, the Dutch case demonstrates the necessity of developing a more sophisticated theoretical conceptualization of institutional structures. Most scholarship on the welfare state treats the state as a dichotomous variable. It is either strong or weak; strong states can produce big welfare states, but weak states never can. The Dutch corporatist state does not fit comfortably in this formulation. Corporatism by definition is a peculiar mixture and blurring of state and society. When one recognizes this, it becomes more useful to think of the state as a set of institutions that maintain a balance of political forces and bear witness to the historic struggle among political forces. Research into the welfare state would be well served by more study of the historical development of state institutions that would assist in the development of more sophisticated models of types of state.

Indeed, these models should be built upon historical and comparative investigation. One of the early problems a student of Dutch politics confronts is the inappropriateness of most theories of the corporatist state for the Dutch case. In the 1970s and 1980s, when corporatism was *the* theme in western European studies, the models scholars were working with lacked broad empirical relevance. The models of economic corporatism fitted only a few countries. Many of the assumptions about corporatism (e.g., it was a postwar development; it required peak organizations of interests; these interests were functional economic groups) were extrapolated from the German experience. This line of thinking, however, overlooked Germany's checkered history, which may have produced a unique kind of corporatism. Peter Katzenstein (1985) was among the first to discover that in other countries corporatism had a different pattern of development. The Netherlands was one of those countries.

Institutions can be identified by the processes they engender as well as their structures. This study exposes some omissions in our understanding of corporatist structures. In addition, it identifies some errors in our understanding of its processes. Much of the scholarship on corporatism has been guided by a laudable attempt to examine policy in some countries in order to draw lessons that may be applied elsewhere. Much of the study of corporatism was characterized by boasts that it was a more desirable means of reaching decisions on policy because it fostered greater consensus in discussion, bridged the chasm that separates management and labor in more classically liberal societies, and provides a mechanism for the state to "steer" society rather than react to societal pressures.

The Dutch case confirms that all these things are true, but the story is more complicated. The existence of corporatist structures does not necessarily produce more efficient and less divisive policies. To claim that it does would require a denial that disagreement is inherent in the human condition. The history of Dutch corporatism shows that the structures hid much of the political divisiveness that did exist in society. Corporatist institutions are less democratic. In many cases their negotiations occurred behind closed doors. When students of comparative politics were examining the supposed "consociational" decision making in the smaller European countries, they were looking at the traditional institutions, governments and parliaments. There they found a great deal of agreement and dubbed the countries relatively free of conflict. Had they probed further and examined the institutions where decisions were actually made, they would have discovered levels of conflict and disagreement that parallel those in any pluralist society. The lesson from this is twofold. Further research that challenges prevailing assumptions increases our understanding of the empirical world. Also, prescriptive remedies, such as advocating corporatism as a solution to the stagnation of policy in other countries, needs to take greater stock of the relationship between the structure of a policy and the societal context to which it corresponds, before that structure is deemed appropriate for application elsewhere.

The Development of the Dutch Welfare State

These are the three theoretical implications of the study. In addition, the examination of the Dutch experience in the 1980s points to another important topic for further welfare research. The Netherlands, like other countries, is experiencing a crisis of the welfare state. The world economic condition is less rosy. This had raised serious concern over the cost of social welfare programs and engendered efforts to roll back spending levels. What the Dutch case shows — a finding that is probably appropriate to other countries — is that the process of retrenchment bears only paradoxical resemblance to the process of expansion of the welfare state. Though individual strategies, group mobilization, and institutional dynamics combine to characterize the policy-making process, welfare states cannot be dismantled by reversing the process by which they were created. The generous programs were based on a faith in continued economic prosperity. No one anticipated the demographic changes that produced a large percentage of pensioners, or the technological changes that brought on the unemployment problems. Perhaps most important, optimistic policy makers never anticipated that a generous disability program would be used by labor and business to make the state pay the costs of economic dislocation.

The changes that accompanied the development of the Dutch welfare state have set constraints on the current attempts to cut back on expenditures. The open policy-making process provides access to groups that oppose welfare retrenchment, among which beneficiaries are not alone. The welfare state has created a tertiary sector of professionals who now have a vested interest in maintaining the programs. Doctors and social workers complain about the current cutbacks and strive to undermine government efforts. In addition, the groups represented on corporatist councils now desire to reassert their position in the policy-making process. Though the institutional changes have circumscribed the role played by corporatist bodies such as the SER, these institutions still exist, and their members wish to reestablish the prerogative they once enjoyed in policy making.

Indeed, the era of retrenchment may be the best opportunity

for a revival of Dutch corporatism. Corporatism characterized policy making when the basic principles of the Dutch welfare state were under discussion. Now that retrenchment has again raised questions about the nature of entitlements, broader societal interests, such as labor and capital, may again become important participants in the debates. But if there is a revival of corporatism, it will be very different from what it once was. Religion has disappeared as the primary line of cleavage among societal groups. Consequently councils such as the SER have come to resemble such tripartite bodies in other European countries where the lines of cleavage are between labor, business, and the state. Also, the disappearance of religion has had its effect in other policy areas where religious forces contributed to the establishment of corporatist practices. In social work church charities are no longer important actors, and even the mobilizing agencies that operated in the 1970s are being replaced by agencies that have a more managerial orientation.

This is the history of the development of the Dutch welfare state. The pattern of its development was different from the norm. It came about later than in other European countries but then developed more quickly. Despite the efforts on the part of Dutch policy makers to borrow ideas from neighboring countries, it also has many unique features. Politics explains much of what is unique about the Dutch case. Yet the politics of social welfare in the Netherlands illustrates some basic themes common to the history of all welfare states. In all countries welfare policy is a major area that defines the relationship between the state and society. Consequently it is a battleground for contending forces that strive to imprint policy with their own vision of the role the state should assume in ordering civil society. The institutional context in which these contests occur aids some groups and impedes others. Attitudes may change, and this may bring about changes in policy, though institutional constraints may frustrate some of the attempted reforms. Institutions are also capable of changing, and when they do, they produce a situation ripe for dramatic changes in public policy. The Dutch case is an excellent illustration.

Appendices   Bibliography   Index

Appendix One
Chronology of Social Legislation

PENSIONS

1913 Invalidity Law (Invaliditeitswet)

1919 Voluntary Retirement Insurance Act (Wet op de Vrijwillige Ouderdomsverzekering)

1947 Emergency Retirement Pensions Act (Noodwet Ouderdomsvoorziening)

1957 Public Retirement Pensions Act (Algemene Ouderdomswet)

1959 Public Widows and Orphans Act (Algemene Weduwen en Wezenwet)

1967 Repeal of the Invalidity Law (replaced by the Worker's Disability Act)

1978 Repeal of the Voluntary Retirement Insurance Act

1980 Social Security Harmonization Act (Wet Aanpassingsmechanismen)

PUBLIC ASSISTANCE

1854 Poor Law (Armenwet)

1912 New Poor Law (Nieuwe Armenwet)

1965 Public Assistance Act (Algemene Bijstandswet)

1974 Decree for National Benefit Uniformity (Besluit Landelijke Normering)

1979 Amendments to the Public Assistance Act (reductions in administration, financing, and services)

1980 Social Security Harmonization Act (Wet Aanpassingsmechanismen)

Appendix One

DISABILITY BENEFITS

1901 Workmen's Compensation Act (Ongevallenwet)

1913 Invalidity Act (Invaliditeitswet)

1919 Seaman's Compensation Act (Zee-Ongevallenwet)

1921 New Workmen's Compensation Act (Nieuwe Ongevallenwet)

1922 Agricultural Workmen's Compensation Act (Land en Tuinbouw Ongevallenwet)

1930 Illness Act (Ziektewet)

1967 Disability Security Act (Wet op de Arbeidsongeschiktheids Verzekering)

1976 Public Disability Act (Algemene Arbeidsongeschiktheidswet)

1979 Equalization of Disability Benefit Rights for Men and Women (Herziening AAW Gelijkerechten Man-Vrouw)

1980 Social Security Harmonization Act (Wet Aanpassingsmechanismen)

UNEMPLOYMENT INSURANCE

1917 Unemployment Decree (Werkloosheidsbesluit)

1935 Unemployment Insurance Fund Act (Wet op de Werkloosheidssubsidiefonds)

1944 Special Decree for Unemployment Provisions (Buitengewoon Besluit Werklozenzorg)

1952 Unemployment Act (Werkloosheidswet)
Social Employment Provisions Act (Wet Sociale Werkvoorzieningen)

1965 Extra Unemployment Provisions Act (Wet Werkloosheidsvoorziening) replaces the Social Provisions for the Unemployed (1952)

1980 Social Security Harmonization Act (Wet Aanpassingsmechanismen)

COMPENSATION FOR MEDICAL EXPENSES

1941 Illness Fund Decree (Ziekenfondsen Besluit)

1950 Preventative Illness Fund Act (Wet op Het Praeventiefonds)

1965 Illness Fund Act (Ziekenfondswet) replaced Illness Fund Decree

Appendix One

1968   Public Exceptional Medical Expenses Act (Algemene Wet Bijzondere Ziekenkosten)

CHILDREN'S ALLOWANCES

1940   Wage-Earner's Children's Allowance Act (Kinderbijslagwet voor Loontrekkenden)

1952   Emergency Children's Allowance for the Self-Employed (Noodwet Kinderbijslag voor Kleine Zelfstandigen)

1963   Public Children's Allowance Act (Algemene Kinderbijslagwet)

1980   Integration of the three programs into a New Children's Allowance Act

LEGISLATION PERTAINING TO SOCIAL INSURANCE ADMINISTRATION

1913   Councils Act (Radenwet) awarded public status to producer groups

1920   Institutionalization of the National Insurance Bank (Wet op de Rijksverzekeringsbank)

1933   Institutionalization of the Councils of Labor (Wet op de Rijksverzekeringsbank en de Raden van Arbeid)

1952   Social Insurance Organization Act (Organizatiewet Sociale Verzekering)

1956   Institutionalization of the Social Insurance Bank and the Councils of Labor (Wet op de Sociale Verzekeringsbank en de Raden van Arbeid)

Appendix Two
Major Political Parties

CONFESSIONAL PARTIES

KVP	Catholic Peoples' party (post–World War II)
ARP	Antirevolutionary party (fundamentalist Protestant)
CHU	Christian Historical Union (progressive Protestant)
CDA	Christian Democratic Appeal (merger of KVP, ARP, CHU)

LEFT PARTIES

PvdA	Labor party (post–World War II)
D '66	Democrats '66 (left-wing splinter from Labor party)
DS '70	Democrat-Socialists '70 (right-wing splinter from Labor party)

RIGHT PARTIES

VVD	Liberal party (post–World War II)
SGP	Dutch Reformed Political party (ultra-fundamentalist)

Appendix Three
Cabinets, 1945–1989

Source: H. Daalder and C. Schuyt, eds. 1990. *Compendium Voor Politiek en Samenleving in Nederland*, A0500:88–113. Alphen aan den Rijn: Samsom.

SCHERMERHORN-DREES

Duration:	24-6-1945 to 3-7-1946
Composition:	6 PvdA, 3 KVP, 3 independent, 1 liberal, 1 ARP, 1 socialist

Major ministers
Prime Minister:	W. Schermerhorn (PvdA)
Home Affairs:	L. J. M. Beel (KVP)
Social Affairs:	W. Drees (PvdA)

BEEL I

Duration:	3-7-1946 to 7-8-1948
Composition:	5 KVP, 6 PvdA, 3 independent

Major ministers
Prime Minister:	L. J. M. Beel (KVP)
Home Affairs:	L. J. M. Beel (to 15-9-1947, KVP)
	P. J. Witteman (to 7-8-1948, KVP)
Social Affairs:	W. Drees (PvdA)

DREES–VAN SCHAIK

Duration:	7-8-1948 to 15-3-1981
Composition:	5 PvdA, 6 KVP, 1 CHU, 1 VVD, 2 independent

Major ministers
Prime Minister:	W. Drees (PvdA)
Home Affairs:	J. H. van Maarseveen (to 15-6-1949, KVP)
	J. R. H. van Schaik (to 20-9-1949, KVP)
	F. G. C. J. M. Teulings (to 15-3-1951, KVP)
Social Affairs:	A. M. Joekes (PvdA)

Appendix Three

DREES I
Duration: 15-3-1951 to 2-9-1952
Composition: 5 PvdA, 6 KVP, 1 VVD, 2 CHU, 1 independent

Major ministers
Prime Minister: W. Drees (PvdA)
Home Affairs: J. H. van Maarseveen (to 18-11-1951, KVP)
F. G. C. J. M. Teulings (to 6-12-1951, KVP)
L. J. M. Beel (to 2-9-1952, KVP)
Social Affairs: A. M. Joekes (PvdA)

DREES II
Duration: 2-9-1952 to 13-10-1956
Composition: 5 PvdA, 6 KVP, 2 ARP, 2 CHU, 1 independent

Major ministers
Prime Minister: W. Drees (PvdA)
Home Affairs: L. J. M. Beel (to 7-7-1956, KVP)
J. C. van Oven (to 13-10-1956, PvdA)
Social Affairs: J. G. Suurhoff (PvdA)
Social Work: L. J. M. Beel (to 9-9-1952, KVP)
F. J. F. M. van Thiel (to 13-10-1956, KVP)

DREES III
Duration: 13-10-1956 to 22-12-1958
Composition: 5 PvdA, 5 KVP, 2 ARP, 2 CHU

Major ministers
Prime Minister: W. Drees (PvdA)
Home Affairs: J. G. Suurhoff (to 29-10-1956, PvdA)
A. A. M. Struycken (to 22-12-1958, KVP)
Social Affairs: J. G. Suurhoff (PvdA)
Social Work: M. A. M. Klompé (KVP)

BEEL II
Duration: 22-12-1958 to 19-5-1959
Composition: 6 KVP, 2 ARP, 2 CHU

Major ministers
Prime Minister: L. J. M. Beel (KVP)
Home Affairs: A. A. M. Struycken (KVP)
Social Affairs: L. J. M. Beel (KVP)
Social Work: M. A. M. Klompé (KVP)

DE QUAY
Duration: 19-5-1959 to 24-7-1963
Composition: 6 KVP, 3 VVD, 2 ARP, 2 CHU

232

Appendix Three

Major ministers
  Prime Minister: J. E. de Quay (KVP)
  Home Affairs: E. H. Toxopeus (VVD)
  Social Affairs: J. M. A. von Rooij (to 3-7-1961, KVP)
                    V. G. M. Marijnen (to 17-7-1961, KVP)
                    G. M. J. Veldkamp (to 24-7-1963, KVP)
  Social Work: M. A. M. Klompé (KVP)

MARIJNEN
  Duration: 24-7-1963 to 14-4-1965
  Composition: 6 KVP, 3 VVD, 2 ARP, 2 CHU

Major ministers
  Prime Minister: V. G. M. Marijnen (KVP)
  Home Affairs: E. H. Toxopeus (VVD)
  Social Affairs: G. M. J. Veldkamp (KVP)
  Social Work: J. S. Schouwenaar-Franssen (VVD)

CALS
  Duration: 14-4-1965 to 22-11-1966
  Composition: 6 KVP, 5 PvdA, 3 ARP

Major ministers
  Prime Minister: J. M. L. Th. Cals (KVP)
  Home Affairs: J. Smallenbroek (to 31-8-1966, ARP)
                    I. Samkalden (to 5-9-1966, PvdA)
                    P. J. Verdam (to 22-11-1966, ARP)
  Social Affairs: G. M. J. Veldkamp (KVP)
  Social Work: M. Vrolijk (PvdA)

ZIJLSTRA
  Duration: 22-11-1966 to 5-4-1967
  Composition: 5 ARP, 8 KVP

Major ministers
  Prime Minister: J. Zijlstra (ARP)
  Home Affairs: V. J. Verdam (ARP)
  Social Affairs: G. M. J. Veldkamp (KVP)
  Social Work: M. A. M. Klompé (KVP)

DE JONG
  Duration: 5-4-1967 to 6-7-1971
  Composition: 6 KVP, 3 VVD, 3 ARP, 2 CHU

Major ministers
  Prime Minister: P. J. S. de Jong (KVP)
  Home Affairs: H. K. J. Beernink (CHU)

Social Affairs:	B. Roolvink (ARP)
Social Work:	M. A. M. Klompé (KVP)

BIESHEUVEL I
Duration:	6-7-1971 to 20-7-1972
Composition:	3 ARP, 6 KVP, 3 VVD, 2 CHU, 2 Democrat-Socialists '70

Major ministers
Prime Minister:	B. W. Biesheuvel (ARP)
Home Affairs:	W. J. Geertsema (VVD)
Social Affairs:	J. Boersma (ARP)
Social Work:	P. J. Engels (KVP)

BIESHEUVEL II
Duration:	20-7-1972 to 11-5-1973
Composition:	6 KVP, 3 ARP, 2 CHU, 3 VVD

Major ministers
Prime Minister:	B. W. Biesheuvel (ARP)
Home Affairs:	W. J. Geertsema (VVD)
Social Affairs:	J. Boersma (ARP)
Social Work:	P. J. Engels (KVP)

DEN UYL
Duration:	11-5-1973 to 19-12-1977
Composition:	7 PvdA, 2 Radical Political Party, 1 Democrats '66, 4 KVP, 2 ARP

Major ministers
Prime Minister:	J. M. den Uyl (PvdA)
Home Affairs:	W. F. de Gaay Fortman (ARP)
Social Affairs:	J. Boersma (ARP)
Social Work:	H. W. van Doorn (Radical Political Party)

VAN AGT I
Duration:	19-12-1977 to 11-9-1981
Composition:	10 CDA, 6 VVD

Major ministers
Prime Minister:	A. A. M. van Agt (CDA)
Home Affairs:	H. Wiegel (to 22-2-1980, VVD)
	G. M. V. van Aardenne (to 5-3-1980, VVD)
	A. P. J. M. M. van der Stee (to 11-9-1981, CDA)
Social Affairs:	W. Albeda (CDA)
Social Work:	M. H. M. F. Gardeniers-Berendsen (CDA)

Appendix Three

VAN AGT II
Duration: 11-9-1981 to 29-5-1982
Composition: 6 CDA, 6 PvdA, 3 Democrats '66

Major ministers
    Prime Minister: A. A. M. van Agt (CDA)
    Home Affairs: E. van Thijn (PvdA)
    Social Affairs: J. M. den Uyl (PvdA)
    Social Work: A. A. van der Louw (PvdA)

VAN AGT III
Duration: 29-5-1982 to 4-11-1982
Composition   9 CDA, 5 Democrats '66

Major ministers
    Prime Minister: A. A. M. van Agt (CDA)
    Home Affairs: M. Rood (Democrats '66)
    Social Affairs: L. de Graaf (CDA)
    Social Work: H. A. de Boer (CDA)

LUBBERS I
Duration: 4-11-1982 to 14-7-1986
Composition: 8 CDA, 6 VVD

Major ministers
    Prime Minister: R. F. M. Lubbers (CDA)
    Home Affairs: J. G. Rietkerk (to 20-2-1986, VVD)
                        F. Korthals Altes (to 12-3-1986, VVD)
                        R. W. de Korte (to 14-7-1986, VVD)
    Social Affairs: J. de Koning (CDA)
    Social Work: L. C. Brinkman (CDA)

LUBBERS II
Duration: 14-7-1986 to 7-11-1989
Composition: 9 CDA, 5 VVD

Major ministers
    Prime Minister: R. F. M. Lubbers (CDA)
    Home Affairs: C. P. van Dijk (to 3-2-1987, CDA)
                        J. de Koning (to 6-5-1987, CDA)
                        C. P. van Dijk (to 7-11-1989, CDA)
    Social Affairs: J. de Koning (to 3-2-1987, CDA)
                        L. de Graaf (to 6-5-1987, CDA)
                        J. de Koning (to 7-11-1989, CDA)
    Social Work: L. C. Brinkman (CDA)

Appendix Four
Composition of Parliaments, 1946–1989

Party	1946	48	52	56	56	59	63	67	71	72	77	81	82	86
KVP	32	32	30	33	49	49	50	42	35	27				
ARP	13	13	12	10	15	14	13	15	13	14				
CHU	8	9	9	8	13	12	13	12	10	7				
CDA											49	48	45	54
SGP	2	2	2	2	3	3	3	3	3	3	3	3	3	3
PvdA	29	27	30	34	50	48	43	37	39	43	53	44	47	52
CPN	10	8	6	4	7	3	4	5	6	7	2	3	3	
PvdV/VVD	6	8	9	9	13	19	16	17	16	22	28	26	36	27
Other		1	2			2	8	19	28	27	15	26	16	14
Total seats	100	100	100	100	150	150	150	150	150	150	150	150	150	150

Source: H. Daalder and C. Schuyt, eds. 1990. *Compendium Voor Politiek en Samenleving in Nederland*, A0600:24–25. Alphen aan den Rijn: Samsom.

Bibliography

Adriaansens, H. P., and A. C. Zijderveld. 1981. *Vrijwillig Initiatief en de Verzorgingsstaat.* Deventer: Van Loghum Slaterus.

Akkermans, T., and P. W. Nobelen, eds. 1983. *Corporatisme en Verzorgingsstaat.* Leiden: Stenfert Kroese.

Albeda, W. 1982. "Christendemocratie en de ideologie van de verzorgingsstaat." *Beleid & Maatschappij* 1982 (2): 58–64.

Alber, Jens, Gösta Esping-Andersen, and Lee Rainwater. 1987. "Studying the Welfare State: Issues and Queries." In *Comparative Policy Research: Learning from Experience,* ed. Meinolf Dierkes, Hans N. Weiler, and Ariane Berthoin Antal. Aldershot, England: Gower.

Alford, John, and Robert Friedland. 1985. *Powers of Theory.* New York: Cambridge University Press.

Almond, Gabriel. 1988. "The Return to the State." *American Political Science Review* 82 (3): 853–74.

Amelink, H. 1950. *Onder Eigen Banier.* Utrecht: Christelijk Nationall Vakverbond.

Anderson, Charles. 1979. "The Place of Principles in Policy Analysis." *American Political Science Review* 73 (3): 711–23.

Ashford, Douglas. 1986. *The Emergence of the Welfare State.* Oxford: Basil Blackwell.

Badie, John, and Pierre Birnbaum. 1983. *Sociology of the State.* Chicago: University of Chicago Press.

Bakvis, Herman. 1981. *Catholic Power in the Netherlands.* Kingston, Ont.: McGill-Queen's University Press.

Bank, Jan. 1989. "De Loyaliteit van Marga Klompé." In *Herrineringen aan Marga Klompé,* ed. Michel van der Plas. Amsterdam: Arbor.

Bates, Robert H. 1988. "Contra Contractarianism: Some Reflections on the New Institutionalism." *Politics and Society* 16 (2–3): 387–401.

Bax, Mart. 1985. "Religious Infighting and the Formation of a Dominant Catholic Regime in Southern Dutch Society." *Social Compass* 32 (1): 57–72.

Becker, Uwe, and Kees van Kersbergen. 1986. "Der Christliche Wohlfahrtsstaat der Niederlande: Ein kritischer beitrag zur vergleichenden politikforschung." *Politische Vierteljahrschrift* 27 (1): 51–77.

Bibliography

Bendix, Reinhard. 1978. *Kings or Peoples: Power and the Mandate to Rule*. Berkeley & Los Angeles: University of California Press.

Bennett, Colin J. 1991. "Review Article: What Is Policy Convergence and What Causes It?" *British Journal of Political Science* 21: 215–33.

Berger, J. A. 1936. *Van Armenzorg tot Werklozenzorg*. Amsterdam: De Arbeiderspers.

Beus, J. W. de. 1983. "De Contractie van Sociale Zekerheid als Politiek Strijdpunt." *Beleid en Maatschappij* 1983 (1–2): 39–51.

———. 1984. "Oorsprong en Wederkeer van de Liberalen." In *De Interventiestaat*, ed. J. W. de Beus and J. A. van Doorn. Meppel: Boom.

Beus, J. W. de, and J. A. van Doorn, eds. 1984. *De Interventiestaat*. Meppel: Boom.

Bik, J. M. 1988. "Kabinetscrisis? Vergeet het maar." *NRC Handelsblad*, 26 March, 9.

Birch, Anthony H. 1984. "Overload, Ungovernability, and Delegitimation: The Theories and the British Case." *British Journal of Political Science* 14:135–60.

Birnbaum, Pierre. 1982. "The State versus Corporatism." *Politics and Society* 11 (4): 477–501.

———. 1988. *States and Collective Action: The European Experience*. Cambridge: Cambridge University Press.

Blanken, Maurice. 1976. *Force of Order and Methods: An American View into the Dutch Directed Society*. The Hague: Martinus Nijhoff.

Blanpain, Jan, with Luc Delesie and Herman Nys. 1978. *National Health Insurance and Health Resources*. Cambridge, Mass.: Harvard University Press.

Blom, R., and M. Blom-Jorna. 1978. "Welzijn Beleid: Op het kruispunt 4de & 5de macht." *Tijdschrift voor Agologie* 3:146–63.

Boorstin, Daniel. 1960. *America and the Image of Europe*. New York: Meridian Books.

Bosmans, J. 1990. *Staatkundige Vormgeving in Nederland: De Tijd na 1940*. Assem: Van Gorcum.

Bovend'Eert, P. P. 1988. *Regeerakkoorden en Regeringsprograms*. The Hague: SDU-Uitgeverij.

Bovens, M. A. 1985. "Sturing van Corporatieve Actoren." In *Het Schip van Staat: Beschouwingen over recht, staat en sturing*, ed. M. A. Bovens and W. J. Witteveen, 261–74. Zwolle: Tjeenk Willink.

Bowles, Samuel, and Herbert Gintis. 1987. *Democracy and Capitalism: Property, Community, and the Contradictions of Modern Social Thought*. New York: Basic Books.

Braakman, T., M. C. van Schendelen, and R. Ph. Schotten. 1984. *Sociale Zekerheid in Nederland*. Utrecht: Spectrum.

Bibliography

Breton, Maria. 1982. "Changing Relationships in Dutch Social Services." *Journal of Social Policy* 11 (1): 59–80.

Briggs, Asa. 1985. "The Welfare State in Historical Perspective." In *The Collected Essays of Asa Briggs*, vol. 2. Urbana: University of Illinois Press.

Broekman, H., H. Nijenhuis, and D. Schouwman. 1982. "Verzuiling, provinciale coordinatie en sociale planning: De positie en rol van de provinciale opbouworganen na de tweede wereldoorlog." *Tijdschrift voor Agologie* 3:156–84.

Cameron, David. 1978. "The Expansion of the Public Economy: A Comparative Analysis." *American Political Science Review* 72: 1243–61.

Castles, Francis G. 1986. "Social Expenditure and the Political Right: A Methodological Note." *European Journal of Political Research* 14:669–76.

Castles, Francis G., and R. D. McKinlay. 1979. "Public Welfare Provision, Scandinavia, and the Sheer Futility of the Sociological Approach to Politics." *British Journal of Political Science* 9 (2): 157–71.

Cawson, Alan. 1982. *Corporatism and Welfare: Social Policy and State Intervention in Britain.* London: Heinemann.

College van Advies der Anti-Revolutionaire Partij. 1963. *Het Ontwerp-Algemene Bijstandswet.* The Hague.

Collier, David, and Richard E. Messick. 1975. "Prerequisites versus Diffusion: Testing Alternative Explanations of Social Security Adoption." *American Political Science Review* 69:1299–1315.

Couwenberg, S. W. 1953. *Het Particuliere Stelsel: De Beharting van Publieke Belangen door Particuliere Lichamen.* Cuyk: Van Lindert.

———. 1972. "Op- en Neergang der Christen-democratie." *Politiek Perspectief* 1 (4): 3–23.

Cox, Robert H. 1992a. "After Corporatism: A Comparison of the Role of Medical Professionals and Social Workers in the Dutch Welfare State." *Comparative Political Studies* 24 (4): 532–52.

———. 1992b. "Can Welfare States Grow in Leaps and Bounds? Non-Incremental Policymaking in the Netherlands." *Governance* 5 (1): 68–87.

Craig, Peter, and M. L. Harrison. 1984. "Corporatism and Housing Policy: The Best Possible Political Shell." In *Corporatism in the Welfare State*, ed. M. L. Harrison. Aldershot, England: Gower.

Daalder, Hans. 1981. "Consociationalism, Center, and Periphery in the Netherlands." In *Mobilization, Center-Periphery Structures, and Nation-Building: A Volume in Commemoration of Stein Rokkan*, ed. Per Torsvik. Bergen: Universitetsforlaget.

———. 1985. "Sturing, het Primaat van de Politiek en de Bureaucratische Cultuur in Nederland." In *Het Schip van Staat: Beschouwingen*

Bibliography

over recht, staat en sturing, ed. M. A. Bovens and W. J. Witteveen, 197–207. Zwolle: Tjeenk Willink.

Dam, J. C. van. 1964. "Dienst der Overheid: De Sociale Arbeid der Gemeente." In *Maatschappelijk Werk: Krachten, Terreinen, Methoden. Deel I: Maatschappij en Maatschappelijk Werk*, ed. J. M. Broekman. Assen: Van Gorcum.

Dam, J. C. van, J. Loeff, P. J. Roscam-Abbing, and J. in 't Veld. 1949. *Taak en Onderlinge Verhouding van Kerk, Particulier Initiatief en Overheid ten Aanzien van de Maatschappelijk Zorg.* Publication no. 1. Nederlandse Vereniging voor Maatschappelijk Werk. Haarlem: Tjeenk Willink.

Daudt, H. 1982. "Political Parties and Government Coalitions in the Netherlands Since 1945." *Netherlands Journal of Sociology* 18: 1–23.

"Decentralisatie." 1963. *De Magistratuur* 29 (3): 24–25.

Dejong, Gerben. 1984. *Independent Living and Disability Policy in the Netherlands: Three Models of Residential Care and Independent Living.* New York: World Rehabilitation Fund, International Exchange of Experts and Information in Rehabilitation.

Dercksen, Willem, Pim Fortuyn, and Teun Jaspers. 1982. *Vijfendertig Jaar SER-adviezen: Deel I – 1950–1964.* Deventer: Kluwer.

Diamant, Alfred. 1981. "Bureaucracy and Public Policy in Neocorporatist Settings: Some European Lessons." *Comparative Politics* 14 (1): 101–24.

Doorn, J. A. van. 1964. "Professionalisering in het Maatschappelijk Werk." In *Maatschappelijk Werk: Krachten, Terreinen, Methoden. Deel I: Maatschappij en Maatschappelijk Werk*, ed. J. M. Broekman. Assen: Van Gorcum.

———. 1978. "Welfare State and Welfare Society: The Dutch Experience." *Netherlands Journal of Sociology* 14:1–18.

———. 1984. "De Onvermijdelijke Presentie van de Confessionelen." In *Interventiestaat*, ed. J. W. de Beus and J. A. van Doorn. Meppel: Boom.

Dyson, Kenneth F. 1980. *The State Tradition in Western Europe.* Oxford: Martin Robertson.

Eijk, N. W. van. 1957. *Onze Algemene Ouderdomsverzekering.* IJmuiden: Vermande Zonen.

Elias, Norbert. 1969. *Über den Prozess der Zivilisation: Soziogenetische und Psychogenetische Untersuchungen, Zweiter Band.* Bern: Francke Verlag.

Esping-Andersen, Gösta, and Walter Korpi. 1984. "Social Policy as Class Politics in Post-War Capitalism: Scandinavia, Austria, and Germany." In *Order and Conflict in Contemporary Capitalism*, ed. John H. Goldthorpe. Oxford: Clarendon Press.

Esveld, N. E. van. 1956. *De Uitdaging van het Sociale Vraagstuk: Het*

Bibliography

Antwoord Ener Verantwoordelijke Samenleving. Assen: Van Gorcum.

Etzioni-Halevy, Eva. 1983. *Bureaucracy and Democracy: A Political Dilemma.* London: Routledge & Kegan Paul.

Fernhout, Roel. 1980. "Incorporatie van Belangengroeperingen in de Sociale en Economische Wetgeving." In *Corporatisme in Nederland: Belangengroepen en Democratie,* ed. H. J. Verhallen, R. Fernhout, and P. E. Visser. Alphen aan den Rijn: Samsom.

Ferrera, Maurizio. 1990. "Reforming the Reform: The Italian *Servizio Sanitario Nazionale* in the 1980s." Paper presented at the Seventh International Conference of Europeanists, Washington, D.C., 23–25 March.

Flora, Peter. 1986. "Introduction." *Growth to Limits: The Western European Welfare States since World War II. Vol. 2, Germany, United Kingdom, Ireland, Italy.* Edited by Peter Flora. Berlin: Walter de Gruyter.

Flora, Peter, and Jens Alber. 1981. "Modernization, Democratization, and the Development of Welfare States in Western Europe." In *The Development of Welfare States in Europe and America,* ed. Peter Flora and Arnold Heidenheimer, 37–80. New Brunswick, N.J.: Transaction Books.

Fortanier, G. F., and J. J. Veraart. 1975. *Arbeidsrecht.* The Hague: VUGA.

Furniss, Norman, and Timothy Tilton. 1977. *The Case for the Welfare State.* Bloomington: Indiana University Press.

Gerschenkron, Alexander. 1962. "Reflections on the Concept of 'Prerequisites' of Modern Industrialization." In *Economic Backwardness in Historical Perspective: A Book of Essays.* Cambridge, Mass.: Harvard University Press.

Gladdish, Ken. 1990. "Parliamentary Activism and Legitimacy in the Netherlands." *West European Politics* 13 (3): 103–19.

Gleick, James. 1987. *Chaos: Making a New Science.* New York: Penguin Books.

Goldthorpe, John. 1984. "The End of Convergence: Corporatist and Dualist Tendencies in Modern Western Societies." In *Order and Conflict in Contemporary Capitalism,* ed. John Goldthorpe, 315–43. Oxford: Clarendon Press.

Gosker, R. 1970. "Voorgeschiedenis van de Sociale Verzekering." In *De Groei van de Sociale Verzekering in Nederland,* R. Gosker, ed. Amsterdam: Vereniging van Raden van Arbeid.

Goudsblom, Johan. 1967. *Dutch Society.* New York: Random House.

Grimmer, Klaus. 1978. "Die Funktion der Staatsidee und die Bedingungen ihrer Wirklichkeit." *Archiv für Rechts- und Socialphilosophie* 64 (1): 63–79.

Guasco, R. A. de, R. H. van der Meer, J. A. Huij, and D. Baars. 1979.

Bibliography

Het Sociaal Verzekeringsrecht in Nederland. Alphen aan den Rijn: Samson.

Harrison, M. L., ed. 1984. *Corporatism in the Welfare State.* Aldershot, England: Gower.

Haveman, Robert H., Victor Halberstadt, and Richard V. Burkhauser. 1984. *Public Policy Toward Disabled Workers: Cross-National Analyses of Economic Impacts.* Ithaca: Cornell University Press.

Heclo, Hugh. 1974. *Modern Social Politics in Britain and Sweden.* New Haven, Conn.: Yale University Press.

Heidenheimer, A. 1983. "Secularization Patterns and the Westward Spread of the Welfare State, 1883-1983: Two Dialogues about How and Why Britain, the Netherlands, and the United States Have Differed." *Comparative Social Research* 6:3-38.

————. 1989. "Professional Knowledge and State Policy in Comparative Historical Perspective: Law and Medicine in Britain, Germany, and the United States." *International Social Science Journal* 122 (November): 529-53.

Heuvel, Hans van den, and Jacques van Maarseveen. 1986. "Van Armenzorg naar Verzorgingsstaat." *Intermediar* 22 (49): 47-51.

Hirschman, Albert. 1970. *Exit, Voice and Loyalty: Responses to Decline in Firms, Organizations, and States.* Cambridge, Mass.: Harvard University Press.

Hoogland, E. B. Baron Wittert van. 1940. *De Parlamentaire Geschiedenis der Social Verzekering, 1890-1940,* Deel II. Haarlem: Tjeenk Willink.

Hoogstraten, J. M. van. 1924. "Vrijwillige Ouderdomsverzekering: Van sociaal belang tot staatsbedrijf." *De Werkgever* 1924 (December): 1-20.

Huysman, A. D. 1986. "Partij van de Vrijheid Gaf het Liberalisme een Sociaal Gezicht: Vrijheid, Verantwoordelijkheid, Sociale Gerechtigheid Vormen nog Steeds de Pijlers." *NRC Handelsblad,* 11 October, 8.

Idenburg, Ph. A. 1977. "Vragen en Kanttekeningn bij een Voortgaande Discussie." In *Overheid en Partikulier Initiatief.* The Hague: Nationale Raad voor Maatschappelijk Welzijn.

Institutie voor Toegepaste Sociologie. 1979. *Decentralisatie en de Verhouding Overheid Particulier Initiatief.* Nijmegen.

Janssen, Gerald, and Theo Berben. 1982. *De Vakbeweging en de Sociale Zekerheid in Nederland na 1945.* Nijmegen: Doctoraal Scriptie.

Joekes, A. M., and A. A. van Rhijn. 1952. *Nota Inzake de Toekomstige Ouderdomsvoorziening.* The Hague: Staatsdrukkerij.

Jong, Jan de, and Bert Pijnenburg. 1986. "The Dutch Christian Democratic Party and Coalitional Behaviour in the Netherlands: A Pivotal Party in the Face of Depillarisation." In *Coalitional*

Bibliography

Behaviour in Theory and Practice: An Inductive Model for Western Europe, ed. Geoffrey Pridham, 145–70. Cambridge: Cambridge University Press.

Jonge, J. A. de. 1971. "Industrial Growth in the Netherlands, 1850–1914." *Acta Historiae Neerlandica* 5:159–212.

Katzenstein, Peter J. 1985. *Small States in World Markets: Industrial Policy in Europe.* Ithaca, N.Y.: Cornell University Press.

Keizer, Madelon de. 1979. *De Gijzelaars van Sint Michielsgestel: Een Elite-beraad in Oorlogstijd.* Alphen aan den Rijn: Sijthoff.

Keman, J. E., and J. J. Woldendorp. 1985. "Neo-Korporatisme en de Loonpolitiek in Nederland, 1965–1981." In *Het Neo-Korporatisme als Nieuwe Politieke Strategie: Krisisbeheersing met en (door) Overleg,* ed. Hans Keman, Jaap Woldendorp, and Dietmar Braun, 139–62. Amsterdam: Kaal Boek.

Kesselman, Mark. 1982. "Socialism without the Workers: The Case of France." *Kapitalistate* 10 (1982): 397–438.

Kieve, R. A. 1981. "Pillars of Sand: A Marxist Critique of Consociational Democracy in the Netherlands." *Comparative Politics* 14 (2): 313–37.

Kleine Gids voor de Nederlandse Sociale Zekerheid. 1986. Amsterdam: Vereniging van Raden van Arbeid.

Klompé, M. A. 1984. "Kerk en Politiek." *Christen-Democratische Verkenningen* 4 (7–8): 365–67.

Komdeur, B. 1986. "De ARP en de Opbouw van de Welvaartsstaat, 1945–1958: Ontwikkeling in het Antirevolutionaire Denken Over de Rol van de Overheid in het Sociaal-Economisch Leven." Doktoraalscriptie Contemporaine Geschiedenis. Utrecht: Rijksuniversiteit Utrecht.

Kooten, Gerrit van. 1988. *Stakingen en Stakers: Een Theoretische en Empirische Verkenning van Fluctuaties in Stakingsactiviteit in Nederland van 1951 to en met 1981.* Delft: Eburon.

Korpi, Walter. 1980. *The Working Class and Welfare Capitalism.* London: Routledge & Kegan Paul.

Korpi, Walter, and Michael Shalev. 1980. "Strikes, Power, and Politics in the Western Nations, 1900–1976." *Political Power and Social Theory* 1:301–34.

Kramer, Ralph. 1981. *Voluntary Agencies in the Welfare State.* Berkeley and Los Angeles: University of California Press.

Kranenburg, Mark. 1986. "Bezuiniging Via de Spreekkamer." *NRC Handelsblad,* 25 January, p. 7.

Krasner, Stephen, D. 1984. "Approaches to the State: Alternative Conceptions and Historical Dynamics." *Comparative Politics* 16 (January): 223–46.

———. 1988. "Sovereignty: An Institutionalist Perspective." *Comparative Political Studies* 21 (1): 66–94.

Bibliography

Kreisi, Hanspeter. 1988. "Local Mobilization for the People's Petition of the Dutch Peace Movement." In *From Structure to Action: Comparing Social Movement Research across Cultures*, ed. Bert Klandermans, Hanspeter Kreisi, and Sidney Tarrow. Greenwich, Conn.: JAI Press.

Kroniek van Nederland. 1987. "Noodwet Regelt Staatspensionen." Amsterdam: Elsevier.

Kruijt, J. P. 1957. "Sociologische Beschouwingen over Zuilen en Verzuiling." *Socialisme en Democratie* 12 (1): 11–29.

Kuhn, Thomas S. 1970. *The Structure of Scientific Revolutions.* 2d ed. Chicago: University of Chicago Press.

Lehmbruch, Gerhard. 1979. "Consociational Democracy, Class Conflict, and the New Corporatism." In *Trends toward Corporatist Intermediation*, ed. P. C. Schmitter and G. Lehmbruch. Beverly Hills, Calif.: Sage.

Lehning, Percy B. 1984. "Socialisten Tussen Plan en Macht." In *De Interventiestaat*, ed. J. W. de Beus and J. A. van Doorn. Meppel: Boom.

Leibfried, Stephan. 1978. "Public Assistance in the United States and the Federal Republic of Germany." *Comparative Politics* 10 (October): 59–75.

Lewis, Paul Martin. 1981. "Family, Economy, and Polity: A Case Study of Japan's Public Pension Policy." Ph.D. Dissertation. Berkeley, University of California, Berkeley.

Lier, Theo van. 1981. "Op Weg naar de Verzorgingsstaat (1950–1960)." In *Van Brede Visie tot Smalle Marge: Acht Prominente Socialisten Over de SDAP en de PvdA*, ed. Jan Bank and Stef Temming. Alphen aan den Rijn: Sijthoff.

Lijphart, Arend. 1975. *The Politics of Accommodation: Pluralism and Democracy in the Netherlands.* 2d ed. Berkeley and Los Angeles: University of California Press.

———. 1984. "Time Politics of Accommodation: Reflections — Fifteen Years Later." *Acta Politica* 19 (1): 9–18.

———. 1985. "Non-Majoritarian Democracy: A Comparison of Federal and Consociational Theories." *Publius* 15 (2): 3–16.

Lindblom, Charles. 1959. "The Science of Muddling Through." *Public Administration Review* 19:79–88.

———. 1982. "The Market as Prison." *Journal of Politics* 44:324–36.

Linder, J. J. 1975. "De Vijfde Macht in Welzijnsland." *Jeugd en Samenleving* 5:833–43.

Lipschits, I. 1969. *Links en Rechts in de Politiek.* Meppel: Boom.

Lorwin, Val. 1974. "Segmented Pluralism: Ideological Cleavages and Political Cohesion in the Smaller European Democracies." In *Consociational Democracy: Political Accommodation in Segmented Societies*, ed. Kenneth McRae. Toronto: McClelland & Stewart.

Bibliography

Lowi, Theodore. 1972. "Four Systems of Policy, Politics, and Choice." *Public Administration Review* 32:298–310.

Luebbert, Gregory. 1991. *Liberalism, Fascism, or Social Democracy: Social Classes and the Political Origins of Regimes in Interwar Europe.* New York: Oxford University Press.

Lukes, Stephen J. 1974. *Power: A Radical View.* London: Macmillan Press.

Lutz, J. L. 1989. "Emulation and Policy Adoptions in the Canadian Provinces." *Canadian Journal of Political Science* 22:147–54.

Mannoury, J. 1967. *Hoofdtrekken van de Sociale Verzekering.* Alphen aan den Rijn: Samsom.

——. 1972. "Enkele Legislatieve Aspecten van het Groot-amendement-Kuyper op de Ongevallenwet 1901." In *Sociale Politiek Opnieuw Bedacht,* ed. P. A. Steenkamp and G. M. Veldkamp. Deventer: Kluwer.

Martin, Ross M. 1983. "Pluralism and the New Corporatism." *Political Studies* 31:86–102.

Miedema, S. 1957. "De Kosten van de Verzuiling." *Socialisme en Democratie* 12 (1): 46–59.

Mierlo, Hans van. 1986. "Depillarization and the Decline of Consociationalism in the Netherlands." *West European Politics* 9 (1): 97–119.

Ministerie van Welzijn, Volksgezondheid en Cultuur. 1990. *Werken aan Zorgvernieuwing.* Rijswijk: Ministerie WVC.

Montesquieu, Baron de. 1949. *The Spirit of the Laws,* translated by Thomas Nugent. New York: Hafner Press.

——. 1973. *The Persian Letters,* translated by C. J. Betts. Harmondsworth, Middlesex: Penguin Books.

Moore, Barrington, Jr. 1977. *Injustice: The Social Bases of Obedience and Revolt.* White Plains, N.Y.: M. E. Sharpe.

Moseley, Hugh. 1983. "Social Security in the United States and the Federal Republic of Germany." *Policy Studies Journal* 11:493–503.

Moulijn, C. D. 1948. "Rooms-Katholieke Cultuurpenetratie." *Wending* 2:717–28.

MvT-AOW. 1955. "Memorie van Toelichting, Algemene Ouderdomsverzekering." *Bijlagen van de Handelingen van de Tweede Kamer.* Zitting 1954–55. 4009, no. 3.

MvT-Noodwet. 1946. "Memorie van Toelichting, Noodregeling Ouderdomsvoorziening." *Bijlagen van de Handelingen van de Tweede Kamer.* Zitting 1946–47. 362, no. 3.

MvT-Verhaalsrecht. 1960. "Memorie van Toelichting, Beperking van het Verhaalsrecht, Bedoeld in Hoofdstuk V der Armenwet." *Bijlagen van de Handelingen van de Tweede Kamer.* Zitting 1959–60. 5864, no. 3.

Nijenhuis, H. 1978. "De Verhouding Overheid-particulier Initiaitef op

Bibliography

het Terrein van Armenzorg en Maatschappelijk Werk: Een Historische Schets." *Tijdschrift voor Agologie* 1978 (3): 131–45.

Nijenhuis, H., and D. Schouwman. 1980. "Nederlands Volksherstel en Zijn Invloed op het Opbouwwerk in Nederland." *Tijdschrift voor Agologie* 1980 (3–4): 139–63.

Nordlinger, Eric. 1981. *On the Autonomy of the Democratic State.* Cambridge, Mass.: Harvard University Press.

NRC Handelsblad. 1986. "Tweede Kamer Tegen Gelijke Hehandeling Bejaarden AOW." 1986 (30 January): 3.

———. 1986. "Veel Kritiek op Plannen Tegen Fraude." 1986 (31 January): 3.

———. 1988. "Spanning stijgt tussen CDA en kabinet over bezuinigingsplannen." 1988 (25 March): 1, 3.

Offe, Claus. 1981. "The Attribution of Public Status to Interest Groups: Observations on the West German Case." In *Organizing Interests in Western Europe,* ed. Susan Berger. Cambridge: Cambridge University Press.

———. 1984. *Contradictions of the Welfare State.* Edited by John Keane, Cambridge, Mass.: MIT Press.

Olson, Mancur. 1965. *The Logic of Collective Action: Public Goods and the Theory of Groups.* Cambridge, Mass.: Harvard University Press.

———. 1982. *The Rise and Decline of Nations: Economic Growth, Stagflation, and Social Rigidities.* New Haven, Conn.: Yale University Press.

Orloff, Ann, and Theda Skocpol. 1984. "Why Not Equal Protection? Explaining the Politics of Public Social Welfare in Britain and the United States, 1880–1920s." *American Sociological Review* 49 (6): 726–50.

Oud, P. J. 1990. *Staatskundige Vormgeving in Nederland: 1840–1940.* Assen: Van Gorcum.

Oude Engberink, G. 1984. *Minima Zonder Marge.* Rotterdam: Gemeentelijke Sociale Dienst.

Panitch, Leo. 1980. "Recent Theorizations of Corporatism: Reflections on a Growth Industry." *Comparative Political Studies* 19 (1): 61–90.

Peper, Abraham. 1972. *Vorming van Welzijnsbeleid: Evolutie en evaluatie van het opbouwwerk.* Meppel: Boom.

———. 1978. "Beheersproblemen in de Welzijnsector." In *De Stagnerende Verzorgingstaat,* ed. J. A. van Doorn and C. J. Schuyt. Meppel: Boom.

Rapport — Inzake de Herziening van de Sociale Verzekering. 1948. Uitgebracht door een commissie, bestande uit vertegenwoordigers van de Minister van Sociale Zaken en van de Stichting van den Arbeid. The Hague: Staatsdrukkerij.

Bibliography

Rein, Martin. 1983. "Value-Critical Policy Analysis." In *Ethics, the Social Sciences, and Policy Analysis*, ed. D. Callahan and B. Jennings. New York: Plenum Press.

Rengelink, A. W. 1969. "Geschiedenis van de Invaliditeits-, Ouderdoms- en Overlijdensverzekering." In *De Groei van de Sociale Verzekering in Nederland*. Amsterdam: Raden van Arbeid.

Ridder, G. A. de. 1954. "Sociale Rechtvaardigheid." *Vrijheid en Democratie* 1954 (20 March): 1.

Rieken, J. G. 1985. *Bestuur en Organisatie in Sociale Zekerheid en Arbeidsvoorziening*. Deventer: Kluwer.

Ringnalda, G. 1965. "Formatuer en Informateur." *Acta Politica* 1 (1): 77–112.

Roebroek, Joop, and Göran Therborn. Forthcoming. "The Netherlands." In *Growth To Limits: The Western European Welfare States since World War II*, vol. 4 ed. Peter Flora. Berlin: De Gruyter.

Romme, C. P. 1950. *Staatspensionnering Ouderdomsverzekering*. Publication of Algemene R. K. Ambtenarenvereninging.

Rose, Richard. 1991. "What Is Lesson-Drawing?" *Journal of Public Policy* 11:3–30.

Rossem, G. van. 1962. "Arbeidsongeschiktheidsverzekering en Zelfstandigen." *Gids voor Personeelsbelied, Arbeidsvraag stelling, Sociale Verzekering*. 1962 (7): 156–59.

Rothstein, Bo. 1990. "Marxism, Institutional Analysis, and Working Class Power: The Swedish Case." *Politics and Society* 18 (3): 317–46.

Rozehnal, Alois. 1972. *Unfulfilled Promises: Social Insurance in Czechoslovakia*. Rome: Accademia Cristiana Cecoslovacca.

Ruppert, M. 1965. *De Welvaartstaat: Een inleidende beschouwing*. Kampen: J. H. Kok.

Sartori, Giovanni. 1966. "European Political Parties: The Case of Polarized Pluralism." In *Political Parties and Political Development*, ed. Joseph LaPalombara and Myron Weiner. Princeton, N.J.: Princeton University Press.

—————. 1970. "Concept Misformation in Comparative Politics." *American Political Science Review* 54:1033–53.

Scharpf, Fritz W. 1991. *Crisis and Choice in European Social Democracy*, translated by Ruth Crowley and Fred Thompson. Ithaca, N.Y.: Cornell University Press.

Schattschneider, E. E. 1960. *The Semi-Sovereign People*. Hinsdale, Ill.: Dryden.

Schendelen, M. C. van. 1983. "Crisis of the Dutch Welfare State." *Contemporary Crises*. 7:209–30.

Scheyde, E. H. 1967. "De Organisatie van de G. M. D. en de Samenwerking met de Behandelende Artsen." *Medische Contact* 4 (5): 93–99.

Schmitter, P. 1979. "Still the Century of Corporatism?" In *Trends toward*

Bibliography

Corporatist Intermediation, ed. P. Schmitter and G. Lehmbruch. Beverly Hills, Calif.: Sage.

Scholten, G. H. 1968. *De Sociaal-Economische Raad en de Ministeriële Verantwoordelijkheid.* Meppel: J. A. Boom & Zoon.

Scholten, Ilja. 1980. "Does Consociationalism Exist? A Critique of the Dutch Experience." In *Electoral Participation: A Comparative Analysis*, ed. Richard Rose. London: Sage.

————. 1987. "Corporatism and the Neo-Liberal Backlash in the Netherlands: Integrated Labour Relations, Public Policy Making, and Administration." In *Political Stability and Neo-Corporatism in Europe: Societal Cleavages and Corporatist Integration*, ed. Ilja Scholten. London: Sage.

Schoonenberg, J. 1930. *Particulier Initiatief in de Arbeidersverzekering: Ontwikkeling van de Positie der Bijzondere Uitvoeringsorganen in de Wetgeving.* Amsterdam: H. J. Paris.

Schuyt, K., and R. van de Veen, eds. 1986. *De Verdeelde Samenleving: Een Inleiding in de Ontwikkeling van de Nederlandse Verzorgingsstaat.* Leiden: Stenfert Kroese.

SER-Advies. 1954. *Advies Inzake de Wettelijke Ouderdomsvoorziening.* The Hague: Sociaal-Economische Raad.

————. 1965. *Advies Inzake Arbeidsongeschikthiedsverzekering voor Andere dan Loontrekkenden.* The Hague: Sociaal-Economische Raad.

SER-Bulletin. 1990. "Sociale Partners Stellen Zich Corporatistisch Op." 1990 (June): 5–6.

Sewell, William H., Jr. 1985. "Ideologies and Social Revolutions: Reflections on the French Case." *Journal of Modern History* 57 (1): 57–85.

Skocpol, Theda. 1980. "Political Responses to Capitalist Crisis." *Politics and Society* 10 (2): 155–201.

————. 1985. "Bringing the State Back In: Strategies of Analysis in Current Research." In *Bringing the State Back In*, ed. Peter Evans and Theda Skocpol, 3–44. Cambridge: Cambridge University Press.

Smith, M. L. 1988. "Ideas for a New Regime in the Netherlands after the Defeat of 1940." In *Modern Dutch Studies*, ed. Michael Wintle. London: Athlone Press.

Social-Economic Council. 1984. *Advies Hoofdlijnen Gewizigd Stelsel van Sociale Zekerheid bij Werkloosheid en Arbeidsongeschiktheid.* The Hague.

Sociale Zekereheid. 1945. Rapport van de Commissie, ingesteld bij Beschikking van den Minister van Sociale Zaken van 26 Maart 1943, met de opdracht algemeene richtlijnen vast te stellen voor de toekomstige ontwikkeling der sociale verzekering in Nederland. 3 vols. The Hague: Algemene Landsdrukkerij.

Staatsblad. Handelingen van de Tweede Kamer. Various years.

Bibliography

Staatscommissie Vervanging Armenwet. 1954. *Eindrapport*. The Hague: Staatsdrukkerij.

Stephens, John. 1979. *The Transition from Capitalism to Socialism*. London: Macmillan Press.

Stuurman, Siep. 1983. *Verzuiling, Kapitalisme en Patriarchaat: Aspecten van de ontwikkeling van de moderne staat in Nederland*. Nijmegen: Socialistiese Uitgeverij.

Swaan, Abram de. 1988. *In Care of the State: Health Care, Education, and Welfare in Europe and the U.S.A. in the Modern Era*. New York: Oxford University Press.

Tempel, J. van den. 1946. *Nederland in London: Ervaringen en Beschouwingen*. Haarlem: Tjeenk Willink.

Tex, Ursula den, and Elma Verhey. 1987. "Het Einde van de WAO: Verslag Vanuit het Uitkeringskantoor te Dordrecht." *Vrij Nederland* 1987 (14 November supplement).

Therborn, Göran. 1989. "Pillarization and Popular Movements: Two Variants of Welfare State Capitalism: The Netherlands and Sweden." In *The Comparative History of Public Policy*, ed. Francis Castles. New York: Oxford University Press.

Toirkens, José. 1988. *Schijn en Werkelijkheid van het Bezuinigingsbeleid 1975–1986*. Deventer: Kluwer.

Vaandrager, A. B. 1968. *Overheid en Sociale Zekerheid voor Boeren en Tuinders: Verkenningen rondom de integratie van de zelfstandige agrarische beroepsbevolking in het kader van het sociale zekerheidsbeleid in Nederland*. Deventer: Kluwer.

Valentin, Finn. 1978. "Corporatism and the Danish Welfare State." *Acta Sociologica* 1978 (supplement): 73–95.

Valk, Loes van der. 1986. *Van Pauperzorg tot Bestaanzekerheid: Een Onderzoek Naar de Ontwikkeling van de Armenzorg in Nederland Tegen de Achtergrond van de Overgang naar de Algemene Bijstandswet, 1912–1965*. Delft: Eburon.

Veld, R. J. in 't. 1989. *De Verguisde Staat*. The Hague: VUGA.

Veldkamp, G. M. 1949. *Individualistische Karaktertrekken in de Nederlandse Sociale Arbeidsverzekering: Een Critisch Onderzoek naar de Grondslagen der Sociale Arbeidsverzekering*. Alphen aan den Rijn: Samsom.

———. 1980. *Inleiding tot de Sociale Zekerheid: En de toepassing ervan in Nederland en Belgie, Deel II*. Deventer: Kluwer.

Verkade, Willem. 1965. *Democratic Parties in the Low Countries and Germany: Origins and Historical Developments*. Leiden: Universitaire Pers.

Vijf en Zestig Jaren Sociale Verzekering in Nederland 1901–1966. 1966. The Hague: Ministerie van Sociale Zaken.

Visser, J. C. 1970. "Geschiedenis van Ongevallenwet en Ziektewet (3)." *Het Ziekenfonds* 44 (1): 63–69.

Bibliography

Vliet, Ineke van. 1986. "Sociale Zekerheid in de Klem." In *De Verdeelde Samenleving: Een Inleiding in the Ontwikkeling van de Nederlandse Verzorgingsstaat*, ed. Kees Schuyt and Romke van der Veen, 97–123. Leiden: Stenfert Kroese.

Vries, J. de. 1985. *De Algemene Bijstandswet*. Alphen aan den Rijn: Samsom.

Vries, W. de. 1970. *De Invloed van Werkgevers en Werknemers op de Totstandkoming van de Eerste Sociale Verzekeringswet in Nederland (de Ongevallenwet 1901)*. Deventer: Kluwer.

Waals, D. van der. 1975. *Balans van een Halve Eeuw Sociale Ontwikkeling*. Deventer: Kluwer.

Walker, Jack L. 1969. "The Diffusion of Innovation among the American States." *American Political Science Review* 63 (3): 880–99.

Wassenberg, Arthur. 1982. "Neo-Corporatism and the Quest for Control: The Cuckoo Game." In *Patterns of Corporatist Policy-Making*, ed. G. Lehmbruch and P. Schmitter. London: Sage.

Weber, Max. 1958. "Politics as a Vocation." In *From Max Weber: Essays in Sociology*, ed. H. H. Gerth and C. Wright Mills. New York: Galaxy Books.

Weir, Margaret, and Theda Skocpol. 1983. "State Structures and Social Keynesianism: Responses to the Great Depression in Sweden, Britain, and the United States." *International Journal of Comparative Sociology* 24 (1–2): 4–29.

Wetenschappelijk Raad voor het Regeringsbeleid. 1985. *Waarborgen voor Zekerheid: Een Nieuw Stelsel van Sociale Zekerheid in Hoofdlijnen*. The Hague: Staatsuitgeverij.

Wilensky, Harold L. 1975. *The Welfare State and Equality: Structural and Ideological Roots of Public Expenditure*. Berkeley and Los Angeles: University of California Press.

———. 1981. "Leftism, Catholicism, and Democratic Corporatism: The Role of Political Parties in Recent Welfare State Development." In *The Development of Welfare States in Europe and America*, ed. P. Flora and A. Heidenheimer. New Brunswick, N.J.: Transaction Books.

Windmuller, J. P. 1969. *Labor Relations in the Netherlands*. Ithaca, N.Y.: Cornell University Press.

Winter, Reiner de. 1972. "Naar een Volksverzekering Inzake Arbeidsongeschiktheid." *Ars Aequi* 21 (9): 448–50.

Wissen, G. J. van. 1982. *De Christen-democratische Visie op de Rol van de Staat in het Sociaal-economisch Leven*. Amsterdam: Rodopi.

Wolfe, Alan. 1977. *The Limits of Legitimacy: Political Contradictions of Contemporary Capitalism*. New York: Free Press.

Wolinetz, Stephen B. 1983. "Neo-Corporatism and Industrial Policy in the Netherlands." Paper presented at the annual meeting of

Bibliography

the Canadian Political Science Association, Vancouver, B.C., 6–8 June.
————. 1989. "Socio-Economic Bargaining in the Netherlands: Redefining the Post-War Policy Coalition." *West European Politics* 12 (1): 79–98.
————. 1990. "The Dutch Election of 1989: Return to the Centre-Left." *West European Politics* 13 (2): 280–85.
Wolman, Harold. 1992. "Understanding Cross National Policy Transfers: The Case of Britain and the U.S." *Governance* 5 (1): 27–45.
Zahn, Ernest. 1989. *Regenten, Rebellen en Reformatoren: Een Visie op Nederland en de Nederlanders.* Amsterdam: Contact.
Zweeden, A. F. van. 1983. "Van Nachterwakersstaat naar Verzorgingsmaatschappij." In *Onzekere Zekerheid: Het sociale zekerheidsstelsel in stroomversnelling,* ed. F. G. van den Heuvel. The Hague: VUGA.

BIBLIOGRAPHIC NOTE ON ARCHIVAL SOURCES

Much of the information concerning opinions of private agencies, discussions among ministerial personnel, and meetings between ministerial staff and private agencies was found in Dutch governmental archives. All files pertaining to the Public Retirement Pensions Act and the Public Disability Act are housed in the Historical Archive of the Ministry of Social Affairs and Employment. These files are arranged chronologically, which makes quick perusal difficult. The files for the Public Assistance Act were arranged topically at the Archive of the Ministry of Public Health, Housing, and Hygiene. However, at the time I conducted the research, all files pertaining to the Public Assistance Act were in the process of being transfered to the Royal Library in the Hague.

I consulted the following archival files:

Public Retirement Pensions Act
Totstandkoming Noodwet Ouderdomsvoorziening. 4 parts.
Totstandkoming van de Algemene Ouderdomswet. 10 parts.

Public Disability Act
Totstandkoming van de Algemene Arbeidsongeschiktheidswet. 15 parts.

Public Assistance Act
Staatscommissie Vervanging Armenwet. "Benoeming en ontslag der leden (1947–1952)."
Commissie onderzoek financiële gevolgen van de nieuwe Armenwet. (1954/1955).
Financiële Bijstand. "(Uitvoering) Armenwet en (totstandkoming van) Bijstandswet, etc. (1955–1965)."

Bibliography

Ontwerp Algemene Bijstandswet. "Werkstukken inzake de conferenties in Gerner en Duinoord ter vaststelling van het definitief ontwerp (1961/2)."

Voorontwerp Algemene Bijstandswet. "Adviezen Ontvangen van Provinciale Opbouworganen, Instellingen van het Maatschappelijk Werk, diverse andere Instellingen, Overzicht en Commentaren (1961–62)."

Nationale Raad voor Maatschappelijk Werk. "Subsidierings adviescommissie, correspondentie en begaderstukken (1962/1963)."

Algemene Bijstandswet. "Administratieve Regelen Bijstand (1964/1968)."

Voorontwerp Algemene Bijstandswet. "Correspondentie met ambtgenoten en staatssecretarissen (1961/62)."

Voorontwerp Algemene Bijstandswet. "O.A. adviezen ontvangen van Sociale Raden, Provinciale Besturen (1961/62)."

Voorontwerp Algemene Bijstandswet. "C. A. Aanbieding aan H. M. de Koningin en toezending om advies aan Raad van State (1962/63)."

Ontwerp-Algemene Bijstandswet. "Tweede Behandeling in de Ministerraad (Mei-Juni 1962)."

Reacties op het Totstandkomen van de Algemene Bijstandswet. (1962/1966).

Ontwerp-Algemene Bijstandswet. Adviezen en Commentaren op voorontwerp, afkomstig van Overheidsinstanties en particuliere instellingen.

Index

Administrative reorganization, 180
Alber, Jens, 10, 20
Anti-Revolutionary Party, 126–27, 158
Association of Subsidized and Premium Funded Enterprises, 74
Austria, 62
Autonomy: of private and religious charities, 84; of the state, 18, 22, 29, 56

Beel, L. J., 105, 110–12, 129
Belgium, 96
Bendix, Reinhard, 34, 216
Beveridge Model, 100, 203, 204
Beveridge Report: 97, 101, 128; impact in Netherlands, 215; universalization, 24
Beveridge, William, 33
Bipartism, 70
Bismarck, Otto Von, 22, 30, 33, 59, 84–85, 91, 97
Bismarck system, 203
Boorstin, Daniel, 33
Bourgeois Rebellion (1848), 62
Budget deficit, 175
Business Councils (*Bedrijfsraden*), 93–94

Calvinism, 64
Cameron, David, 10, 12
Catholicism: political doctrine, 60–65; social question, 47; SER Report, 126
Catholic Labor Movement, 103
Catholic Party: 29, 61, 93, 103, 105, 106, 129; coalition, 14–15; tensions with Labor Party, 136; Social Insurance Initiatives, 144–50; resistance to welfare reforms, 111–12; radicalization of, 136; corporatism

in Austria, Belgium, 47; conception of solidarity, 167; change in position on social welfare, 135–41; principle of solidarity, 122
Central Administrative Office (Gemeenschappelijk Administratie Kantoor), 78
Centralization, 18–19
Change, 43
Chaos theory, 38
Charities: professionalization of, 74, 138–39; state supervision, 113; subsidization, 113, 115
Church, 40
Christian Democratic Appeal (CDA), 61
Christian Historical Union (CHU), 61
Christian tradition, 63
Civil servants: 54, 57; and drafting of Public Disability Act, 159–60
Coalitions, 61
Codetermination (*medezeggenschap*), 88
Collective action: 37, 41; religious organizations, 39, 218; consequences of, 40
Collier, David, 32
Compromise of 1917, 66
Confessional parties, 175
Confessional politics: and Dutch corporatism, 208; and expansion of welfare state, 219
Confessional Unions, 85
Conservatism, 62
Consociational politics, 49, 60, 221
Constitutional Monarchy (1848), 61
Control, 42
Convergence: policy borrowing, 8, 26; social security-redistribution, 30; of welfare states, 5, 6, 21, 30, 32, 203

Index

Convergence in policy, 214
Corporatism: 22, 25, 45; advantages for members, 195–96; changes in, 184–85; challenges to, 211–13; confessional view of, 67; confessional influence, 91; and conflict, 29; criticisms of, 196; depoliticization of issues, 49; decision-making, 133; development of, 48; definition, 7, 44; grassroots, 89; institutions-tripartism, 131; liberal/social, 85; as an obstacle to retrenchment, 200; and policy-making, 19, 50, 200, 205–06; effects on policy-making, 200; rationalization and coordination, 23; relevance to Netherlands/religious organizations in, 29, 204; and slow growth of Dutch welfare state, 207–08; socialist view of, 67, 99; and state society relations, 206; state role in, 67; 1960's transformations, 52; undemocratic aspects of, 221
Corporatist institutions: 25, 46; number of, 68; conflict resolution, 49; development, 68; duration, 71; specialization-differentiation, 68; transformation, 70
Cost of welfare state, 26
Councils of Labor (*Raden van Arbeid*), 77
Critical Junctures, 18–19
Crown Members (*Kroonleden*), 78

Decentralization, 188–89
Democracy, 56
Denmark, 62
Disability programs: increases in benefits and beneficiaries, 151–52; reforms of, 189–94; reasons for adoption, 199
Disability Security Act, 135, 150, 152, 190
Divergence of welfare states, 5, 6, 12, 26, 203
Doorn, Jacques Van, 15
Double dispensation (*dubbelbedeling*), 82
Drees, Willem (Minister of Social Affairs), 75, 99, 103–11, 122, 128–29

Dutch Association for Social Work. *See* Dutch Council for Social Work
Dutch Association for the Handicapped, 74
Dutch Christian Labor Federation, 85
Dutch Council for Social Work, 72, 113–14, 140
Dutch Federation of Trade Unions (NVV) (Nederlands Verbonol van Vakverenigingen), 108

Economic Crisis, 167–68, 174
Education: parochial schools, 66
Elias, Norbert, 41–42
Emergency Retirement Pensions Act (Noodwet Ouderdomsvoorziening), 109–10, 115–20, 124–25, 130
England, 96
Entitlement to Social Insurance, 101–02
Erasmus, 59
Esping-Andersen, Gösta, 20

Federation of Catholic Workers, 85
Flora, Peter, 10
Formateur, 111–12
Fraud in social welfare, 181–82
Functional Decentralization, 67, 99

German Model, 22–23, 30, 47, 91, 97
Germany: *Berufsgenossenschaften*, 87
Gerschenkron, Alexander, 96
Governing agreement (*Regeerakkoord*), 178
Governing crisis of 1973, 163
Government coalition: 112; Red-Roman coalition, 103–05; confessional-liberal coalition, 119
Government in exile, 98–100
Government program (*Regeringsprogram*), 179
Growth of welfare state, 3, 9, 23, 51, 131
Great Britain, 23
Great Depression, 83

Heclo, Hugh, 33
Hirschman, Albert, 39
Historical analysis, 17–18, 41, 220

Index

Ideology: and collective mobilization, 29, 48, 218; dimensions of, 17, 41, 44, 60
Inclusiveness in social insurance, 166–67
Incrementalism, 51, 198
Individual behavior, 21, 39
Industrial insurance boards (bedrijfsverenigingen): 45, 76–78, 87–91, 103, 116–21; and disability program, 162
Industrialization, 31, 96–97
Interest Groups: capital and labor organizations, 47; confessional, 64; private, 45; protestant, 81
Institutional analysis, 17–18, 203, 220
Institutional change, 42–44, 169
Institutional structure, 41
Insurance programs, 86, 88–93, 116
Invalidity Act 1913, 90, 107–08

Joekes, A. M., 119–24
Joint Medical Service, 161–62

Katzenstein, Peter, 85
Keynesian economics, 173
Klompé, Marga (Minister of Social Work), 137–38
Korpi, Walter, 13–14
Krasner, Stephen, 43
Kuhn, Thomas, 27
Kuyper, Abraham, 87–90, 215

Labor councils, 102, 121
Labor unions, 12, 15
Labor organization, 66
Labor Party (PvdA), 14–15, 61, 66, 103–05, 115
Labor Party: commitment to social policy, 215; retirement pension, 97; universal public insurance, 58, 107, 127; universal scheme, 111
Lateness of Dutch welfare state, 96–97
Leftist mobilization, 208
Legislation, 35
Levels of analysis, 8, 28–30, 34, 53
Liberal democracy, 43
Liberal party (VVD): 61; electoral support, 16; platform, 16; position on retrenchment, 179

Liberals, 60–63
Lijphart, Arend, 49, 60
Locke, John, 60
Lowi, Theodore, 58

Medical professionals, 182
Messick, Richard, 32
Ministry of Home Affairs, 72, 105–06
Ministry of Social Affairs, 16, 116, 119, 128, 129
Ministry of Social Work: and poor relief, 112; Catholic party's control of, 129
Mobilization: 26, 31, 41–42, 48, 54–55, 63; religious forces, 81, 94; social-democratic, 47; working classes, 13–14
Monarchy, 64
Montesquieu, Baron Charles-Louis, 41
Multiparty system, 60
Municipal councils, 189

National Insurance Bank (NIB) (Rijksverzekeringsbank): 76–78, 87, 89, 90–91, 94, 102, 107, 109, 116, 121, 125
Nederlands Gemeenschap, 99
Netherlands Union (Nederlandse Unie), 99
Nederlands Volksherstel, 106
Newtonian vision, 38
Nonincremental policy-making, 209–10
Nordlinger, Eric, 35

Offe, Claus, 46
Olson, Mancur, 37–38

Parliamentary government, 62
Pension: new program (1957), 10; disability, 90; retirement, 90
Pillarization: 48, 60, 63, 85, 93; breakdown of, 51, 155–56, 213
Pluralism, 37, 44, 221
Pluralist Lobby, 72–73
Polarization, 48–49
Policy Borrowing: 22, 25, 32, 34–35, 168, 203; elites and, 35; geographic factors, 34; German, Great Britain, 23; ideas, 32–33; mechanisms of, 216–17; and retrenchment, 198

Index

Policy makers: definition of, 54; accommodation, 49; corporatist institutions and, 36, 59; and mobilization, 36; political conflict, 50
Policy process, 31
Political change in Netherlands, 51, 53, 133–34
Political culture, 42
Political ideologies, 68
Political development, 10
Political parties, 169
Political mobilization: 60, 62, 212; in Scandinavia, in Yugoslavia, 60
Poor councils (*Armenraden*), 75, 82
Poor Law of 1912, 75, 82, 106, 139
Poor relief: 94, 103; administration of, 72, 82, 114; and church-state relationships, 80–82, 105–07, 113–15, 130; and private charities, 71, 81, 114; and public assistance, 113
Poverty ("New poor"), 91–92, 187
Power difference model, 13
Power sharing, 49
Private charities, 140–41
Professionals, 51
Professionalization, 213
Proportional representation, 60
Protestants, 60, 122
Protestant parties: Protestant Antirevolutionary Party (ARP), 6, 111–12; Christian Historical Union, 111–12; Staatskundige Gereformeerden, 127
Provincial Reconstruction Organizations (POOs), 75, 106, 112
Public assistance: 1963 program, 21, 24, 71, 136; changes in entitlements, 189; efforts to combat misuse, 185–86; state involvement, 81
Public Assistance Act 1963: 75, 135, 140, 142; effects on private charities, 142–43
Public Disability Act: 135; passage of, 155–62, 164–65; interest groups and, 161
Public insurance: universal benefits, 20, 127; and SER, 123
Public Retirement Pensions Act (1957), 127, 131
Public Widow & Orphans Act, 146

Rational choice, 37, 40
Red-Roman coalitions, 145

Redistribution, 30
Reform, 26
Religion and politics: autonomy of the church, 24; mobilization of, 7–8, 25, 37, 40, 44, 47; parties, 6; toleration, 59; and development of corporatism, 207
Religious business associations, 48
Religious charities, 83–84
Religious cleavages, 14
Religious forces, 59, 63
Religious freedom, 65
Religious parties, 61
Religious trade unions, 48
Rerum Novarum (Leo XIII), 65
Retirement insurance, 94, 108, 120, 122
Retirement pensions, 86, 109, 116–24, 127, 131
Retrenchment: effects on Social Welfare, 175–76, 180, 190–91; effects on solidarity, 199; contrast with welfare state growth, 197, 222; politics of, 173, 177–78, 182–83; and medical professionals, 192
Rieken, J. G., 49
Right of recovery (*Verhaalsrecht*), 83, 113
Romme, C. P., 103–04, 136
Rotterdam Municipal Social Services, 186
Roolrink, B., 157
Roosevelt, Franklin D., 33
Ruding, H., 179

Saint Michiel (Abbey), 98, 100
Sartori, Giovanni, 8, 17, 48, 135
Scientific Council for Government Policy, 190, 198
Schmitter, Phillipe, 67, 71
Second Van Rhijn Commission (Report), 116–17, 119, 131, 148–49
Self-employed, 157–58
Shalev, Michael, 13–14
Shimpei, Goto, 33
Skocpol, Theda, 18
Social democratic unions, 48
Social Economic Council (SER): 45, 79, 123, 125, 127; advice on public disability, 150; conflict with Ministry of Social Affairs, 150–51; Report on Retrenchment, 190; dis-

Index

cussion on disability reform, 195; Report on Public Disability, 156; Report on Public Retirement Pensions, 125–26
Social change, 44, 133
Social ideology, 41–42
Social insurance: 20, 22–24, 32, 84, 90, 100–02, 105, 107, 130; after World War II, 77; models, in the U.S. and Great Britain, 100, 102; financing, 86, 93, 102; religious interests, 103, 110, 130; state involvement, 77, 91
Social Insurance Council (Sociale Verzekeringsraad), 45, 78–79, 118, 162
Social Insurance Organization Act (1952), 78, 120
Social legislation, 85
Social movements, 51
Social mobilization, 212
Social question, 86–87, 94
Social reform, 84, 98
Social renewal, 188
"Social risk," 151
Social work, 75
Socialism, 66
Socialists, 22, 60
Socialist, 67, 99
Social security. *See* Social insurance
Social welfare: administrative structure, 94; Catholic/Calvinist doctrine (confessional)-church concern, 65; decentralization, 101; entitlements; reforms, 104; Reforms-studies/theorizing, 100; state involvement — strong, limited, 97; state involvement, 99; universal scheme, 97, 104
Societal corporatism, 71
Sovereignty, 64
State: 37, 44, 63; consociational corporatist, 44; definition of, 56; unitary, 62
State corporatism, 71
State-Society Relations, 184
Stephens, John, 14–15
Subsidiarity, 65
Subsidization, 82
Suurhoff, J. G., 124–25, 128, 217
Sweden, 18, 47
Switzerland, 13

Taxation, 30
Technological development, 31
Thatcher, Margaret, 211
Theory of the state, 56
Thiel, F. J., van, 112, 114, 136
Thorbecke, Johan, 62
Trade unions, 156, 193
Tripartism, 47, 70, 99

Unemployment, 31, 92
Unintentional consequences, 165–68
Unionization, 96
United provinces, 59
United States, 18, 19, 31, 33
Urbanization, 31

Values, 32, 41–42, 62–63
Van Rhijn, A. A., 100, 116, 124
Van Rhijn Commission, 100–03, 103–04, 107, 116
Veldkamp, Gerhard (Minister of Social Work), 141, 146–49
Voluntary Retirement Insurance Act, 107–08
Voluntary Old Age Pensions Act (Wet op de Vrijwillige Ouderdomsverzekering 1919), 90
Vos, Hein, 121–22, 124

Wagner Report, 100–01
War Victim's Assistance Program, 107, 112
Wassenberg, Arthur, 50
Weber, Max, 42
Weltanschauung, 48
Welfare Policy, 12, 211
Welfare Reform: corporatist institutions, 129; in Great Britain, 128; and growth of the welfare state, 132
Wilensky, Harold, 9–10, 47
Willem II, King, 62
Wolfson, Dik, 196
Wolinetz, Stephen, 159
Workmen's Compensation Act of 1901 (*Ongevallenwet*), 76, 87–89
World War I, 92
World War II, 20, 24–26, 98

Zijlstra, J., 126

257

Pitt Series in
Policy and Institutional Studies
Bert A. Rockman, Editor

The Acid Rain Controversy
James L. Regens and Robert W. Rycroft

Advising West European Governments: Inquiries, Expertise, and Public Policy
B. Guy Peters and Anthony Barker, Editors

Affirmative Action at Work: Law, Politics, and Ethics
Bron Raymond Taylor

Agency Merger and Bureaucratic Redesign
Karen M. Hult

The Aging: A Guide to Public Policy
Bennett M. Rich and Martha Baum

Arms for the Horn: U.S. Security Policy in Ethiopia and Somalia, 1953–1991
Jeffrey A. Lefebvre

The Atlantic Alliance and the Middle East
Joseph I. Coffey and Gianni Bonvicini, Editors

The Budget-Maximizing Bureaucrat: Appraisals and Evidence
André Blais and Stéphane Dion, Editors

Careers in City Politics: The Case for Urban Democracy
Timothy Bledsoe

Clean Air: The Policies and Politics of Pollution Control
Charles O. Jones

The Competitive City: The Political Economy of Suburbia
Mark Schneider

Conflict and Rhetoric in French Policymaking
Frank R. Baumgartner

Congress and Economic Policymaking
Darrell M. West

Congress Oversees the Bureaucracy: Studies in Legislative
Supervision
Morris S. Ogul

Democracy in Japan
Takeshi Ishida and Ellis S. Krauss, Editors

Demographic Change and the American Future
R. Scott Fosler, William Alonso, Jack A. Meyer, and Rosemary Kern

The Development of the Dutch Welfare State: From Workers' Insurance to Universal Entitlement
Robert H. Cox

Economic Decline and Political Change: Canada, Great Britain,
and the United States
Harold D. Clarke, Marianne C. Stewart, and Gary Zuk, Editors

Executive Leadership in Anglo-American Systems
Colin Campbell, S.J., and Margaret Jane Wyszomirski, Editors

Extraordinary Measures: The Exercise of Prerogative Powers in
the United States
Daniel P. Franklin

Foreign Policy Motivation: A General Theory and a Case Study
Richard W. Cottam

"He Shall Not Pass This Way Again": The Legacy of Justice
William O. Douglas
Stephen L. Wasby, Editor

History and Context in Comparative Public Policy
Douglas E. Ashford, Editor

Homeward Bound: Explaining Changes in Congressional
Behavior
Glenn Parker

How Does Social Science Work? Reflections on Practice
Paul Diesing

Imagery and Ideology in U.S. Policy Toward Libya, 1969–1982
Mahmoud G. ElWarfally

The Impact of Policy Analysis
James M. Rogers

Interests and Institutions: Substance and Structure in American Politics
Robert H. Salisbury

Iran and the United States: A Cold War Case Study
Richard W. Cottam

Japanese Prefectures and Policymaking
Steven R. Reed

The Japanese Prime Minister and Public Policy
Kenji Hayao

Making Common Sense of Japan
Steven R. Reed

Making Regulatory Policy
Keith Hawkins and John M. Thomas, Editors

Managing the Presidency: Carter, Reagan, and the Search for Executive Harmony
Colin Campbell, S.J.

The Moral Dimensions of Public Policy Choice: Beyond the Market Paradigm
John Martin Gillroy and Maurice Wade, Editors

Native Americans and Public Policy
Fremont J. Lyden and Lyman H. Legters, Editors

Organizing Governance, Governing Organizations
Colin Campbell, S.J., and B. Guy Peters, Editors

Party Organizations in American Politics
Cornelius P. Cotter et al.

Perceptions and Behavior in Soviet Foreign Policy
Richard K. Herrman

Pesticides and Politics: The Life Cycle of a Public Issue
Christopher J. Bosso

Policy Analysis by Design
Davis B. Bobrow and John S. Dryzek

The Political Failure of Employment Policy, 1945–1982
Gary Mucciaroni

Political Leadership: A Source Book
Barbara Kellerman, Editor

Political Leadership in an Age of Constraint: The Australian Experience
Colin Campbell, S.J., and John Halligan

The Political Psychology of the Gulf War: Leaders, Publics, and the Process of Conflict
Stanley A. Renshon, Editor

The Politics of Expert Advice: Creating, Using, and Manipulating Scientific Knowledge for Public Policy
Anthony Barker and B. Guy Peters, Editors

The Politics of Public Utility Regulation
William T. Gormley, Jr.

The Politics of the U.S. Cabinet: Representation in the Executive Branch, 1789–1984
Jeffrey E. Cohen

Politics Within the State: Elite Bureaucrats and Industrial Policy in Authoritarian Brazil
Ben Ross Schneider

The Presidency and Public Policy Making
George C. Edwards III, Steven A. Shull, and Norman C. Thomas, Editors

Private Markets and Public Intervention: A Primer for Policy Designers
Harvey Averch

The Promise and Paradox of Civil Service Reform
Patricia W. Ingraham and David H. Rosenbloom, Editors

Public Policy in Latin America: A Comparative Survey
John W. Sloan

Reluctant Partners: Implementing Federal Policy
Robert P. Stoker

Researching the Presidency: Vital Questions, New Approaches
George C. Edwards III, John H. Kessel, and Bert A. Rockman, Editors

Roads to Reason: Transportation, Administration, and Rationality in Colombia
Richard E. Hartwig

The SEC and Capital Market Regulation: The Politics of Expertise
Ann M. Khademian

Site Unseen: The Politics of Siting a Nuclear Waste Repository
Gerald Jacob

The Speaker and the Budget: Leadership in the Post-Reform
House of Representatives
Daniel J. Palazzolo

The State Roots of National Politics: Congress and the Tax
Agenda, 1978–1986
Michael B. Berkman

The Struggle for Social Security, 1900–1935
Roy Lubove

Tage Erlander: Serving the Welfare State, 1946–1969
Olof Ruin

Thatcher, Reagan, Mulroney: In Search of a New Bureaucracy
Donald Savoie

Traffic Safety Reform in the United States and Great Britain
Jerome S. Legge, Jr.

Urban Alternatives: Public and Private Markets in the Provision
of Local Services
Robert M. Stein

The U.S. Experiment in Social Medicine: The Community Health
Center Program, 1965–1986
Alice Sardell